INDIA AND SOUTH ASIA

Exploring Regional Perceptions

INDIA AND SOUTH ASIA

Exploring Regional Perceptions

Editor

VISHAL CHANDRA

INSTITUTE FOR DEFENCE STUDIES & ANALYSES
NEW DELHI

PENTAGON PRESS

India and South Asia: Exploring Regional Perceptions
Vishal Chandra (Editor)

First Published in 2015

ISBN 978-81-8274-812-5

Published by
PENTAGON PRESS
206, Peacock Lane, Shahpur Jat,
New Delhi-110049
Phones: 011-64706243, 26491568
Telefax: 011-26490600
email: rajan@pentagonpress.in
website: www.pentagonpress.in

Branch Office
Flat No.213, Athena-2,
Clover Acropolis,
Viman Nagar,
Pune-411014

In association with
Institute for Defence Studies and Analyses
No. 1, Development Enclave,
New Delhi-110010
Phone: +91-11-26717983
website: www.idsa.in

Printed at Aegean Offset Printers, Greater Noida, U.P.

Contents

Foreword

The Institute for Defence Studies and Analyses (IDSA) has been organising an annual South Asia Conference which brings together experts from India and all the other SAARC countries to exchange views on major issues of common interest to the region. Commencing the 6th South Asia Conference in the year 2012, scholars from Myanmar have also been participating. Every year, the papers presented at the Conference are collated and published as an edited book for future reference by researchers and students. The present volume is the product of the 7th South Asia Conference on the theme "India and South Asia: Exploring Regional Perceptions" that was held in New Delhi on October 30-31, 2013. The present volume, edited by Mr. Vishal Chandra, Associate Fellow at the Institute, brings together the papers presented at the Conference. Scholars and experts from Afghanistan, Bangladesh, Bhutan, India, Maldives, Myanmar, Nepal, Pakistan and Sri Lanka had shared their perspectives on the theme of the Conference.

It is an established fact that South Asia is one of the least integrated regions of the world. Mutual suspicions and negative perceptions about one another have played a big part in keeping the region out of step with the global trend towards greater regional integration. Difference in size, population and economy relative to India, although important, still does not offer full explanation for India being seen as an overbearing 'big brother'. There are issues specific to each country; sometimes related to identity and domestic politics, and other times because of unresolved bilateral disputes or the felt need to involve external powers to balance a bigger neighbour and/or benefit by playing one against the other.

The participants at the Conference discussed the reasons for the prevailing- many a time negative- perceptions among the SAARC partners vis-à-vis India and vice versa. They also discussed the inadequacy of the effort on India's part to be more sensitive to the natural fears and apprehensions of smaller countries, and being unable to reinforce its image of being a developmental partner for them. The participants also rightly brought out the need for greater people-to-people contacts and ease of travel within the region so that perceptions are not shaped and exploited by the vested interests. It was also felt by most participants that there was inadequate emphasis on studying the neighbours in all the countries of the region. This lacuna has to be filled for correcting perceptions.

It is a fact that India, with 80 per cent of the regional GDP and 70 per cent of South Asia's population, has an important role to play in making regional cooperation possible by improving its relationship further with all its neighbours. Greater effort—going beyond public diplomacy, to clear and improve perceptions among its neighbours will be in the interest of India and the region. Exchange of researchers and students and research about one another should be focused upon.

I commend Mr. Vishal Chandra for having brought out this useful volume. It is hoped that the book would raise awareness about the importance of perceptions in shaping relationships between India and its neighbours and would be found useful by scholars, researchers and policy makers alike.

New Delhi

Brig. Rumel Dahiya, SM (Retd.)
Deputy Director General, IDSA

Acknowledgements

This edited volume is an outcome of the 7th South Asia Conference which was held on October 30-31, 2013 at the Institute for Defence Studies and Analyses (IDSA) in New Delhi. Participants from all the South Asian countries deliberated upon the theme of the annual conference, titled, "India and South Asia: Exploring Regional Perceptions", and made a valuable contribution by way of revisiting, reinterpreting and often deconstructing various narratives and perceptions—national and sub-national, historical and contemporary, and social and economic—embedded within the South Asia region.

The emerging or changing intra-regional perceptions were also put to scrutiny during the two-day deliberation. The participants not only highlighted and discussed various critical aspects relating to the conference theme, but also suggested the way forward on managing diverse and often negative and regressive perceptions prevalent within the region.

Apart from expressing my sincere gratitude to the distinguished participants from Afghanistan, Pakistan, Nepal, Bhutan, Bangladesh, Sri Lanka, Maldives and Myanmar, I must acknowledge the valuable contribution made by the Indian scholars too. The moderators for different sessions of the conference—Professor S.D. Muni, Ambassador Veena Sikri, Ambassador Sheel Kant Sharma, General (Retd.) Ashok K. Mehta and Dr. Arvind Gupta—played a significant role in the smooth conduct of the proceedings. Their known scholarship in the subject further enriched the discussion and debate that followed at the end of each session.

I am indebted to my former Director General Dr. Arvind Gupta for his constant support and guidance in organising the 7th South Asia Conference.

This book would not have been possible without the trust and encouragement of my Deputy Director General Brig. Rumel Dahiya, SM (Retd.). His personal attention and advice especially as I was finalising the manuscript of this book is deeply appreciated. I am also grateful to my colleague Dr. Ashok Kumar Behuria, Coordinator of the South Asia Centre at IDSA, for his support.

I would be failing in my duty if I do not acknowledge several of my other colleagues who contributed in their respective capacities to the success of this conference. I would particularly like to thank my colleague Ms. Gulbin Sultana, who tirelessly worked and ably assisted me in successfully organising the conference. Mr. Aditya Valiathan Pillai, research intern at the time of the conference, too deserves my special praise for responsibly carrying out the assigned tasks. I also wish to sincerely thank my colleagues Ms. Sumita Kumar, Dr. Smruti S. Pattanaik, Dr. Priyanka Singh, Dr. Anand Kumar, Mr. Shyam Hari, Dr. Nihar Nayak, Ms. Shruti Pandalai, Ms. Eshita Mukherjee, Mr. Amit Kumar, Dr. Saurabh Mishra, Dr. Saroj Bishoyi, Mr. Parveen Bhardwaj, Mr. Shreyas Deshmukh, Dr. Yaqoob ul Hassan, Ms. Pranamita Baruah, Mr. Avinash Godbole, Ms. Daneesh Sethna, Ms. Gunjan Singh, Mr. Rajorshi Roy and many others for their kind support and cooperation.

I am also grateful to my colleague Mr. Vivek Kaushik, Associate Editor, Publication Division, for ensuring timely copy-editing of all the chapters. I must also place my special thanks to the publisher, Pentagon Press, for bringing out this edited volume in a professional manner.

I present this volume to the interested readers with the hope that it would contribute to the ongoing debate and discourse on the future of the South Asia region. We at IDSA certainly feel encouraged to take forward this process of dialoguing at the intra-regional level with greater enthusiasm and intellectual vigour. This is very much reflected in the proposed idea to upgrade our annual 'South Asia Conference' to the level of 'South Asia Dialogue' in the coming years.

New Delhi **Vishal Chandra**

Abbreviations

AAGR	Average Annual Growth Rate
ACU	Asian Clearing Union
ADB	Asian Development Bank
AGP	Asom Gana Parishad
AI	Amnesty International
AIF	ASEAN Infrastructure Fund
AL	Awami League
ANSF	Afghan National Security Forces
APEC	Asia Pacific Economic Cooperation
APTA	Asia-Pacific Trade Agreement
ASEAN	Association of South East Asian Nations
BCIM	Bangladesh, China, India and Myanmar
BHU	Banaras Hindu University
BIMSTEC	Bay of Bengal Initiative for Mutli-sectoral Technical and Economic Cooperation
BIPPA	Bilateral Investment Promotion and Protection Agreement
BIS	Bureau of Industrial Standards
BJP	Bharatiya Janata Party
BLA	Baloch Liberation Army
BNP	Bangladesh Nationalist Party
BSF	Border Security Force
BSTI	Bangladesh Standard and Testing Institution
BTV	Bangladesh Television
CA	Constituent Assembly
CEC	Committee on Economic Cooperation
CENTO	Central Treaty Organisation
CNAS	Centre for Nepal and Asian Studies

COMPOSA	Coordination Committee of Maoist Parties and Organisations in South Asia
CoNI	Commission of National Inquiry
CPA	Comprehensive Peace Agreement
CSN	Centre for the Study of Nepal
CVD	Countervailing Duty
DKD	Delhi-Kolkata-Dhaka
EAS	East Asia Summit
ECO	Economic Cooperation Organisation
ECOSOC	Economic and Social Council
ECOTA	ECO Trade Agreement
EU	European Union
FICCI	Federation of Indian Chambers of Commerce and Industry
FTA	Free Trade Agreement
GATT	General Agreement on Tariffs and Trade
GDP	Gross Domestic Product
GNH	Gross National Happiness
GTAP	Global Trade Analysis Project
HRW	Human Rights Watch
ICG	International Crisis Group
ICSSR	Indian Council for Social Science Research
ICWA	Indian Council of World Affairs
IDSA	Institute for Defence Studies and Analyses
IFAD	International Fund for Agricultural Development
IFC	International Financial Corporation
INA	Indian National Army
INIA	Ibrahim Nasir International Airport
ISFTA	India-Sri Lanka Free Trade Agreement
ITC	International Trade Centre
ITEC	Indian Technical and Economic Cooperation
ITI	Istanbul-Tehran-Islamabad
JIB	Jamat-e-Islami Bangladesh
JNU	Jawaharlal Nehru University
JP	Jumhoree Party
LBA	Land Boundary Agreement
LDCs	Least Developed Countries
LoE	Letter of Exchange
LTTE	Liberation Tigers of Tamil Eelam
MACL	Maldives Airports Company Limited

MAHB	Malaysia Airports Holdings Berhad
MDP	Maldivian Democratic Party
MEA	Ministry of External Affairs
MFN	Most Favoured Nation
MoU	Memorandum of Understanding
NAFTA	North American Free Trade Agreement
NAM	Non Aligned Movement
NC	Nepali Congress
NDMA	Non-Discriminatory Market Access
NLD	National League for Democracy
NLDCs	Non Least Developed Countries
NSB	National Statistics Bureau
NTB	Non-Tariff Barrier
NTC	Non-Tariff Commission
ODA	Official Developmental Assistance
OHCHR	Office of the High Commissioner for Human Rights
PBC	Pakistan Business Council
PDP	People's Democratic Party
PPM	Progressive Party of Maldives
PPP	Pakistan Peoples' Party
PSQCA	Pakistan Standards and Quality Control Authority
PWG	People's War Group
R-CEP	Regional Comprehensive Economic Partnership
RLP	River Linking Project
RMG	Readymade Garment
RTA	Regional Trade Agreement
RTCEC	Round Table on Commercial and Economic Cooperation
SAARC	South Asian Association for Regional Cooperation
SADC	South African Development Community
SAFTA	South Asian Free Trade Area
SAIL	Steel Authority of India Limited
SAPTA	SAARC Preferential Trading Arrangement
SARSO	SAARC Standards Organisation
SASC	South Asia Studies Centre
SATIS	SAARC Agreement on Trade in Services
SCO	Shanghai Cooperation Organisation
SDF	SAARC Development Fund
SDG	SAARC Development Goals
SDR	Special Drawing Rights

SEATO	South East Asia Treaty Organisation
SEWA	Self-Employed Women's Association
SICO	SAARC Industrial Cooperation
SIS	School of International Studies
SPA	Seven Party Alliance/Strategic Partnership Agreement
SPS	Sanitary and Phytosanitary
TAR	Tibet Autonomous Region
TMC	Trinamool Congress
TNA	Tamil National Alliance
TPP	Trans-Pacific Partnership
TTIP	Transatlantic Trade and Investment Partnership
UGC	University Grants Commission
ULFA	United Liberation Front of Assam
UN	United Nations
UNCTAD	UN Conference on Trade and Development
UNDP	United Nations Development Programme
UNESCAP	United Nations Economic and Social Commission for Asia and the Pacific
UNICEF	United Nations Children's Fund
UNMIN	United Nations Mission in Nepal
UNSG	United Nations Secretary General
UPA	United Progressive Alliance
US	United States
USK	United States of Kashmir
WHO	World Health Organisation
WITS	World Integrated Trade Solution
WTO	World Trade Organisation

About the Contributors

Pratyoush Onta is Chair, Martin Chautari, Kathmandu. He has a Ph.D in History from the University of Pennsylvania (1996). He has written about Nepali nationalism, Gurkha history, institutions, area studies, politics of knowledge production and media. He has written, edited and co-edited several books including *Nepal Studies in the UK* (2004), *Social History of Radio Nepal* (2004, in Nepali), *Social Scientific Thinking in the Context of Nepal* (2004, in Nepali), *Radio Journalism: News and Talk Programs in FM Radio* (2005, in Nepali), *Growing Up with Radio* (2005, in Nepali), *Mass Media in Post-1990 Nepal* (2006), *Ten Years of Independent Radio: Development, Debates and the Public Interest* (2008, in Nepali), *Autocratic Monarchy: Politics in Panchayat Nepal* (2012) and *Post-1990 History of Nepali Magazines* (forthcoming, in Nepali). He is also the founding editor of two journals - *Studies in Nepali History and Society* (est. 1996) and *Media Adhyayan* (est. 2006, in Nepali).

Yaqoob Khan Bangash is Chairman, Department of History, Forman Christian College, Lahore, Pakistan. His research interests lie in the formation of post colonial states, questions of identity, rise of regional nationalisms and insurgency, and human rights. His first book is entitled *Subjects to Citizens: Accession and Integration of the Princely States of Pakistan, 1947-55* (forthcoming, to be published by Oxford University Press). He also writes regularly for *The Express Tribune, The News* and various other news magazines of South Asia. He has also previously published in the *Journal of Imperial and Commonwealth History* and *South Asia Research.*

M. Humayun Kabir is Vice President, Bangladesh Enterprise Institute (BEI), Dhaka. A career diplomat, he retired as Secretary, Ministry of Foreign Affairs of Bangladesh, in September 2010. His last foreign assignment was in Washington, D.C., where he served as Bangladesh Ambassador to the United States. He has also served as Ambassador to Nepal and High Commissioner to Australia and

New Zealand and as Deputy High Commissioner in Kolkata, India. He also advises UNDP and other business consultancies in Bangladesh and abroad.

Dayan Jayatilleka was Sri Lanka's Ambassador Extraordinary and Plenipotentiary to France, Portugal and Spain as well as Permanent Delegate to UNESCO until January 2013. He was Ambassador/Permanent Representative of Sri Lanka to the United Nations in Geneva (2007-09) and was a Vice-President of the UN Human Rights Council. He was appointed Chairman of the Governing Body of the International Labour Organisation (ILO) in 2007. He was Minister of Planning and Youth Affairs in the North-East Provincial Council of Sri Lanka (1988-89). His select publications include: *The Travails of a Democracy: Unfinished War, Protracted Crisis* (1995) and *Fidel's Ethics of Violence: The Moral Dimension of the Political Thought of Fidel Castro* (2007). His latest book is *Long War, Cold Peace: Conflict and Crisis in Sri Lanka*, Vijitha Yapa Publishers, 2013.

Partha S. Ghosh is Senior Fellow at the Nehru Memorial Museum and Library, New Delhi and editor of *India Quarterly*. Until recently, he was Professor of South Asian Studies at Jawaharlal Nehru University, New Delhi and the Indian Council for Cultural Relations Chair on Indian Studies at Victoria University of Wellington, New Zealand. Earlier, he was Visiting Professor at the OKD Institute of Social Change and Development, Guwahati; Research Director at the Indian Council of Social Science Research; Humboldt Fellow at the Heidelberg University; Ford Visiting Scholar at the University of Illinois at Urbana-Champaign and a Visiting Fellow at the Centre for Policy Research, New Delhi. His academic interests include South Asian politics, ethnicity, majority-minority relations, inter-state migrations and domestic politics-foreign policy interface.

Dinesh Bhattarai was Nepal's Ambassador/Permanent Representative to the United Nations including the World Trade Organisation and International Organisations in Geneva, Rome, and Vienna from 2007 to 2012. He was Ambassador of Nepal to the Swiss Confederation and concurrently accredited to Italy and Croatia. He was First Secretary (Political Affairs) at the Embassy of Nepal in New Delhi from 1991-1994 and Deputy Chief of Mission at the Embassy of Nepal in Washington, D.C., from 1998-2003, in which he served as *Charge d'Affaires* a.i. from 2000-01. He did his Post Graduate Diploma in International Relations and Development from the Institute of Social Studies (ISS), The Hague. He obtained his Ph.D in International Relations from Jawaharlal Nehru University, New Delhi. He has co-authored the book, *Nepal-India: Democracy in the Making of Mutual Trust*, Nirala Publications, 1993.

M. Ashique Rahman is Research Fellow, Bangladesh Institute of International and Strategic Studies (BIISS), Dhaka. As a Fulbright Scholar, he obtained his Master's degree in International Relations from Boston University, Massachusetts in 2010. He was also awarded the VLIR-UOS Scholarship by the Belgian Government to attend the International Training Programme (ITP) on "Governing for Development" at the University of Antwerp, Belgium. Earlier, he completed his Master of Social Sciences (MSS) and Bachelor of Social Sciences (BSS) in Political Science from the University of Dhaka. His areas of expertise are US-South Asia relations, South Asian politics, inter-state relations and security in South Asia and conventional arms control. He is also Assistant Editor of the *BIISS Journal*.

Davood Moradian is Director General of the Afghan Institute of Strategic Studies (AISS), Kabul. He has worked with the Afghan Government since 2006 in different capacities, including as Chief of Programmes at former President Hamid Karzai's office and as Chief Policy Advisor to Afghanistan's Ministry of Foreign Affairs (2006-2011). He has also taught International Relations at the University of St. Andrews, Scotland and the American University of Afghanistan.

Mohamed Naahee Naseem was a Journalist with Minivan News in Male, Maldives. He had reported on the political crisis in the Maldives that began following the controversial transfer of power in February 2012. He has also appeared at private local broadcaster *Raajje Television* as a news analyst in its current affairs programme *Sungadi*. He is also currently involved in formulating the Press Club of Maldives (PCM), an NGO that focuses on supporting and promoting journalism in the Maldives, while also creating a platform that would support local journalists in their career development. Earlier, he had briefly worked for *Miadhu Daily*, a local newspaper. He is also pursuing his Bachelor's degree in Sharia and Law (LLB Hon.) at the Faculty of Sharia and Law, The Maldives National University.

Denzil Abel is Member, Myanmar Institute of Strategic and International Studies (MISIS), Yangon, Myanmar. He holds a Mater's degree in International Public Policy from the School of Advanced International Studies, Johns Hopkins University. He has served in various positions in the Myanmar Foreign Service (1972 -2005), as SO and ASEAN Plus Three Specialist, ASEAN Secretariat (2006-08), as Strategic Support Manager, ASEAN High Level Task Force for Cyclone Nargis Operation (2009-2010) and as Senior Advisor to the UN-Habitat Myanmar (2011).

Pema Tenzin is Regional Head of Kuensel Corporation, Kanglung, Trashigang, Bhutan. He has a Bachelor's degree in Business Management from Bangalore University, India. He has attended several international and regional training programmes and seminars on business, leadership, natural resources and cooperation in Norway, Bhutan and India. The co-author of his chapter in the book, **Chhimi Dorji**, is an Executive Engineer with the Royal Government of Bhutan, Thimphu.

Nagesh Kumar is Head, UNESCAP South and South-West Asia Office, New Delhi. In October 2011, he was appointed as Director, Subregional Office for South and South-West Asia based in New Delhi. Earlier, he was Director of the Macroeconomic Policy and Development Division of ESCAP in Bangkok and also served as the Acting Deputy Executive Secretary of ESCAP (September 2010-June 2011). Prior to joining ESCAP in May 2009, he had served as Director-General of Research and Information System for Developing Countries (RIS), New Delhi. He has also served on the faculty of the United Nations University-Institute for New Technologies (now UNU-MERIT), Maastricht, The Netherlands (1993-98); boards of the International Centre for Trade and Sustainable Development (ICTSD), Geneva; South Asia Centre for Policy Studies (SACEPS), Kathmandu; Institute of Studies in Industrial Development, New Delhi and the Export-Import Bank of India. His recent books include: *Asia's New Regionalism and Global Role* (ISEAS, Singapore, 2008); *International Competitiveness and Knowledge-based Industries in India* (Oxford University Press, 2007); *Towards an Asian Economic Community* (Singapore and New Delhi: 2005); *Globalization and the Quality of Foreign Direct Investment* (Oxford University Press, 2002). He co-founded the *South Asia Economic Journal* in 2000 and writes a monthly column in *Business Standard*, a leading financial daily published from New Delhi.

Gabriel Ian Lynn Ockersz is former Director, Bandaranaike Centre for International Studies (BCIS), Colombo, Sri Lanka. He is presently Associate Editor/Business Editor, *The Island*, a Colombo based newspaper. He was previously an Associate Editor with *The Island*. Prior to it, he worked with *The Sun* and *The Daily News*. He has been a regular contributor to the national press since 1982 on subject areas ranging from domestic and international politics to personality profiles, arts and culture, including weekly columns in *The Daily News* titled "Asia Watch" and "Global Scrutiny" and in *The Island* under the title "World Scan". Currently, he is also working as Visiting Lecturer at the University of Colombo. Previously, he also served as Lecturer at Aquinas College and the Diplomatic Training Institute, Colombo; and the Kelaniya University and Open University of Sri Lanka. He has two publications to his credit: "Flame and Sparks", a collection of poems of socio-religious significance (October 2002) and "The Peace

Thou Gives", a collection of devotional poems (July 2010). He was conferred the title "Catholic Writer 2004" by the Catholic Writers' Association of Sri Lanka. He was appointed as a member of Advisory Body by Ministry of Constitutional Affairs in the 1990s to help find political solution to the ethnic conflict.

S.D. Muni is Distinguished Fellow, Institute for Defence Studies and Analyses (IDSA), New Delhi. Earlier, he was Research Professor at the Institute of South Asian Studies of the National University of Singapore. He served as India's Ambassador to Laos PDR (1997-99) and as India's Special Envoy to Southeast Asian countries on the issue of UN Security Council reform (2005-06). In 2005, the Sri Lankan President bestowed upon him the country's highest civilian honour for a foreign national, the 'Sri Lanka Ratna'. He has taught International Studies for 34 years at Jawaharlal Nehru University, New Delhi and has visited on research assignments to various universities and think tanks in the US, UK, Europe, Japan, Australia, West Asia and Southeast Asia. He has authored and edited more than two dozen books and monographs on Indian and Asian foreign and security policies. His latest publications include *India and China: The Next Decade* (co-edited, 2009), *India's Foreign Policy: The Democracy Dimension* (2009), *The Emerging Dimensions of SAARC* (2010), *A Resurgent China: South Asian Perspectives* (co-edited, 2012) and *Asian Strategic Review* (co-edited, 2013).

I.N. Mukherji is former Chairman of South Asian Studies and Dean of School of International Studies, Jawaharlal Nehru University and Senior Consultant at Research and Information System for Developing Countries, New Delhi. After retiring as professor from JNU in 2008, he became the Regional Editor (India) of the *South Asia Economic Journal*. He is in the Governing Body of the Centre for International Relations and Community Well Being, Gurgaon. He has completed 22 research projects sponsored by the Committee on Studies for Cooperation in South Asia (CSCD), World Bank, UNESCAP, IDRC, FAO, ADB, ICSSR and SANEI among others. His core interest relates to trade and development issues in South Asia. Two of his recent publications are: "Deepening Economic Cooperation between India and Sri Lanka" (with Kavita Iyenger; Asian Development Bank, Manila, 2013) and "SAFTA and Food Security in South Asia-An Overview", in *Regional Trade Agreements and Food Security in Asia*, Food and Agriculture Organisation of the United Nations Regional Office for Asia and the Pacific, Bangkok, 2012.

Shahmahmood Miakhel is Country Director, United States Institute of Peace (USIP), Kabul, Afghanistan. Prior to joining USIP in 2009, he worked as Governance Adviser/Deputy Head of Governance Unit for the United Nations Assistance Mission in Afghanistan (UNAMA). From 2003-05, he served as the deputy interior minister of Afghanistan. He has also worked as a reporter for Pashto and Dari services of *Voice of America* (1985-1990) and as deputy director of SOS/Belgium, an international organisation assisting Afghan refugees in Pakistan. He has also worked for UNDP/UNOPS programme in Afghanistan as Senior Liaison Officer to establish District Rehabilitation *Shuras* (DRS) in eastern and south-eastern provinces of Afghanistan. He was elected to the Emergency *Loya Jirga* in 2002, the Peace *Jirga* between Afghanistan and Pakistan in August 2007 and Consultative Peace *Jirga* in June 2010. He has published books in Pashto and English: "Emergency Loya Jirga and the Election Process in the Eastern Provinces of Afghanistan"; "In the Light of Truth," a personal account of the *mujahideen* uprising in the Kunar Province and refugee life in Pakistan; "Ministry of Interior: Challenges and Achievements", a personal account (2003-05); and "Understanding Afghanistan: Collection of Articles" (2001-12).

Phae Thann Oo is a retired ambassador and had served in various capacities in the Myanmar Ministry of Foreign Affairs. As a career diplomat, he served at the Myanmar Embassy in Paris, Singapore, Ottawa, Seoul and Dhaka. He also served as Director General in the Department of Political Affairs of the Ministry of Foreign Affairs. As Myanmar Delegate, he attended a number of annual UNGA meetings in New York and some UN special summit meetings, such as United Nations Conference on Economic Development (Earth Summit) in Rio, Brazil (1992) and the UNFCCC Summit Meeting in Kyoto, Japan (1999). As Secretary, National Commission for Environmental Affairs, he participated in environmental conferences on climate change, desertification and sustainable development. He has also served as Myanmar SOM leader at ASEAN meetings and summits.

List of Map, Tables and Figures

Figures

Chapter 12

Chapter 15

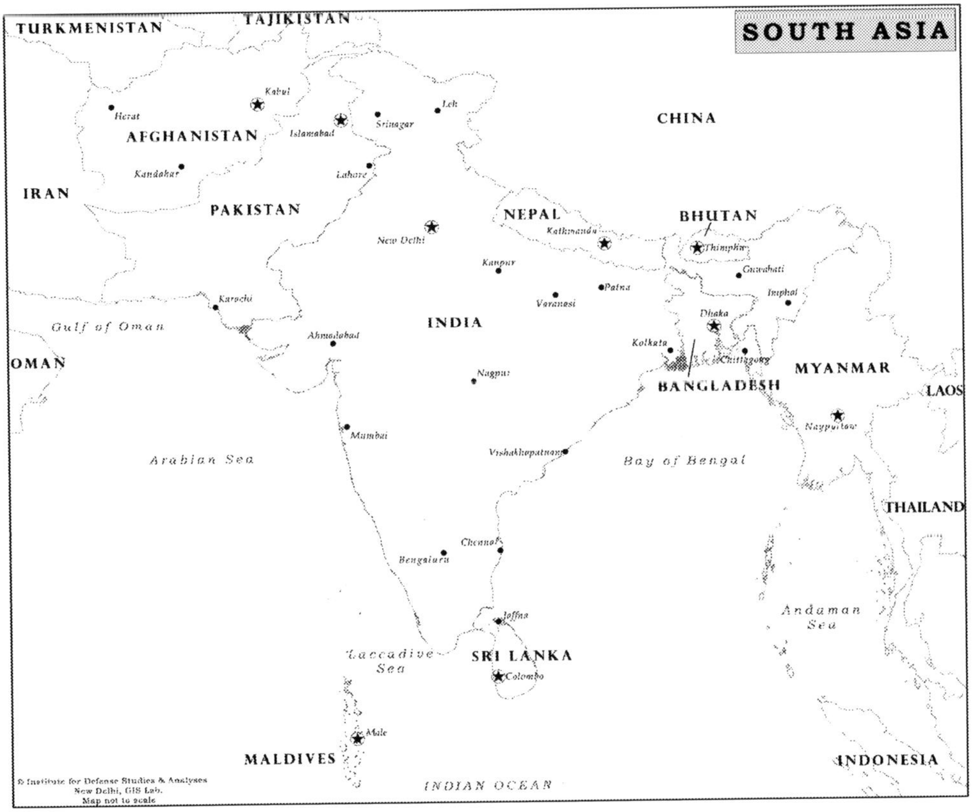
SOUTH ASIA
TURKMENISTAN
TAJIKISTAN
Kabul
Herat
AFGHANISTAN
Islamabad
Srinagar
Leh
CHINA
Kandahar
Lahore
IRAN
PAKISTAN
NEPAL
BHUTAN
New Delhi
Kathmandu
Thimphu
Kanpur
Guwahati
Patna
Imphal
Karachi
Varanasi
Dhaka
Gulf of Oman
INDIA
Ahmadabad
Kolkata
Chittagong
OMAN
MYANMAR
Nagpur
BANGLADESH
LAOS
Mumbai
Arabian Sea
Vishakhapatnam
Bay of Bengal
THAILAND
Chennai
Bengaluru
Andaman Sea
Jaffna
Laccadive Sea
SRI LANKA
Colombo
Male
MALDIVES
INDONESIA
INDIAN OCEAN
© Institute for Defense Studies & Analyses
New Delhi, GIS Lab.
Map not to scale

Welcome Remarks by Dr. Arvind Gupta, Director General, IDSA at the 7th Annual South Asia Conference, October 30, 2013*

Hon'ble Raksha Mantri
Delegates to the conference
Members of the Executive Council
Members of the Strategic Community
Members of the Media
IDSA Colleagues
Ladies and Gentlemen

Good Morning,

It gives me great pleasure to welcome you to the 7th South Asia Conference being organised by the IDSA on the theme "India and South Asia: Exploring Regional Perceptions".

I am most grateful to the Hon'ble Defence Minister for having agreed to inaugurate this conference. His invaluable support to this project over the last several years has resulted in institutionalising the South Asia Conference as an annual event of the IDSA.

In the last seven years the conference has emerged as a platform for scholars and experts from India and SAARC countries for exchange of views on a variety of issues concerning South Asia.

The previous six conferences have discussed themes such as "Economic Cooperation for Security and Development in South Asia", "Changing Political

*Dr. Arvind Gupta was Director General, IDSA from 2012 to 2014. He is currently Deputy National Security Advisor, Government of India.

Context in India's Neighbourhood and Prospects of Security and Regional Cooperation", "South Asia 2020: Towards Cooperation or Conflict?", "The Common Challenge of Terrorism in South Asia and Prospect of Regional Cooperation", "Cooperative Security Framework for South Asia", and "Prospects for Stability and Growth in South Asia".

Despite the best efforts of the leaders, regional cooperation in South Asia remains at a level much below the desirable. The SAARC was established in 1985 and BIMSTEC in 1997. These are important regional organisations but the progress towards regional cooperation has been slow.

The present situation in the region is not comforting either. Democracy has set in but the democratic institutions remain weak. Terrorism continues to be a serious threat. The aspirations of the youth are growing. This will have serious consequences for stability in our countries. Radicalisation of societies is happening at a disturbing pace. One can count several other disconcerting trends.

There are many reasons why South Asia has been lagging behind in the efforts towards regional cooperation. One of the reasons is the negative perceptions the countries of the region have about each other. Many countries of the region have had a turbulent past. Conflicts and wars have continued to shape negative perceptions about each other. Very often the discourse about India in the neighbouring countries is coloured by its predominant size, colonial legacy, and historical baggage. These factors also come in the way of fostering a positive image about each other.

But, we should not overlook our strengths and positive stories from the region. This will help generate better perceptions about each other.

The region has not remained static. Democracy has taken hold in this part of the world. South Asian countries have also done relatively well economically. Our young people and the new generation are less affected by the negative past. Thanks to the ICT revolution and the onset of social media, we know each other better than before. The Indian economy has grown significantly in size since 1991 and is on course to become a global economy. The countries of the region are beginning to realise the sizable benefits they will acquire if their economies are linked with the Indian economy.

The region has tremendous soft power which can be harnessed for mutual benefit. All our countries have great civilisational past and can boast of cultural richness which is the envy of others. We have young and talented populations.

India is the largest country in the region. This conference will seek to explore various perceptions about India in each of the neighbouring South Asian countries. Which are the key forces that shape or perpetuate the prevailing perceptions? What is the role of the media? Why has the region failed to connect to India with its rising political and economic profile? We will also explore how best India can manage or improve the perceptions among its South Asian neighbours. These and other questions mentioned in the concept note of the conference, will inform the discussions over the next two days.

There are grounds for hope that negative discourse about each other may change. However, our wishing so will not make it happen. We all have to make a positive and sustained effort towards changing the discourse.

This conference is informed by the assumption that perceptions play a significant role in the South Asian politics. Adversarial and negative perceptions come in the way of regional cooperation and integration. Hyperactive 24x7 media plays a role in perpetuating cynicism. A cooperative approach to resolving regional issues remains elusive. But this need not be so. An effort to forge positive perceptions about each other must be made.

I am grateful to the delegates from Afghanistan, Bangladesh, Bhutan, Maldives, Myanmar, Nepal, Pakistan and Sri Lanka for traveling to New Delhi for this conference. I wish you a pleasant stay in India.

Thank you.

Inaugural Address by Hon'ble Defence Minister at the 7th South Asian Conference on "India and South Asia: Exploring Regional Perceptions"

Hon'ble Defence Minister, Shri A. K. Antony*

October 30, 2013

Director General IDSA, Shri Arvind Gupta,
Excellencies,
Distinguished Delegates,
Scholars of IDSA,
Ladies and Gentlemen,

At the outset, I extend a warm welcome to all the delegates and participants representing their nation for the 7th South Asia Conference. IDSA's efforts to bring together delegates from different countries in the South Asian region are commendable. The Conference is an occasion to discuss issues of mutual interest and concern at Track II level. Such initiatives have immense potential to generate ideas and concepts that can create a momentum for regional peace and cooperation.

Despite sharing commonalities of history, geography and culture, the South Asian region has lagged in generating impulses for regional cooperation. In fact, it is one of the least integrated regions of the world. Its share in the world economy is quite small. This often leads to misunderstandings.

---

*Shri A.K. Antony was President of IDSA from 2007 to 2014.

The share of the South Asian region in global trade is only 1.7 per cent. Intra-regional trade accounts for mere 6 per cent of the total trade for the countries of the region. In comparison, intra-regional trade in the case of NAFTA, EU and ASEAN stands at 62, 58 and 26 per cent, respectively. Therefore, it becomes evident that a lot of effort is required to enable regional integration in true sense of the term.

In this context, the theme of this year's conference, "India and South Asia: Exploring Regional Perceptions", is quite meaningful and relevant. As the largest country in the region, India has an important role to play in making regional cooperation possible. It accounts for 80 per cent of the regional GDP and 70 per cent of South Asia's population. The nation's economy has been growing steadily in recent years. India has made conscious efforts to strengthen its relationship with its neighbours. Its bilateral relations with some of the neighbouring countries have also made significant progress.

However, the cumulative effect of all this on regional cooperation is yet to be felt. This requires a careful analysis. The Conference must make an effort to study and analyse regional perceptions about India and its role in South Asia.

In international relations, perceptions often prove to be as important as reality. In regions plagued by conflict and underdevelopment, mistrust has an impact on the behaviour amongst states. In such a scenario, perceptions often get divorced from the reality. Perceptions of countries about each other in the region are not too favourable for regional cooperation. South Asia has been in a state of turmoil for long. Fears, be they real or perceived, can at times, shape policies of state.

India enjoys a unique position in South Asia. As the largest country with a stable democratic system and vast resources, it is often called upon to play a stabilising role in the region. However, India's natural predominance is viewed with concern by some states. Such concerns about Indian intentions are far from real and often misplaced.

Over the years, India has assumed a responsibility to improve its relationship with neighbours. This policy has paid off at bilateral level. India's relationship with some countries has undergone a dramatic transformation. However, its relationship with some other countries continues to be problematic. Nevertheless, India has always remained committed to further and maintain peace and friendly relations with all its neighbours.

India has always tried its best to reach out to all its neighbours and engage them through political, economic, defence and developmental cooperation. India has forged several development-based partnerships across the globe in recent years. Most of India's developmental assistance, which is to the tune of $1 billion per year, is focused on its immediate neighbourhood. India's efforts in the reconstruction of Afghanistan are well known. It is the fifth largest bilateral donor in Afghanistan.

India has also been playing a major role in strengthening regional infrastructure and in supporting efforts aimed at human resource development. India has unilaterally relaxed its visa policies to enable the people of the region to avail of its improved healthcare systems. It offers thousands of scholarships to students from neighbouring countries to receive education in its premier educational institutes.

India continues with its efforts to strive to achieve better economic relationship with all the countries. We expect that an improvement in India's bilateral relationships with the countries of the region will have a beneficial impact on the process of regional integration.

Against this backdrop, perceptions of neighbours about India and the region become quite important. We hope that the perception about India will change gradually, as we make earnest efforts to build trust and mutual confidence. India has to factor in expectations of people from different states, while framing its policy towards the region. In fact, not only India, but all the states of the region will have to deal with mutual perceptions, while conducting their foreign policies towards each other. The issue that we need to focus on is how to make perceptions favourable to bring about a positive change in the region. In this context, think tanks, civil societies, intelligentsia and media have a crucial and a responsible role to play.

As a first step, we should draw inspiration from the common strands of history and culture. At the same time, we must respect cultural differences and emphasise on inter-cultural learning. The soft power that each country has, should be harnessed to bring people together. The entire region has many heritage sites that connect various nations through history. These states are endowed with immense cultural capital. We have to use this capital to build bridges with one another. Recently, India and Bangladesh held joint celebrations of the 150th birth anniversary of Rabindranath Tagore. It reminded the two countries of their common literary traditions. Such efforts should be strengthened and carried forward.

States should evolve policies that will strengthen people-to-people contacts. They should encourage students to travel across borders, and enable contacts among academics, scientists, journalists, sportsmen, businessmen, poets and writers. Public diplomacy has a major role to play in this regard. Institutions like IDSA must strengthen the linkages with their counterparts in the region and develop collaborative research. Only then can nations think of changing negative perceptions about each other.

Your inputs during the conference will be immensely useful. The basic purpose of this conference should be to cull out the views of the scholars and acquaint ourselves with their concerns, hopes and expectations.

I am sure that the deliberations at the conference will throw up useful and practical ideas for action. These could be strung together as policy inputs for governments in the region. This will go a long way in connecting the various tracks of dialogue. Hopefully, they will be of great value for policy makers in various countries of the region.

I wish all the participants at the Conference and the deliberations all success.

Thank You. Jai Hind!

Introduction

Vishal Chandra

India, in view of its geographical expanse, vast population, and massive natural resources, is often seen as overbearing in the region. Its smaller neighbours have responded to the natural asymmetry more or less in similar ways in their bilateral engagements with India. At a more nuanced level, a perceived sense of insecurity vis-à-vis India often gives way to aggressive posturing particularly by countries still grappling with complex issues pertaining to formation of national identity and state consolidation. Unresolved border issues leading to protracted territorial disputes, including concerns over sharing of river waters and maritime resources, coupled with huge imbalances in trade, are often used for cultivating negative stereotypes and unfounded or inflated threat perceptions. Some of these issues have largely shaped the general (mis)perception and the prevalent social and political narratives about India in its immediate neighbourhood.

As the only country having borders with all other South Asian countries, most of whom do not share borders with one another—and the largest one at that in terms of size and population—India has often been the target of persistent criticism despite the fact that it has sought to build a friendly or at least a working relationship with all its neighbours by taking non-reciprocal economic and political initiatives in the last two decades.

Perceptions play a very significant role in the South Asian politics. They have largely shaped and influenced state policies and politics among South Asian countries, especially in relation to India and vice versa, over the years. State policies have at times been hostage to negative or adversarial perceptions, well-entrenched in the popular psyche. As one delves into the complexities involved in the shaping of perceptions among countries in South Asia, one realises that it is an extremely dynamic process that has evolved differently in different countries. Perceptions among states are not static and have often changed with the shift in global as well as regional and domestic politics. There are myriad stakeholders—with their sectional interests and concerns—playing their role explicitly or implicitly in shaping and influencing mutual perceptions among countries in South Asia. Modern communications technology and expanded media networks have often reinforced old perceptions and inhibited the process of regional cooperation and integration.

India, on its part, too faces a complex set of challenges due to the fact that negative perceptions about it are engendered by powerful vested interests in the neighbouring states. Most of its neighbours are also in a state of major social-political ferment and transition, and are up against a wide array of internal challenges. Due to their tense and fragile ties with India, most of them have not been able to participate in, and benefit from, the Indian economy which is growing at a rapid pace.

Regional initiatives and groupings, such as the South Asian Association for Regional Cooperation (SAARC), have had varying success in building an abiding cooperative framework to address issues of common concern to the countries of the region. There can be no doubt that over the centuries the region has acquired an inherently diverse and yet a distinct multi-layered geo-cultural identity. The impact of British colonialism in the evolution of the South Asian region has proved to be enduring and irreversible. The European concepts of political organisation, territoriality and nationality have left an indelible mark on state formation in the post-colonial period.

The emergence of new states in the post-colonial period, with exclusive notions of identity, citizenship and nationality within fixed well-defined borders, and geo-political and economic asymmetry among them, has imparted an altogether new dynamics to the region. In such a setting, perceptions about each other changed as old historical narratives were replaced by exclusive, imagined and sponsored histories, often categorised in terms of 'us' and 'them.' This has also resulted in general apathy and lingering tension among the states despite a shared sense of history and geography amongst the people of the region.

In view of the asymmetry in size and capabilities, India too faces a major policy dilemma when it comes to responding to any crisis in its immediate neighbourhood, lest it stokes 'anti-India' sentiments and further complicates the situation. Interestingly, India, at the same time, is not expected to remain a mute spectator either. The challenges of how India should respond or what should be the nature and level of its intervention, if needed, has often confounded India's policy and decision makers.

Although there are certain realities and factors that are unalterable, such as the shared geography or the fundamentals of geo-economics—irrespective of how national interests are defined or on what terms states or their key institutions interact within the region—a regional approach to addressing regional issues remain elusive. India's thrust on strengthening intra-regional trade through increased connectivity and unilateral concessions, has at best yielded mixed results. South Asia largely remains mired in protracted conflicts and chronic socio-economic challenges, which require each country in the region to constantly evaluate its position and policy in relation to India and vice versa.

On the basis of the findings of the last six annual conferences that the Institute for Defence Studies and Analyses (IDSA) has been organising since 2007, it was felt that a detailed assessment of various perceptions about India that prevails in its immediate neighbourhood is critical for policy makers to devise appropriate measures to enable and strengthen the process of regional cooperation. Thus, the 7th Annual South Asia Conference was organised with the objective of identifying the various strands of political and economic perceptions about India prevalent among its South Asian neighbours, and vice versa, as well as to find the way forward.

The two-day conference sought to examine and address the following set of queries and issues:

(i) What are the various perceptions about India in each of the neighbouring South Asian countries? How do other countries in the region look at India's economic power? Is India perceived as a reluctant or an unreliable partner in the development of the region? Has India failed to relate and connect to its immediate neighbourhood?

(ii) Which are the key institutions and forces shaping perceptions about India in the neighbouring countries? What has been the role of media in shaping or perpetuating the prevalent perceptions? How perceptions have defined or transformed the inter-state relations in South Asia?

(iii) What are the Indian perceptions of its 'neighbourhood' and its approaches to the individual countries in South Asia? Has the region failed to connect to India, and to identify with its rising political and economic profile?

(iv) How best India can manage or improve its perceptions among its South Asian neighbours? What role India should play to make regional cooperation a success? What should be India's long-term approach in this regard?

This edited volume is an outcome of the two-day deliberations among participants from all the South Asia countries—Afghanistan, Pakistan, Nepal, Sri Lanka, Bhutan, Maldives, Bangladesh and India—and, also Myanmar. In order to present the study in a simple, lucid and reader-friendly manner, the book comprising sixteen chapters is divided into three parts corresponding to the sub-themes of the conference.

The book ends with a separate section on 'The Way Forward: Key Recommendations', which brings forth some of the key suggestions and recommendations that emerged from the roundtable discussion that took place at the end of the conference.

The chapters in the first part of the book try to identity key drivers, institutions and stakeholders and their role in shaping of perceptions among states in South Asia. The second part explores how mutual perceptions have influenced the inter-state relations in South Asia. Chapters in the third and final part of the book examine various perceptions about regional cooperation among the South Asian states, including the growing Chinese thrust in the region.

Pratyoush Onta in his paper, "Does Academia Matter to the Shaping of Mutual Perceptions in South Asia?," deals with fundamental issues pertaining to the state of South Asian Studies in the countries of the region including the state of academic research in India and Nepal. He argues that ideally, academia should matter to the shaping of informed mutual perceptions among the countries in South Asia, but that is not the case presently. According to Onta, being surrounded by India on three sides, it is imperative for Nepal to closely study India. However, due to lack of adequate infrastructure and environment, and the poor state of social science research in academic institutions, the India Studies in Nepal has not flourished. There have been no serious efforts in Nepal at the government level to establish research centres which could study various aspects of the Indian society.

On the other side, Nepal Studies in India too has suffered in terms of quality in recent years due to financial mismanagement and various institutional constraints. In fact, the funding for area studies in general is shrinking in India. Even the academic exchange programmes conducted under the SAARC framework have failed to generate quality scholarship. In this regard, Onta suggests that a long-term solution would require investments in both institutions – universities and research centres – and academics in each of the countries of South Asia. He further urges that governments, regional organisations and international agencies must support long-term research initiatives which could lead to better knowledge exchange and cooperation within the region. Without this, academia cannot either be strengthened or expected to play a key role in influencing perceptions and ideas about each other.

Yaqoob Khan Bangash's paper, titled, "'Not India': Pakistan, India and the Self" captures the historical processes of perception formation about India in Pakistan, as part of its continuing quest for an identity distinct from India. He argues that Pakistan's identity as 'Not India' has been a defining feature of its identity and which still shapes its outlook towards India. He states that Pakistan's definition of itself as the 'Muslim' country, and India as the 'Hindu' country, resulted in Pakistani textbooks treating Indians and Hindus as synonyms. The perpetual enmity between Hindus and Muslims was emphasised and perpetuated through textbooks to illustrate the historic need for Pakistan. The paper also reflects on the role of media in constantly reinforcing the anti-India perception. Bangash further argues that what Pakistan thinks of India is critically tied to what it thinks of itself and what is happening in the country. The perception that India has still not come to terms with the partition is still quite widespread in Pakistan.

Referring to possible decline in the level of animosity towards India, the paper states that the people of Pakistan think more in terms of moving on rather than remaining confined to historical issues. Bangash asserted that interest in Kashmir issue too is on the wane among people in general. A section of media in Pakistan has diversified and organisations such as the *Jang* Group and its media channel, the *Geo TV*, have shown commitment to building peace and trust between the people of the two countries. However, there are still strong anti-India constituencies within Pakistan which remain severely opposed to such peace initiatives.

As a way forward, Bangash suggests that India should help in promoting stability in Pakistan. India must also assure Pakistan that it does not have any intention of undoing the partition. Only a stable, secure and a confident Pakistan would be able to engage with India without the baggage of the past. On the other hand, Pakistan needs to take a more nuanced view of India. Bangash further suggested that Pakistan's textbooks should be more inclusive in terms of teaching the rich non-Muslim heritage of the Subcontinent. The textbooks must also restart teaching the history of ancient as well as post-independence modern India.

Humayun Kabir's paper, titled, "Changing Relations between Bangladesh and India: Perceptions in Bangladesh," dwells on the perception parameters between India and Bangladesh which, in his opinion, are defined by geography, processes of identity formation, asymmetric power setting, policy initiatives and rising economic profile of India. He explains how the interplay of these complex factors has had significant consequences for the bilateral relationship and formation of perceptions in Bangladesh. He argues that in order to further enhance the relationship both countries needed to be creative and adopt innovative measures to bring about greater cooperation between the two neighbours. There is an increasing realisation within Bangladesh that India is focussing more on pursuing its traditional realist agenda than forging a stronger partnership with Bangladesh for harnessing new opportunities.

Dayan Jayatilleka in his paper, "The Geo-strategic Matrix and Existential Dimension of Sri Lanka's Conflict, Post War Crisis and External Relations," takes a Southern or Southernist perspective which is, in his opinion, quite distinctive. He argues that the third-worldist perspective, later known as the perspective of the global south, or a southern perspective, is quite specific in terms of the narrative and the causal relationship, and things look differently when viewed from the south. He shared his perspectives on Sri Lanka as India's southern periphery and Tamil Nadu as its inner periphery, and the relationship between the two peripheries and the political dynamics involved therein. The intrusive role of a sub-state unit raises concerns whether India's policy-making is constrained by the stridency shown by Tamil Nadu politicians. In Sri Lanka, it is usually felt that Tamil Nadu factor is overrated in Indian policy circles.

Jayatilleka further argues that Sri Lanka's relationship with India is a vital constituent of its management of the internal ethnic relationships, just as its relationship with its own Tamil minority is intrinsic to the management of the larger and essential relationship with India. In his opinion, there is an existential imperative of dual co-existence: Sri Lanka's co-existence with India and Sinhala co-existence with the Tamils.

Partha S. Ghosh in his paper, "Perceptions and Memories: Making Sense of Bangladesh's India Outlook", contests the argument that the Bangladeshi society is divided between the 'Bengali nationalists' and the 'Bangladeshi nationalists'. In his opinion, the above argument is not completely valid as there is an overlap between the two. According to Ghosh, the history of the Indian Subcontinent in the last 150 years has witnessed three social trends vying for pre-eminence in the South Asian politics—Hindu nationalism, Muslim nationalism and the composite Hindu-Muslim nationalism. The paper tries to understand the respective influences of these trends on Bangladesh politics vis-à-vis India and West Bengal in the context of three events: partition of Bengal in 1905, partition of India in 1947, and the creation of Bangladesh in 1971.

According to Ghosh, from the perspective of memory-policy interface, Bangladesh faces two challenges—how to work out its Pakistan outlook, on the one hand, and how to define its India outlook, on the other. Ghosh asserts that as long as Bangladesh's Pakistan outlook remains blurred, its India outlook cannot be any clearer. In fact, memories of 1947 and 1971 would keep haunting all the three countries and in three different ways. In South Asia, the debate over partition has not ended and all the states are passing through a complex process of state formation. Ghosh concludes that perceptions and memories of Bangladesh about India are contradictory. Bangladesh largely suffers from its collective memory of the past. Most Indians have no clue about the realities of Bangladesh, which is, in his opinion, simply a potential den of future Taliban. Bangladesh too remains largely ignorant about society and politics in India. Both the countries certainly need to know much more about each other.

The next paper, "Changing Dynamics in Nepal-India Relations", by Dinesh Bhattarai notes that probably no two neighbouring countries in the world share so many similarities and interact so comprehensively on a daily basis, both at the government and people's level, than Nepal and India. However, despite having historically deep-rooted, interdependent and multi-faceted bilateral relations, the two countries have recurring irritants, constraints and complexities born out of misperceptions and conflicting narratives of the emerging dynamics. The gap between fact and fiction has blurred the necessary debate on core issues in Nepal-India relations, and has added new complexities to it.

Referring to the global power shift towards the Asia-Pacific region due to phenomenal economic growth of both China and India, and the US' Asia 'pivot' strategy, the paper intends to look at how the emerging dynamics are shaping Nepal-India relations. Bhattarai notes that the simultaneous rise of both China and India, which together have 40 per cent of the world's population, has shifted the gravity of geo-politics and geo-economics to the region. Nepal, in his opinion, needs to work wisely amidst its interminable political transition, to benefit from its proximities to these economic powerhouses. Bhattarai argues that increased global attention to the region also presents Nepal with several challenges. For instance, Nepal's proximity and affinity to Tibet has made it a meeting point of overlapping and intersecting interests of various kinds including that of the European Union and the US.

While arguing that it is a geographical reality that Nepal shares border with both India and China, the two fastest growing economies in the world, he points out that Nepal, which is making a democratic transition, remains one of the poorest countries of the world. Though the living standards of the people around the country are rising, Nepal has been left untouched by this economic development as remittances still constitute about 25 per cent of its GDP. Talking of perception and reality, he referred to the growing gap in Nepal-India relations. As a result, Nepal sees India's hand in all its problems. He also questions the conduct of a section of the Nepali leadership particularly from the leftist parties who often equate nationalism to anti-Indianism and thrive on blind jingoism when out of power. He concluded by highlighting the need for increased people-to-people contact to dispel misunderstandings about each other. He suggested that socio-economic transformation in Nepal should be expedited within the democratic framework. Leaders of both India and Nepal should talk frankly and address issues of mutual concern. Also, Nepali leaders should be sensitive to India's legitimate concerns.

M. Ashique Rahman in his paper, "Rising India and Bangladesh-India Relations: Mutual Perceptions and Expectations", argues that relationship with India constitutes the most important cornerstone of Bangladesh's foreign policy.

After giving a brief overview of Bangladesh-India relations since 1971, the paper examines the processes of perception formation in Bangladesh vis-à-vis India. Rahman refers to the widening expectation-achievement gap particularly in the context of India's rising economic and political profile. In his opinion, India's emergence as a major global power has imparted a new dimension to the expectations and desires of its smaller neighbours which expect India to follow a friendlier neighbourhood policy while making utmost efforts to resolve all outstanding bilateral issues with them. However, the experience of last few years show, in spite of improving bilateral relations, India could not deliver on some of the issues or could not provide concessions in some areas that affect people's perceptions about India, often contributing to the persistence of negative perceptions among its smaller neighbours. Negative perceptions in turn help reinforce anti-India sentiments, further constraining efforts to improve bilateral relations including between India and Bangladesh.

He further states that media plays a very significant role in shaping public perception and talks about the role of Indian media and civil society in perception-formation. Rahman asserts that resolving outstanding bilateral issues is the foremost way of addressing the adverse perceptions persistent in both the countries. India seems to lack a proper awareness of the politics and processes of perception formation in Bangladesh. Also, India often appears convinced that economics would remove the negative perceptions and take the Bangladesh-India relations forward on a sustainable basis, but such a perception fails to factor in the political divisiveness in Bangladesh. Rahman argues that political opposition as a major actor and institution in the processes of perception formation has to be recognised and incorporating them in the policy making process could help the incumbent government in advancing Bangladesh-India relations.

Davood Moradian in his paper, "Indo-Afghan Relationship: Afghan Expectations and Indian Reluctance", states that while Afghan-India relations have all elements of a truly historical and strategic partnership, both the countries have failed to fully utilise their identical security and economic interests to their mutual advantage. He blames Delhi's cautious geo-strategic mindset and its entrenched bureaucracy for a significant gap between the reality and the potential of Afghanistan-India partnership, followed by West's Pakistan-centric understanding of the region and Kabul's transitioning political and institutional landscape. However, India, being a growing economy, is perceived to be in a much better position to help Afghanistan in reviving its war-shattered economy as the Western forces withdraw.

While referring to the signing of Strategic Partnership Agreement between the two countries in 2011, the paper suggests that Afghanistan chose India as a strategic partner for three reasons: firstly, due to shared values, as both are pluralistic and multi-cultural societies; secondly, convergence of security interests since both India and Afghanistan face similar threat from terrorism, and, finally, due to complementary economic interests. Moradian argues that India has been keen to be seen as a development partner and not as a strategic partner, even though the two countries have signed a Strategic Partnership Agreement. According to him, India does not seem to be too much interested in security cooperation which is the basis of any strategic relationship. He further states that India's reluctance to engage Afghanistan on security issues show that India does not have an independent foreign policy.

Moradian gives five reasons for India's reluctance to engage Afghanistan– Gandhian legacy of non-violence, transition to a rising power, lack of confidence about its own capacities, resource constraint, and institutional inefficiency of the Indian bureaucracy. He concludes by suggesting that India's policy should be more dynamic and adaptable. There is need for India and Afghanistan to build greater trust in each other. Moradian also referred to the socialisation gap between the people of the two countries. He emphasised that India can help transform Afghanistan into a moderate, stable and a developing country.

The paper by Mohamed Naahee Naseem, "Shift in Maldivian Perception Towards India During the 2012 Political Crisis", explains how the Maldivian political crisis following the unprecedented transfer of power in February 2012 impacted the Maldivian perception of India. According to Naseem, India has undoubtedly emerged as a strong regional partner in the development of the Maldives in the last few decades. The paper discusses the 2012 political crisis following the fall of the Nasheed Government and how allegations of Indian involvement in the domestic politics of the country came up. While acknowledging the significance of India for the Maldives, he points out that the Maldives has benefited from the Gujral Doctrine. However, Naseem asserts, it does not exempt Maldives from its obligation towards protecting Indian investments and Indian people working and residing in the country. The paper concludes by suggesting that since media has a critical role to play in shaping up perceptions, a stronger coordination by the Indian High Commission with the Maldivian media would be extremely helpful. It would go a long way in dispelling misperceptions or negative perceptions about India.

Denzil Abel in his paper, "Myanmar's Perception of India", points out that presently Myanmar does not see itself as a South Asian country and feels more like an observer in South Asia's intra-regional interaction. Myanmar and its people are currently more oriented towards Southeast Asia. This is despite the fact that Myanmar and India have had deep historical and cultural linkages since times immemorial. The age-old religious and cultural linkages with India are very much embedded in Myanmar's consciousness and identity.

The paper also provides an overview of how Myanmar's perception of India has evolved from the British colonial era to the present times. The several ups and downs in bilateral relations including various developments that often created negative perceptions about India have been discussed in the paper. Abel points out that the luminaries of India's freedom struggle were held in high esteem in Myanmar. He particularly refers to the 'golden age' of India-Myanmar relations when immediately after independence the two countries enjoyed a high level of political understanding and commonality of interests. The relationship thereafter has been one of neglect on both sides due to fundamental differences on several issues. Abel notes that meanwhile China's influence surged dramatically within Myanmar.

However, the India-Myanmar relations gradually began to gain momentum after India came up with its Look East Policy in 1992. The military regime in Myanmar too saw an opportunity to rebuild bilateral ties while simultaneously redressing the imbalance that had crept in due to China's growing influence in the region. Abel notes that the visit of President U. Thein Sein to India in October 2011 and the then Indian Prime Minister Manmohan Singh to Myanmar in May 2012, has laid the foundation for a much closer and realistic relationship between the two countries.

As for the bilateral trade, the paper points out that India is seen as a less attractive market by Myanmar's business community in view of poor connectivity and lack of infrastructure, compared to markets in China, Southeast Asia, Japan and Korea. Similarly, the defence cooperation between the two countries is much less compared to what Myanmar has with China. China has also stepped up its cultural diplomacy, while India with its far deeper historical and cultural linkages with the people of Myanmar remains reticent. The paper concludes with the observation that the democratic transition currently underway in Myanmar provides a huge opportunity for the two countries to make a new beginning. Both Myanmar and India share similar perceptions on the need for greater regional or sub-regional cooperation as well.

The next paper, titled, "Bhutan and Its International Collaborations-2013" by Pema Tenzin and Chhimi Dorji provides an extensive introduction to Bhutan and highlights India's role and contribution in harnessing and realising the country's energy potential. India is largely seen as a development partner, and, particularly in view of the country's landlocked feature, is regarded as critical to capacity building and sustaining the economic development of the country. Indian aid comprises almost 70 per cent of the total foreign aid that the country receives each year. India also remains the largest trading partner of Bhutan.

Nagesh Kumar's paper, "South Asian Economic Integration: Potential, Challenges and the Way Forward", argues that regionalism is a rising trend in international politics but South Asia has been slow in exploiting the potential of regional economic integration. South Asia economies have largely been relying on rising demand for its products in the advanced economies to support its growth over the past two decades. However, the region faces a dramatically altered economic context in the aftermath of the global financial crisis of 2008-09 and there is a need to look for alternative engines of growth.

The paper summarises major initiatives for regional economic integration undertaken in South Asia, their limitations and challenges. It also puts forth some proposals on how to exploit the potential of regional economic integration in a mutually beneficial, inclusive, balanced and sustainable manner. According to Kumar, regional economic integrations have proved successful as smaller and poorer economies too have benefited from integrations and thereby received aid and expertise for development. He further argued that regionalism is said to be effective in tackling several vulnerabilities and risks especially when it comes to various non-traditional security threats arising in the region. An integrated South Asia will be able to play its due role in the broader Asia and the Pacific markets. The paper also discusses in detail the various factors leading to low level intra-regional trade in South Asia and suggests measures to harness the potential of regional economic integration in South Asia. The South Asian states are emerging as dynamic players in the world economy as the total trade is expected to triple from $1 trillion currently to $3 trillion by 2017.

According to Kumar, the bulk of intraregional trade potential remains unexploited in SAARC and needs to be explored further. Smaller and poorer economies will benefit from liberalisation of trade under SAFTA. India-Sri Lanka FTA, for instance, has helped in balanced expansion of bilateral trade. Recent developments in the trade related to service sector have been helpful. Development of trade corridors and hubs helps in infrastructure development of the region and also that of nearby zones and should be given prime consideration. Regionalism assumes criticality in external context and there is a need to expedite the implementation of regional trade agreements. Gap in the development of infrastructure needs to be closed in the South Asia states and there is an urgent need to promote cross border movements of goods and travel within the region.

Kumar is of the opinion that obstacles facing increased subregional cooperation are not economic, but rather are political in nature. Overcoming these political barriers are of increasing relevance and importance, given the geopolitical situation prevailing in the subregion and faltering demand in the subregion's principal trading partners in the developed world. Perhaps, new opportunities have opened up for the South Asian region. The paper concludes arguing in favour of letting economics and regional cooperation to finally take the centre stage in South Asia.

Gabriel Ian Lynn Ockersz in his paper, "Stepped-Up Inter-State Dialogue as a Key to Improving SAARC Development", argues that perceptions could prove to be of vital importance, perhaps more decisive in their impact than reality, when it comes to inter-state ties in South Asia. Referring to the India-Sri Lanka ties, he stated that often India is viewed through lenses which are centuries-old. He asserts that what is true of Indo-Lanka ties is also true of India's relations with many of its neighbours in the post-independence times. Divisive issues between India and some of its neighbours have restrained SAARC from evolving into a successful exercise in regional cooperation. SAARC currently is functional only to the level to which its member states deem it to be.

Ockersz emphasises the need for change of mindset through a process of informed public education to overcome historical prejudices and misperceptions prevalent in the region. He also stresses on the value of confidence building measures and sustained but constructive dialogue among the South Asian states. Increased democratisation in South Asia too has opened up opportunities for countries to give a new direction to their troubled bilateral ties. At the broader level, SAARC also need to put to good use the relatively widespread spirit of democracy in the region. He also urges the SAARC to take on itself a humanising and civilising mission in the region.

The paper proposes the need to evolve 'development conversation' in each of the South Asian states to highlight the value of good neighbourliness, with material benefits that could be reaped from it clearly underscored for the purpose of winning public support. While emphasising the need for both India and its neighbours to recognise each other's sensitivities and core concerns, the paper argues that SAARC must facilitate constructive inter-state dialogue which should be held in a spirit of openness and in informal settings. Ockersz further stated that India's neighbours need to have a more constructive approach towards India if the emerging economic strengths of this region are to be tapped in an equitable manner.

S.D. Muni in his paper, titled, "China and South Asian Cooperation Under SAARC", focuses on China's role in the South Asian regional cooperation and how it is being perceived within South Asia. The paper identifies three specific reasons for China's growing engagement and interest in the South Asia region: China's sense of vulnerability in relation to the security in its western periphery, comprising Tibet and Xinjiang, which borders Nepal and Pakistan, respectively; search for opportunities of investments and access to new markets and natural resources; and, multiple strategic objectives ranging from keeping India boxed within South Asia to securing transit and access points in the Indian Ocean/Bay of Bengal region. In relation to the last point, the paper makes reference to China's investments in developing ports like Humbantota in Sri Lanka, Chittagong in

Bangladesh, Gwadar in Pakistan, Kyaukpyu in Myanmar and building economic/ transit corridors in Pakistan and Myanmar. The new Maritime Silk Road and Silk Road Economic Belt proposed by China could also be added to it.

The paper states that some of the South Asian countries, particularly Pakistan and Nepal, have long supported the idea of China playing a role in the region, much before the SAARC was established in 1985. They not only looked at China as a potential counterweight to India in South Asia, but also as a potential development partner in view of its growing economic strength. China along with several other countries was granted an Observer status in SAARC in 2005. The paper brings out the reasons for India's resistance to China's full entry into the SAARC. The paper notes that that since 2005 China has taken several initiatives to improve its credentials for closer engagement with the SAARC.

Meanwhile, as stated in the paper, India's resistance too seems to have diluted. Today, China and India are observers in the SAARC and the SCO, respectively; and this reflects the changing perception of India and China towards each other regarding their role in regional forums. In fact, India has actively taken advantage of China's economic growth as the trade between the two states have flourished. The paper also notes that India and China have agreed to work together to develop the BCIM Economic Corridor. Another reason behind the Indian shift is also the initiative to develop India's Northeast region and link it with the Look East Policy.

The paper asserts that China cannot be simply wished away, particularly its growing economic and strategic interest in the South Asia region. India is learning slowly and hesitatingly to cope with the growing Chinese presence in the region. China's full membership of SAARC would raise several complex issues, which might further divide the regional grouping from within. The paper suggests that the South Asian countries, most of which are in a state of democratic transition, should seriously think through as far as China's growing interest in SAARC is concerned. China is not known to have sympathy either for democracy or for developmental politics. In fact, China is characterised by its preference for strong, assertive, centralised regimes on its periphery.

Indra Nath Mukherji in his paper, titled, "India's Trade with Neighbours: Perceptions and Reality—With Special Reference to India-Pakistan Trade", brings out the role of perceptions in defining Pakistan's trade relations with India. While some of these perceptions cut across other neighbouring countries of India as well, the focus of his paper is primarily on Pakistan. The paper also brings out the background to regional trade liberalisation, particularly the deliberations at the official level meetings under the previous Pakistan People's Party (PPP) Government in Pakistan and the United Progressive Alliance (UPA) Government in India. Mukherji states that a rethink is on among a section of Pakistani stakeholders, strongly asserting that unless a level playing ground is provided by India, the grant of Non-Discriminatory Market Access (NDMA) to India should be kept in abeyance. The paper further discusses reasons for Pakistan's inability to confer the Most Favoured Nation (MFN) status on India.

Mukherji is of the opinion that growing trade imbalance has been one of the major issues in India's trade relations with its neighbours. He also explains why China is making deeper penetration in Pakistan's market, even though Pakistan's trade deficit with China is four times more than that with India. Pakistan's free trade agreement with China offers preferential access to China in those very products which it has restricted to India. While India is prohibited from entering into Pakistan's industrial market, China has been granted duty-free access. The paper concludes by stating that all bilateral perceptions, including those on trade, are ultimately shaped by the overall relations between the concerned countries.

Shahmahmood Miakhel in his paper, titled, "Seizing New Opportunity for Regional Cooperation and Understanding", deals with the issue of myth and (mis)perception as a factor in inter-state relations in the region. Miakhel states that politicians in South Asia have often turned to exploiting historical myths and misperceptions prevalent within the region to either strengthen their position in the domestic politics or to divert the attention of the people from poor governance. While this may be an effective populist tool, it has historically led to fractured regional politics. He further states that these myths have not only become a part of the popular narrative, but have also significantly influenced policy formulation in the region, albeit negatively. It has had an adverse impact on security, economic growth, governance and regional cooperation in the region. He stresses on the need for change in political mindset within the region. The political leadership and elites should move away from the rhetoric of the Cold War or the old Great Game, and look towards developing a new political culture based on the challenges and aspirations of the 21st century.

Miakhel argues that the key to improving inter-state relations in South Asia lie in improving governance in each of the countries, and in enhancing the role of a new generation of leaders who have the energy and vision to look at the region from a fresh perspective. He also emphasises the need for sustained dialogue among the rival countries to address some of the key contentious issues affecting peace and stability in the region. Failure to do so would only reinforce negative perceptions in the region and people would continue to view each other through the prism of historical mistrust and suspicion.

This volume thus raises several issues of concern as far as managing diverse, and often negative, perceptions prevalent among the South Asian countries, particularly in relation to India, are concerned. Several practical suggestions and way forwards relevant to both policy makers and practitioners have been made.

It was often felt that much depends on the overall political intent of various actors and forces shaping the perception including the media, their relation to the state and, more importantly, the orientation of the state elites and structures in respective countries. Nevertheless, a strong urge could be noted within the region, rather a reasonable amount of consensus, on the need to change and resolve negative perceptions. This in itself could be regarded as a positive perception and enough reason to further encourage dialogue among the countries of the region at various levels and in different settings. The urgent need to engage youth and familiarise them with the region, its shared history and culture, has been reiterated time and again by several contributors. Various ideas, ranging from a more inclusive history textbooks to provincialising people-to-people contacts, were put forth to negate and reverse the negative perceptions entrenched in the region in a more effective manner. The value of adopting a regional approach to meeting common challenges too was reiterated by various contributors in their analysis.

Interestingly, several of the contributors to this volume have argued that since India is the pivot of the South Asia region, it is important for the neighbouring countries to factor in India's security needs and concerns in their respective foreign and security policies. India's rise is largely perceived by its neighbours as peaceful and beneficial for the region. However, it has heightened the aspirations and expectations of its neighbours, opening up a new set of opportunities for India to redefine its approach towards its neighbourhood. Some of the contributors saw great merit in India's growing soft power, which in their opinion could be ably used to counter and dispel misperceptions about India among its neighbours in the long run.

China is clearly very much a part of the broader political and development discourse in the region. In all likelihood, its interest and engagement within the region is set to diversify and grow. India will have to find ways to adapt, compete as well as partner with China in the coming years. There is a general perception that India is a reluctant power, and that it must shed its inhibitions and assume a leadership role in the region to enable a genuine process of change in favour of greater regional cooperation and sustained goodwill.

PART I

Shaping of Perceptions in South Asia

1

Does Academia Matter to the Shaping of Mutual Perceptions in South Asia?

Pratyoush Onta

Introduction

Does academia matter to the shaping of mutual perceptions in South Asia? The brief answer to this question is: Academia should matter to the shaping of mutual perceptions in South Asia, but in its current avatar, South Asian academia contributes very little to the shaping of informed mutual perceptions among the countries in the region because of its poor quality. If this conclusion appears a bit too harsh, consider the following thought exercise. Think of any academic from your country of origin who you think is, say, an India (or any other South Asian country) expert in the sense that he/she is a researcher who specialises in any aspect of the Indian (or the respective country's) polity or society. For example, I could not think of any such academic expert based in my home country, Nepal. I would be rather surprised if your answer is any different than mine.

If you do not like the above-mentioned version of the thought exercise, you can ask a slightly different question. For instance, ask yourself if you know an Indian sociologist, anthropologist, historian or political scientist who has spent an academic year in Nepal, Bangladesh, Pakistan, Sri Lanka or Bhutan actively researching—and not just occupying some visiting professorial chair lecturing on the topic of her/his expertise—some aspect of the respective country. Again, for instance, I do not know any Indian post-Ph.D academic researcher from the above-mentioned disciplines who has spent an academic year researching any subject in Nepal during the past 15 years. These thought exercises can be discussed further, but the basic point is that there is a serious lack of such social scientists in the South Asian countries who have researched extensively on various aspects of the other countries in the region. If this inference is correct, we need to reflect on it collectively and take steps within our possibilities to redress it.

I cannot claim expertise on the state of South Asian Studies in all the countries of South Asia. However, I have, in the past, researched and written about the state of mutual area studies in two of the countries of the region, Nepal and India. That research was completed in the year 2000, and two versions of the main write-up based on that work were published in the following two years (2001 and 2002).[1] My research might be a bit dated, but as someone who is interested in the various dimensions of the politics of knowledge generation in and about Nepal,[2] I have, from time to time, looked for evidence and writings that would challenge the conclusions I had reached more than a decade ago. Unfortunately, I have not come across any such evidence or writings. To the contrary, recently published analyses have reconfirmed my findings through variously different analytical[3] and area studies[4] focus.

By reiterating the case of how India is not researched in Nepal and how Nepal is studied in India, this paper argues that the state of South Asian Studies in each of the countries of the region leaves a lot to be desired. It further examines the historical causes and factors that explain the poor state of mutual academic research in countries of the region, and in the process infers that this status quo will have to be greatly improved upon if academia is to matter to the shaping of mutual perceptions in South Asia. Finally, the paper ends by suggesting a few things that could be done to move forward in that direction.

Studying India in Nepal

As a landlocked country that shares borders with India in three directions, Nepal has various imperatives to closely study India, whereas India can "afford" ignorance about Nepal. Logically, this would suggest that the political and academic leadership in Nepal would have identified Indian Studies as a high priority item within academia and that considerably more scholarship on India from Nepal would exist than vice versa. But this is hardly the case. The reasons for this state of affairs would have to be sought in the inadequate academic infrastructure and environment prevalent in the universities in Nepal and the weak state of social science practice in Nepali independent research centres.[5]

Despite platitudes on the sacrosanct nature of India-Nepal relations from 'time immemorial' that have been a fixture of Nepali political rhetoric, I know of no serious Nepali governmental effort to establish, within its own agencies, a research cell of scholars doing work on various aspects of the Indian society. While some desk officers working for the Foreign Ministry of the Nepali Government pay particular attention to a specific country in the region, their expertise is seldom academically grounded. Some such bureaucrats have amassed useful diplomatic experiences through their postings in the neighbouring countries, but they have, with an exception or two, seldom ploughed those experiences for academic and pedagogical purposes.

Tribhuvan University (established in 1959) is the only university in Nepal with social science research programmes that have had something to do with the rest of the region. Within this university, courses in Indian history have been taught at the postgraduate level, and researches on Indian Studies have been conducted at the Centre for Nepal and Asian Studies. This Centre was started on July 16, 1972 as the Institute of Nepal and Asian Studies. In the beginning, the Institute had four faculty members, and it could grant MA and Ph.D degrees by dissertation. Despite its name, due to lack of resources and trained personnel, it initially gave priority to only Nepal Studies in anthropology, sociology, history and linguistics. By the end of the decade, however, the Institute had been downgraded to the Centre for Nepal and Asian Studies (CNAS), and it no longer could grant MA and Ph.D degrees by dissertation. Moreover, it was not until the mid-1980s that it actually began work on Asian Studies under the directorship of late Khadga Bikram Shah, a brother-in-law of the then all-powerful King Birendra. Shah had assembled a remarkable group of Nepali political scientists in CNAS by 1984-85.[6] This effort resulted in several symposia and three major publications: the *Strategic Studies Series* (started in 1984), the *CNAS Year Review* (1986) and the *CNAS Forum Current Issue Series* (1987).

Shah asked Nepali political scientists to focus part of their attention to studying other countries in South Asia, and China and Japan. He started regular interactions amongst these researchers, and several of them began to analyse regional politics, South Asian cooperation, Cold War themes and related issues in seminars and publications. CNAS scholars not only began carrying out country-wise studies but also participated in the academic exercises related to the founding of the official South Asian Association for Regional Cooperation (SAARC). In this connection, a special issue of the *Strategic Studies Series* was published in Spring 1985, and subsequent issues of this journal contained other articles highlighting various perspectives on regional cooperation. In addition, CNAS launched a SAARC documentation series which included an index of relevant articles and books, addresses and statements and chronology of SAARC meetings.[7]

The *CNAS Year Review* contained survey articles similar to those found in the annual country-wise survey edition of the American journal, *Asian Survey*. Starting from 1986, various scholars wrote chapters on the SAARC countries and two or three additional countries outside of the region. India was covered by the political scientist Govinda Malla,[8] whose annual review articles on Indian domestic politics, economy, foreign relations and defence unfortunately were not the kind that could be called informed *academic* analyses. Based largely on Indian newspapers and magazine reports, these reports did not engage with scholarship from India and elsewhere. They were superficial surveys written in a mode devoid of any serious disciplinary perspective. In the three volumes published in this series, Pramod Kantha wrote on Pakistan, Dev Raj Dahal on Bangladesh, Gehendra Lal Malla on Sri Lanka, Pancha N. Maharjan on Maldives and Bharat Sharma and Krishna Hachhethu on Bhutan.

In addition, *CNAS Forum Current Issue Series* carried seminar papers on the 1987 Indian intervention in Sri Lanka, Nepali emigrants in India, Indian workers in Nepal, India-China relations, Nepal-India Relations and related subjects. A major seminar on regional security in South Asia was organised by CNAS in November 1985, and its proceedings were published in a book form.[9] Other publications, both in monograph form and articles were brought out on India, other countries of the South Asian region and on China.

Shah stayed on the job after his first term ended in 1987, but seemed to have lost some of his enthusiasm during his incomplete second term. However, as the Indo-Nepal trade and transit impasse escalated in 1989, he tried to re-invigorate the group of political scientists at CNAS and urged them to write about the subject.[10] But differences between him and some scholars as well as between scholars who took up ultra-nationalist positions and those who were seen to be 'soft' on India grew large. When some articles by Nepali scholars did appear in international publications, Shah again had to face the wrath of the conservatives in the then all-powerful Royal Palace in Nepal for whom the democratic aspirations expressed in those same articles were not palatable. He called an impromptu meeting and returned several of the political scientists he had brought to CNAS to their respective home institutions.[11] With Shah's own subsequent departure from CNAS, the *CNAS Year Review* and *CNAS Forum Current Issue Series* ceased publication. The *Strategic Studies Series* had been stopped in 1987 itself. It is interesting to note that among the political scientists he had cultivated in CNAS, even those who had not been summarily returned in 1989 had mostly left the institution by the mid-1990s. The beginning that had been made on Indian Studies at CNAS could not be sustained.

While Shah was responsible for taking a number of initiatives with respect to South Asian Studies at CNAS, he failed to invest on building the institutional infrastructure that would support these initiatives in CNAS when he was gone. In addition, whatever little South Asian Studies were made possible through his leadership, its overwhelming political science orientation was both its strength and weakness. Scholars from other disciplines were really not central to this CNAS initiative. During the decade after the end of the Panchayat System in 1990, apart from Dhruba Kumar's work on South Asia after the 1998 nuclear explosions by India and Pakistan[12] and on Indo-Nepal relations after the hijacking of an Indian Airlines plane that was on a routine flight out of Kathmandu in December 1999,[13] one can hardly recall any other publications from CNAS on the subject of Indian or South Asian Studies. Today, CNAS has no institutional commitment to studies of the other countries in the South Asian region. Elsewhere at Tribhuvan University, studies on the region have been limited to isolated scholarly efforts by researchers in one or two other departments. In addition to the traditional theme of Indo-Nepal relations,[14] trans-border migration[15] and new dimensions and challenges of regional cooperation[16] have been some of the other subjects in which Nepali scholars have worked in the past two decades.

There are some social science research activities in Nepal outside of Tribhuvan University executed by academic NGOs,[17] but they cannot be described as thriving when it comes to Indian Studies. There is no institutional commitment to studying India in independent Nepali research entities because structurally and resource-wise (both human and financial) they are relatively weak institutions. Whatever research comes out of these organisations is geared mostly toward 'developing' Nepal. This is so partly because unlike the institutions supported by the Indian Council for Social Science Research (ICSSR), there is no state-support extended to autonomous research institutions in Nepal. Hence, they have to rely on doing either contract research (aka consultancies) for foreign donor agencies or the Nepal Government, or research with policy links also supported by the same agencies. However, there are some exceptions. With respect to studies on themes related to Nepal's hydropower possibilities, some independent scholars have highlighted Indian interests in specific hydropower development trajectories in Nepal[18] and studied the institutional forces behind water conflict in the north Indian state of Bihar.[19]

Overall, inadequate research infrastructure nationwide, feeble attempts to establish Indian Studies within Tribhuvan University as discussed above, and the inability of financially weak independent research institutions to carry out robust academic studies on India, account for the current absence of Indian Studies in Nepal.

Studying Nepal in India

Nepal Studies in post-Independence India started in the late 1950s after the establishment of the Indian School of International Studies in Delhi in 1955. The founding of this School was done at a time "when the newly independent India felt the imperative need for competent Indian academic specialists who could regularly watch developments in other areas of the world, interpret their significance, and give a studied second opinion or a critical evaluation of India's own external policies."[20] As one former director of this School, M.S. Rajan, had recalled, its founder A. Appadorai was convinced that "without an institution training specialists on International and Area Studies...it was difficult to promote Indian expertise in these fields."[21] It might also be recalled here that India and particularly former Prime Minister Jawaharlal Nehru was especially keen to foster "friendly relations among the peoples of Asia and to promote the study and understanding of Asian problems" during the 1940s and 1950s.[22]

Accordingly, area studies programs were established in India as a way to respond to all these imperatives. The Department of African Studies was established at the University of Delhi in December 1954, and the Indian School of International Studies was established in October 1955 with sponsorship from the Indian Council of World Affairs (ICWA). In 1963, the University Grants Commission (UGC) of India appointed a committee to prepare a plan for the promotion of area studies in India. The committee recommended that area studies be promoted in a small number of universities and emphasised that the facilitation of relevant reference materials, language training and fieldwork be essential aspects of areas studies programmes. These recommendations were accepted by the UGC, and more than 25 separate area study programmes have been established in more than a dozen Indian universities since the late 1960s.[23]

Within five years of the founding of the Indian School of International Studies, Nepal Studies had started there in the form of research on the political history of Nepal, Indo-Nepal relations and contemporary political developments—three subjects that still dominate the thematic focus of Nepal Studies in India. On the first of these topics, the history of Nepal, Satish Kumar did a dissertation on Nepal under the hereditary rule of the Rana clan.[24] Kanchanmoy Mojumdar analysed India-Nepal relations during the period between 1837 and 1877,[25] and Anirudha Gupta did a dissertation on political developments in Nepal since the end of Rana rule in 1951.[26] But the School was not the only place where research on themes related to Nepal was done in India in the 1950s and 1960s. A few researchers located in traditional departments elsewhere also did research on subjects related to Nepal. One can recall, for instance, the work of historian, K.C. Chaudhuri, on Anglo-Nepal relations until 1816 (when the Treaty of Sagauli ended the Anglo-Nepal war) completed at Calcutta University in the late 1950s.[27] Political scientist, Ramakant, completed a dissertation on the same subject at the University of Allahabad in 1960, focusing on the period between 1816 and 1877.[28] Considering the time at which these researches were completed and given the material and other constraints under which they worked, scholars like Kumar,

Mojumdar, Gupta, Chaudhuri and Ramakant must be credited for setting up initial high standards for Nepal Studies in post-Independence India.[29]

The Indian School of International Studies was merged with the newly founded Jawaharlal Nehru University (JNU) in New Delhi in June 1970, and is now known as the School of International Studies (SIS).[30] Some 45 years later, there are mainly three university-related institutional locations in India where social science research on Nepal is conducted. They are the SIS at the Jawaharlal Nehru University in New Delhi, the South Asia Studies Centre (SASC) of the University of Rajasthan in Jaipur and the Centre for the Study of Nepal (CSN) in Banaras Hindu University (BHU) in Varanasi. At SIS, Nepal has received some attention from researchers affiliated predominantly with its South Asian Studies Division.[31] Several dozen M.Phil. and Ph.D dissertations have been completed from SIS on subjects related to Nepal. Bi-lateral relations, diplomatic history (India-Nepal, Nepal-China) and research on the politics of Nepal since the late Rana era (c. post-1940), informed by perspectives arising from the disciplines of political science, political history and international relations have dominated the themes selected for study by researchers at SIS. It is a pity that SIS scholars have explored very little of the numerous other topics that could be researched about Nepal from other social science disciplinary perspectives, although some effort to study issues related to foreign aid and energy has been made by the Indian economist, Mahendra P Lama.[32]

In Jaipur, Nepal has been studied by researchers affiliated with SASC. It was established in 1963 by S.P. Varma as a programme in the University's Department of Political Science and was adopted by the UGC as a separate Area Studies centre only in 1968.[33] In an unpublished report written in 1981, it is mentioned that when the SASC was established it was decided that it "would not be wedded to any given theoretical framework". Instead, it "had preferred to adopt a multi-disciplinary approach with a view to developing a comprehensive understanding of the socio-economic and political realities of the countries in South Asia."[34] Nepal Studies became a subject pursued at SASC from 1963 itself with the hiring of Ramakant, who as mentioned earlier, had done a dissertation on 19th century Indo-Nepal relations. Some of the early Nepal Studies research students at SASC included S.D. Muni,[35] R.S. Chauhan,[36] and M.D. Dharamdasani, who later headed the Centre for the Study of Nepal at BHU and published several books.[37] Jaipur's SASC has trained several other Nepal experts, almost all of them political scientists. Notable among them is B.C. Upreti who later directed the SASC for many years.[38] Articles on Nepal by SASC's researchers and others have regularly appeared in its journal, *South Asian Studies*, which was established in 1966. Several researchers trained at SASC, and its faculty members have written books on subjects related to Nepal.

In Varanasi, there exists a Centre for the Study of Nepal (CSN) in BHU. The UGC established this Centre in 1976. Its stated objective is to sponsor and promote research on Nepal from a multidisciplinary perspective. CSN has built up a documentation collection of materials on Nepal, and organised several seminars. In the past, CSN has undertaken several research projects on themes including foreign aid in Nepal, Nepal's elites, political ideology of the Nepali leader B.P. Koirala, status of Nepali women in modern Nepali literature, Indo-Nepal trade relations and post-1990 democratic experiments in Nepal. Since 1987, it has published an irregular journal, *Indian Journal of Nepalese Studies*. It has also published several papers on Nepal as part of an Occasional Paper Series.[39]

Accounting for Mediocrity

Scholarship on Nepal that has come out of the SIS in New Delhi, the SASC in Jaipur and CSN in Varanasi covers predominantly contemporary politics and political and diplomatic history (especially Indo-Nepal relations) of Nepal. While substantial in volume, it is rather limited in scope. The predominantly political science orientation, the overall use of only Indian and Nepali newspapers published in the English language as sources and the use of a few key Nepali personalities as regular informants mean that most Indian scholarship on Nepal tend to be restricted to a narrow band—political history, diplomatic history and international relations—within social science research possibilities.[40] The overlap between this scholarship and Indian political interests in Nepal is obvious, and Indian scholars tend to be far less free when it comes to studying subjects and establishing positions that are clearly independent of those forwarded by the Indian Government.[41]

These facts have several corollaries. First, due to their narrow disciplinary interests, Indian researchers of Nepal demonstrate very little awareness of the substantial amount of social science writings (especially anthropological) available on Nepal. This lack of engagement with what other students of Nepal have published from other disciplines overlaps with the formers' lack of interest in theory which has been identified as a vital flaw of area studies in India.[42] Second, Indian scholars exhibit little knowledge of writings available in the languages of Nepal. This is especially significant since English is not the dominant language of public discourse in Nepal, and many Nepali social scientists continue to produce their best work in Nepali or the other languages of Nepal. Third, since there are very few institutional incentives for Indians to study Nepal in innovative ways, competent young researchers are told to "move on" to other areas if they wish to have a viable career. Given this scenario, current Indian scholarship on Nepal does not match the competence level of scholarship demonstrated by the first generation of post-independence Indian scholars of Nepal. Even a quick reading of some of the more recent works on Nepal by Indian scholars should prove this point. At a time when the best Indian scholarship in history, cultural studies, economics and sociology is drawing worldwide attention for its quality, it is depressing to read most Indian works on Nepal.

Why hasn't Nepal Studies in India flourished in terms of quality in recent years? I have tried to answer this question elsewhere in some detail.[43] Here, in brief, the following reasons could be mentioned. The main reason why area studies including Nepal Studies programmes are not thriving in India is their overall poor financial management and administration. The funding for area studies institutions supported by the UGC is shrinking. These institutions are having a hard time meeting the routine costs (namely, salaries, library development, conference organising, etc.) of running their institutions. Funding support for new initiatives or sustained fieldwork in the countries of the researchers' specialisation is simply not available. Due to the inadequacy of the committed monies under the recurring category, area study centres have not been able to provide good language training to their students who are thus handicapped in their ability to access relevant analytical materials in Nepali and other languages of Nepal.[44] Such institutional resource constraints again contribute to the inability of area studies programmes to attract good new students. This situation is true for SIS, SASC and CSN. The latter two have been especially affected by the reduction in funding support from UGC.[45] Funding constraints have also hampered the possibility of productive collaborative work between research institutions in India and Nepal.

Putting it more generally, generating quality Indian scholarship on the rest of the region is not very high in the agenda of Indian formal academic programmes. As stated above, current scholarship is dominated by disciplines such as political science, international relations and economics and a somewhat dated state-centric model of area studies. Academic disciplines such as sociology or anthropology could have contributed to the execution of other types of research by Indian researchers on the other countries of the region, but regretfully these have not been realised.[46] In some cases, the relationship between a set of two countries prevented the free flow of such scholars (e.g., India and Pakistan). In other instances, exaggerated suspicions regarding the motives of Indian social scientists prevented the founding of one such initiative in the 1970s (e.g., India and Nepal).[47]

Based on the above discussion, it is fair to conclude that area studies programmes on the South Asian region are languishing in at least two countries of South Asia, Nepal and India. Zaidi reports much the same in the case of Pakistan when it comes to Indian Studies.[48] Conversations with colleagues from Bangladesh and Sri Lanka over the years have revealed that general academic performance of regional studies programmes in those countries is not any better than that in India. It is clear that not much investment is being made in this field in the universities and the concerned research centres in all of the South Asian countries, despite the relatively high level of noise made in connection with SAARC.

SAARC, Track II and South Asian Academia

It was expected that the founding of SAARC almost 30 years ago would provide a shot in the arm to the field of South Asian Studies in South Asia. That unfortunately has not happened. While general works generated under the auspices of SAARC have added a bit to our understanding of the region, their overall survey-like superficiality has meant that this official initiative has done little to facilitate serious scholarship by members of academia of the region. Other academic exchange programmes have been designed within the SAARC framework, but there is very little record of them having been executed or generated any good scholarship.[49]

Since the early 1990s, commentators have talked about the non-official SAARC process—the so-called track II initiatives—whereby South Asian professionals from various walks of life have begun to meet in different parts of the region under the auspices of various organisations. New networks of social activists, journalists, academics and other professionals have begun to grow as a result of these meetings where it has been said that some nationalist intellectual ghettos are beginning to be broken.[50] However, even then the non-official SAARC process has not charted a new path for social science research and teaching in South Asia. To my knowledge, no foundational texts have emerged from these networks in any of the social science disciplines. The main reason for the absence of an effective regional academia in institutions outside of the universities is the lack of what could be called "regional research imagination" in our collective civil society at large. This manifests itself in the repeated cycles of conferences and seminars (for which money seems to be available) on various themes with South Asia in the title, and in our collective inability to design and carry out region-wide serious research projects with the involvement of researchers from university and non-university based institutions in several countries. While track-II initiatives have involved academics from university departments and centres in the form of resource persons, the output of such initiatives has made very little difference to how the same individuals have taught South Asia in their home institutions. This remains so partly because of the rigidity of university curricula in our region and also because of the lack of concentrated effort on the part of faculty members to innovate new programmes within their universities.

Conclusion

I have argued in this paper that South Asian Studies in South Asia is not in a healthy state at the moment and have suggested that the lack of investment in this field in our universities and research centres is the main reason for the sorry state of affairs. It goes without saying that this will have to be greatly improved upon if academia is to matter to the shaping of mutual perceptions in South Asia.

Given the present scenario regarding area studies in South Asia, conferences of the kind in which this paper was presented must give rise to collaborative networks of scholars and researchers who are willing to create innovative remedial programmes to change the current state of regional scholarship in our countries.

While a long-term solution can only come in the form of investments in our institutions—universities and research centres—and academics in each of the countries of the region,[51] we could perhaps begin producing further analyses of the state of country-specific area studies[52] in each of the countries where such an exercise has not been carried out until now. This would be the kind of academic work that would be needed to put pressure on the individual countries of South Asia to prioritise acquiring knowledge about each other through robust programmes in our universities. It would also enable us to call upon our governments, regional organisations and international agencies to better support long-term regional research initiatives. Given the political and academic morass in much of South Asia, the chances for fresh investments in South Asian Studies in our countries without our collective effort are very small. Nevertheless, we must try if we care about good regional knowledge that helps us understand each other better in the region.

Acknowledgements

The original research for this paper was done in the year 2000 under a fellowship from the Asian Studies in Asia Program of the Council for International Exchange of Scholars and the Institute of International Education. That research and subsequent writing benefited from the generosity of many individuals in India and Nepal. I am grateful to Vishal Chandra for the invitation to participate at the conference 'India and South Asia: Exploring Regional Perceptions' organised by the Institute for Defence Studies and Analyses (IDSA) in October 2013 where I presented an earlier version of this paper. I am thankful to him and Harsha Man Maharjan for the help in locating some recent related writings on the topic. The usual disclaimers apply.

ENDNOTES

1. Pratyoush Onta, "Regional Area Studies in South Asia: Dark Days Ahead," *Nepali Journal of Contemporary Studies,* 1 (2), 2001, pp. 60-89; Pratyoush Onta, "Nepal, India and Area Studies," *Himal Southasia* 15 (1), 2002, pp. 70-75. Also, on track-II initiatives in South Asia and their links with regional academia and national civil society, see Pratyoush Onta, "Where Is the 'SAARC Process' in Academia?," *Himal Southasia,* 11 (3), 1998, pp. 24-27; and Pratyoush Onta, "Old Boys' Do's," *Himal Southasia,* 13 (2), 2000, pp. 46-47.
2. For example, see Pratyoush Onta, *Nepal Studies in the UK: Conversations with Practitioners,* Martin Chautari, Kathmandu, 2004; Pratyoush Onta, "The Landscape of Social Science and Humanities Journals Published from Nepal: An Analysis of its Structural Characteristics," *Studies in Nepali History and Society,* 15 (2), 2010, pp. 331-380; and Pratyoush Onta, "Locating Academic NGOs in the Knowledge Production Landscape," *Dhaulagiri Journal*

of Sociology and Anthropology, 5, 2011, pp. 49-80.

3. For example, see Muthiah Alagappa, "Strengthening International Studies in India: Vision and Recommendations," *International Studies*, 46 (1 & 2), 2009, pp. 7-35; Kanti Bajpai, "Obstacles to Good Work in Indian International Relations," *International Studies*, 46 (1 & 2), 2009, pp. 109-28; Amitabh Mattoo, "The State of International Studies in India," *International Studies*, 46 (1 & 2), 2009, pp. 37-48; T.V. Paul, "Integrating International Relations Studies in India to Global Scholarship," *International Studies*, 46 (1 & 2), 2009, pp. 129-45; and Varun Sahni, "The Fallacies and Flaws of Area Studies in India," *International Studies*, 46 (1 & 2), 2009, pp. 49-68.
4. Tansen Sen, "Is There a Need for China Studies in India?," *Economic and Political Weekly*, 48 (29), 2013, pp. 26-29; and S. Akbar Zaidi, "A Conspicuous Absence: Teaching and Research on India in Pakistan," *Economic and Political Weekly*, 44 (38), 2009, pp. 57-68.
5. Krishna Hachhethu, "Social Sciences in Nepal," *Contributions to Nepalese Studies*, 29 (1), 2002, pp. 49-95.
6. Prayag R. Sharma, "The Late Kumar Khadga Bikram Shah as I Knew Him," in Prem K. Khatry, Ananda P. Shrestha, Anand Aditya, Hari P. Shrestha and Dev Raj Dahal (eds.), *Kumar Khadga Bikram Shah: Man Behind the Persona*, Nepal Mountaineering Association, Kathmandu, 2004, pp. 198-203.
7. *Documentation of SAARC*, Centre for Nepal and Asian Studies (CNAS), Kathmandu, 1988 and *Documentation on SAARC No 2*, CNAS, Kathmandu, 1990.
8. Govinda Malla, "India" in Shambhu R. Simkhada (ed.), *Year Review 1986*, CNAS, Kathmandu, 1986, pp. 59-80; Govinda Malla, "India in 1987: A Year of Great Challenges," in Shambhu R. Simkhada (ed.), *CNAS Year Review 1987*, CNAS, Kathmandu, 1987, pp. 69-108; Govinda Malla, "India in 1988: The Year before the Election," in Anand Aditya (ed.), *CNAS Year Review 1988*, CNAS, Kathmandu, 1988, pp. 52-61.
9. Sridhar Khatri (ed.), *Regional Security in South Asia*, CNAS, Kathmandu, 1987.
10. The most significant article that appeared as a result of this appeal was Kumar's. See Dhruba Kumar, "Beyond 'Blockade': Some Long-term Policy Considerations for Nepal," *CNAS Forum Current Issue Series*, 10, 1989, pp. 1-34. Also, for comparison, see S.D. Muni, "India and Nepal: Erosion of a Relationship," *Strategic Analysis*, 4, reprinted in *CNAS Forum Current Issue Series*, 10, 1989, pp. 35-56.
11. Prayag R. Sharma, no. 6.
12. Dhruba Kumar, "South Asia after the Nuclear Tests: Securing Insecurity," *Occasional Paper*, CNAS, Kathmandu, 1999a; Dhruba Kumar, "Minds at War and Minds at Peace in South Asia," *Occasional Paper*, CNAS, Kathmandu, 1999b.
13. Dhruba Kumar, "Negotiating the Resumption of the Indian Airlines Flights," in Dhruba Kumar (ed.), *Domestic Conflict and Crisis of Governability in Nepal*, CNAS, Kathmandu, 2000, pp. 305-322.
14. Lok Raj Baral (ed.), *Looking to the Future: Indo-Nepal Relations in Perspective*, Anmol Publications, New Delhi, 1996.
15. Lok Raj Baral, *Regional Migrations, Ethnicity and Security: The South Asian Case*, New Sterling Publishers, Delhi, 1990.
16. N.P. Banskota, *Regional Economic Cooperation in South Asia: Nepalese Perspectives*, Daya Publishing House, Delhi, 1990 and Lok Raj Baral, *The Regional Paradox*. Adroit Publishers, Delhi, 2000.
17. Pratyoush Onta, 2011, no. 2.
18. Dipak Gyawali and Ajaya Dixit, "Mahakali Impasse: A Futile Paradigm's Bequested Travails," in *Dhruba Kumar* (ed.), *Domestic Conflict and Crisis of Governability in Nepal*, CNAS, Kathmandu, 2000, pp. 236-304.
19. Dipak Gyawali, "Patna, Delhi and Environmental Activism: Institutional Forces Behind

Water Conflict in Bihar," *Water Nepal,* 6 (1), 1998, pp. 67-115.

20. B. Vivekanandan, "The State of Area Studies in India," in Ankush B. Sawant (ed.), *Area Studies Programmes in Indian Universities: An Appraisal and Review*, Kalinga Publications, Delhi, 1997, p. 41.
21. M.S. Rajan, "Professor A. Appadorai and the Development of International and Area Studies in India: A Personal Memoir" in M.S. Rajan (ed.), *International and Area Studies in India*, Lancers Books, New Delhi, 1997a, p. 168.
22. On various aspects of the history of international and area studies in India, see the articles in M.S. Rajan (ed.), *International and Area Studies in India*, Lancers Books, New Delhi, 1997c; Ankus B. Sawant (ed.), *Area Studies Programmes in Indian Universities: An Appraisal and Review*, Kalinga Publications, Delhi, 1997; B.P. Mishra, "Area Studies: Policy and Methodology," *Occasional Paper No. 10*, Centre for Himalayan Studies, North Bengal University, 1996; Y. Yagama Reddy, *Area Studies: The Proposition, Problems and Prospects*, Centre for Studies on Indochina & South Pacific, Sri Venkateswara University, Tirupati, 1998; and Varun Sahni, no. 3.
23. See Varun Sahni, no. 3, p. 52, Table 1 for a list of area study programmes in various Indian universities.
24. Later published as: Satish Kumar, *Rana Polity in Nepal: Origin and Growth*, Asia Publishing House, New York, 1967.
25. Later revised as: Kanchanmoy Mojumdar, *Anglo-Nepalese Relations in the Nineteenth Century*, Firma K L Mukhopadhyay, Calcutta, 1973.
26. Anirudha Gupta, *Politics in Nepal*, Allied Publishers, Bombay, 1964.
27. K.C. Chaudhuri, *Anglo-Nepalese Relations From the Earliest Times of the British Rule in India Till the Gurkha War*, Modern Book Agency, Calcutta, 1960.
28. Later published as: Ramakant, *Indo-Nepalese Relations 1816 to 1877*, S. Chand & Company, Delhi, 1968.
29. For an exhaustive review of works on area studies in India up to end of the 1960s, see Bimal Prasad and Urmila Phadnis, "Area Studies in India," in *A Survey of Research in Political Science: Volume Five International Studies*, Allied Publishers, New Delhi, 1988, pp. 71-202.
30. M.S. Rajan, "The Merger of the ISIS with the JNU," in M.S. Rajan (ed.), *International and Area Studies in India*, Lancers Books, New Delhi, 1997b, pp. 191-206.
31. For example, S.D. Muni, no. 10; S.D. Muni, *India and Nepal: A Changing Relationship*, Konark Publishers, Delhi, 1995; and Sangeeta Thapliyal, *Mutual Security: The Case of India-Nepal*, Lancer Publishers, New Delhi, 1998. In addition, we might note that while he served in the faculty of the SIS, the late L.S. Baral, a Nepali historian and literary critic, published several articles on politics in Nepal and Nepal's relationship with India and the Non-Aligned Movement. These essays have now been collected in a volume: L.S. Baral in Pratyoush Onta and Lokranjan Parajuli (eds.), *Autocratic Monarchy: Politics in Panchayat Nepal*, Martin Chautari, Kathmandu, 2012.
32. Mahendra P. Lama, "Absorption of Foreign Aid in Nepal: Some Issues," *South Asia Journal,* 4 (3), 1991, pp. 335-46 and Mahendra P. Lama, "Economic Reforms and the Energy Sector in South Asia: Scope for Cross-border Power Trade," *South Asian Survey,* 7 (1), 2000, pp. 3-23.
33. See S.P. Varma, "Area Studies: Concept, Methods and Approach," *South Asian Studies,* 2 (2), 1967, pp. 1-15.
34. Quoted in B. P. Mishra, no. 22, p. 41.
35. S.D. Muni, *Foreign Policy of Nepal*, National Publishing House, Delhi, 1973.
36. R.S. Chauhan, *The Political Development in Nepal 1950-70: Conflict Between Tradition and Modernity*, Associated Publishing House, New Delhi, 1971.
37. M.D. Dharamdasani, *Political Economy of Foreign Aid in the Third World: A Case Study of*

Nepal, Konark Publishing House, Varanasi, 1984a; M.D. Dharamdasani (ed.), *Political Participation and Change in South Asia in the Context of Nepal*, Shalimar Publishing House, Varanasi, 1984b; M.D. Dharamdasani (ed.), *Nepal in Transition*, Rajdhani Publications, Jaipur, 1997; and M.D. Dharamdasani (ed.), *India and Nepal: Big Power-Small Power Relations in South Asia*, South Asian Publishers, New Delhi, 2001.

38. B.C. Upreti, *Indians in Nepal: A Study of Indian Migration to Kathmandu*, Kalinga Publications, Delhi, 1999; B.C. Upreti, *Uneasy Friends: Readings on Indo-Nepal Relations*, Kalinga Publications, Delhi, 2001; B.C. Upreti, *Maoists in Nepal: From Insurgency to Political Mainstream*, Kalpaz Publications, Delhi, 2008; and B.C. Upreti, *Nepal: Transition to Democratic Republican State*. Kalpaz Publications, Delhi, 2010.

39. Further details on the Nepal-related work done at SIS, the Centre in Jaipur and CSN are provided in Pratyoush Onta, no. 1, 2001.

40. Out of the 350 doctoral theses done in SIS during the years 1996-2007, Sahni found out that 287 (82 per cent) were from the discipline of political science. This led him to note: "The domination of political scientists among Indian area specialists, to the virtual exclusion of other social science disciplines, is a major weakness in the development of area studies in India." He considers this to be a symptom of how Indian area studies are "not sufficiently multidisciplinary." See Varun Sahni, no. 3, p. 60. Bajpai also identifies "poor methodological skills of the students and faculty" as one of the main factors for the generation of poor quality scholarship in the field. See Kanti Bajpai, no. 3, p. 116.

41. This seems to be general problem with all area studies scholars in India who, it has been argued recently, "have not liberated themselves intellectually from their dependence on the state, and scholars who take a different view of the world from the government of India can even now invite sanctions in some form or the other." See Amitabh Mattoo, no. 3, pp. 42-43. Bajpai has more to say on this connection as well. See Kanti Bajpai, "International Studies in India: Bringing Theory (Back) Home," in M.S. Rajan (ed.), *International and Area Studies in India*, Lancers Books, New Delhi, 1997, pp. 31-49; and Kanti Bajpai, no. 3, p. 116.

42. Kanti Bajpai, no. 41; Kanti Bajpai, no. 3, p. 116; and Varun Sahni, no. 3.

43. Pratyoush Onta, no. 1, 2001.

44. The lack of fieldwork and language skills are also noted as important flaws of Indian area studies by Sahni, who writes, "If India is to ever build a cadre of genuine area specialists, the sponsoring agencies will have to consider funding scholars to spend up to a year at a time in their area of doctoral study. Language fluency and genuine understanding require a sustained period of immersion in the culture and society that is the object of study." See Varun Sahni, no. 3, p. 61.

45. In addition, it has recently been argued that the UGC's "procedures, practices and interventions are slow, convoluted, politicized and research-unfriendly. The net result has been that a culture of research in International Studies, especially in area studies, that could have been built through UGC support has been effectively retarded." See Amitabh Mattoo, no. 3, p. 42.

46. Bimal Prasad and Urmila Phadnis, no. 29; Nandini Sundar, Satish Deshpande and Patricia Uberoi, "Indian Anthropology and Sociology: Towards a History," *Economic and Political Weekly*, 35 (24), 2000, pp. 1998-2002.

47. Pratyoush Onta, 2001, no. 1.

48. S. Akbar Zaidi, no. 4.

49. Pratyoush Onta, 1998, no. 1.

50. "SAARC Starts to Get Serious," *Himal*, 10 (3), 1997, pp. 14-16; Navnita C. Behera, Paul M. Evans and Gowher Rizvi, *Beyond Boundaries: A Report on the State of Non-Official Dialogues on Peace, Security & Cooperation in South Asia*, University of Toronto-York

University, Ontario, 1997; and Navnita C. Behera, Victor Gunawardena, Shahid Kardar and Raisul A. Mahmood, *People-to-People Contact in South Asia*, Manohar, New Delhi, 2000.

51. Mattoo and Alagappa provide many details on the investments needed in the case of India. See Amitabh Mattoo, no. 3 and Muthiah Alagappa, no. 3. Paul provides other ideas about how Indian scholars of International Relations (IR) have "to integrate in a major way into global IR, especially relating to IR theory." See T.V. Paul, no. 3, p. 141.

52. Pratyoush Onta, 2001, no. 1 and S Akbar Zaidi, no. 4.

2

'Not India': Pakistan, India and the Self

Yaqoob Khan Bangash

Introduction

On August 15, 1947, Pakistan was carved out of the British Indian Empire. While the founder of Pakistan, Mohammad Ali Jinnah, was insistent that the Empire should dissolve into the two 'new' states of India [Bharat] and Pakistan, in reality, Pakistan was seen as the seceding state. Indeed, the Indian Independence Act of July 1947 did indicate that two new states were being created on August 15. Article 1 (1) read: "As from the fifteenth day of August, nineteen hundred and forty-seven, two independent Dominions shall be set up in India, to be known respectively as India and Pakistan."[1] However, independent India retained the seat of British India at the United Nations (UN) and inherited all of the diplomatic and other posts of the empire. Also, since the name 'India' continued with one of the new states, a clear impression of continuity was given. Therefore, while the 'new' India already had an identity (it also inherited the mantle of the British Raj), Pakistan had to articulate its identity anew. Further, while one part of India's new identity had to take into account Pakistan's creation (or secession), for Pakistan, I argue, India was a much more important component of its identity. Pakistan's identity as 'Not India' therefore became a defining feature of its identity, I maintain, and still shapes its outlook.

The Construction of Perception

Pakistan was created on the basis of the Two Nation theory which argued that Hindus and Muslims were separate nations which could not live together. Hence, both required a separate 'homeland'. Jinnah articulated this argument many times, and in his presidential address to the All India Muslim League in March 1940 in Lahore (where the Pakistan Resolution was also passed) said:

> The Hindus and Muslims belong to two different religious philosophies, social customs, and literature[s]. They neither intermarry nor interdine together, and indeed they belong to two different civilisations which are based mainly on conflicting ideas and conceptions. Their aspects [perspectives?] on life, and of life, are different. It is quite clear that Hindus and Mussalmans derive their inspiration from different sources of history. They have different epics, their heroes are different, and different episode[s]. Very often the hero of one is a foe of the other, and likewise their victories and defeats overlap.[2]

Therefore, both communities required a separate country—Pakistan for Muslims and Hindustan for Hindus (in fact for a long time after independence, Pakistan kept referring to India as Bharat, in order to further underscore its 'Hindu' character). The creation of Pakistan, hence, was necessitated by a Hindu India—Pakistan was the Muslim mirror image of a Hindu India.

This notion of Pakistan being purely Muslim was apparent very early in its history. A Hindu member of the Constituent Assembly of Pakistan faced questions when he argued that he was a Hindu but also a Pakistani. Sris Chandra Chattopadhyaya highlighted the convoluted nature of Pakistan's identity in a speech during the debate on the infamous Objectives Resolution in March 1947. He noted:

> Will they both call themselves Pakistanis? Then how will the people know who is Muslim and who is non-Muslim? I say, give up this division of the people into Muslims and non-Muslims and let us call ourselves one nation. Let us call ourselves one people of Pakistan. Otherwise, if you call me non-Muslim and call yourselves Muslim the difficulty will be if I call myself Pakistani they will say you are a Muslim. That happened when I had been to Europe. I went there as a delegate of Pakistan. When I said "I am a delegate of Pakistan" they thought I was a Muslim. They said "But you are a Muslim". I said, "No, I am a Hindu". A Hindu cannot remain in Pakistan, that was their attitude. They said: "You cannot call yourself a Pakistani." Then I explained everything and told them that there are Hindus and as well as Muslims and that we are all Pakistanis. That is the position. Therefore, what am I to call myself?[3]

This dilemma still remains for most non-Muslim Pakistanis.

Pakistan's definition of itself as the 'Muslim' country, and India as the 'Hindu' country, meant that Pakistani textbooks—throughout its history—have treated Indians and Hindus as synonyms. These books have also emphasised the perpetual enmity between Hindus and Muslims, to illustrate the historic need for Pakistan. This focus was not a product of the Islamisation process under General Zia-ul-

Haq as most commentators maintain, and nor does it even find its birth in the radical policies of Zulfikar Ali Bhutto in the 1970s. In fact, this process began as soon as Pakistan was itself created, thereby highlighting its critical role in the creation of Pakistan's identity.

Very soon after its inception, the Government of Pakistan was of the opinion that all curricula should be infused with 'Islamic ideology'. The first minister for education, Fazlur Rahman, noted at the first All-Pakistan Education Conference in November 1947: "It is, therefore, a matter of profound satisfaction to me, as it must be to you, that we have now before us the opportunity of reorienting our entire educational policy to correspond closely with the needs of the times and to reflect the ideas for which Pakistan as an Islamic state stands."[4] He again emphasised in February 1949: "But mere lip-service to Islamic ideology will be as foolish a gesture as Canute's order to the waves of the sea. We must see to it that every aspect of our national activity is animated by this ideology, and since education is the basic activity of the State I realized that a start had to be made there."[5] This 'Islamic ideology' was rooted in the Two Nation theory, and necessitated that the government undertake the project of textbook writing—too dangerous to leave to private enterprise—and therefore a certain view of 'India' and 'Hindus' was perpetuated.

From the beginning, but especially beginning with the government of Zulifkar Ali Bhutto in the 1970s, a negative view of Hindus was reinforced.[6] For example, as early as grade four and grade five, students were taught that "the religion of the Hindus did not teach them good things,"[7] and that the "Hindu has always been an enemy of Islam."[8] At the higher levels, this indoctrination worsens, and even blatant lies are written. For example, the social studies book for class eight notes, "In December 1885, an Englishman...formed a political party named Indian National Congress, the purpose of which was to politically organize Hindus."[9] The same textbook then goes on to simply fabricate facts and notes: "Therefore in order to appease the Hindus and the Congress, the British announced political reforms. Muslims were not eligible to vote. Hindus voters never voted for a Muslim."[10] Even the Pervez Musharraf and post-Musharraf era textbooks which were supposed to be 'Enlightened' exhibit the same antagonism towards Hindus. The 2014-15 social studies textbook for grade eight notes that both the British and the Hindus "conspired against the Muslims to turn them into a poor, helpless and ineffective minority."[11] In the same chapter on the Pakistan Movement, the textbook establishes that: "The introduction of Minto-Morley Reforms was another painful factor for the Hindus. They were not prepared to tolerate any such step which benefitted the Muslims. So they became violent, and freely damaged government and public property."[12] With 'Hindus' being denounced in such clear terms, no wonder there is a very negative perception of the Indian

National Congress (perceived to be completely Hindu) and India in the minds of Pakistanis. Social scientist Rubina Saigol has aptly described the main aim of these textbooks: "It appears that Pakistani public school textbooks were not written to serve the pedagogical imperatives of intellectual development and the inculcation of critical thinking. Rather, they were written to perpetually justify a divisive ideology of rupture which had to be continually reiterated in the construction of national memory."[13]

This hatred towards Hindus was not just confined to the pre-1947 period in Pakistani textbooks and extended to the post-independence period where Pakistani Hindus (especially after the secession of Bangladesh) were dubbed as agents of 'Hindu' India. The social studies textbook for grade five succinctly noted the 'real' reason for the breakup of Pakistan. It stated: "After 1965 war India conspired with the Hindus of Bengal and succeeded in spreading hate among the Bengalis about West Pakistan and finally attacked on East Pakistan in December 1971, thus causing the breakup of East and West Pakistan."[14] Thus, a linear correlation between Hindus and India has cemented anti-India perception in Pakistan for decades.

In all these textbooks, it is never mentioned that presently India has almost the same number of Muslims, if not more, as compared to Pakistan. Obviously, this information would complicate the clear distinction between 'Hindu India' and 'Muslim Pakistan'. When Indian Muslims are mentioned elsewhere in the media, it is often only to highlight their plight, and hence to reinforce the Two Nation theory. Even when there are prominent Indian Muslims, they are dubbed as not 'Muslim enough' by Pakistanis.[15]

Another factor which fuelled anti-India sentiment was and is the fact that except for Jinnah, Liaquat and few other stalwarts and Islamic leaders, all 'heroes' mentioned in textbooks are soldiers who died in wars with India. For example, the Punjab Urdu textbooks from the primary school level upwards contain chapters on military personnel who won Pakistan's highest gallantry award *Nishan-e-Haider* in battles against India. Hence, the Urdu textbook of the Punjab Textbook Board for the year 2014-15 for class four has a chapter on Major Aziz Bhatti (Chapter 12), the textbook for class five has a chapter on Hawaldar Lalik Jan (Chapter 17), Sawar Mohammad Hussain Shaheed is the subject of Chapter 24 in the textbook for class seven, and Chapter nine in the textbook for class eight details the martyrdom of Naik Lal Hussain Shaheed. The promotion of war heroes as general heroes for everyone to emulate has not only limited the number of career paths youth (and parents) consider in Pakistan—the military is always one of the top career paths—but it also solidifies their attitude against the 'enemy' which almost always means India. In fact, a number of times textbooks clarify only later in the chapter that the 'enemy' is India (it is taken for granted that students will automatically assume it is India).

In addition to the promotion of war heroes, in the past few decades, there has been a conscious glorification of war, especially in terms of *Jihad*. For example, in the curriculum document for primary schools in 1995, it was stated that the teachers should strive to create a feeling "among students [that] they are the members of a Muslim nation. Therefore, in accordance with the Islamic tradition, they have to truthful, honest, patriotic and life-sacrificing *mujahids*."[16] Even in the so-called 'Enlightened' period of the rule of General Musharraf, the theme of inculcating the spirit of *Jihad* (clearly referring to war in this sense) continued. The national curriculum directive in 2002 maintained that, "the sense be created among students that they are members of the Islamic Millat. Therefore in accordance with the Islamic tradition, they ought to develop into true, honest patriot, servant of the people and *Janbaz Mujahid* [life giving warrior] in his heart."[17] In higher classes, especially during and after the rule of General Zia ul-Haq, *Jihad* was unabashedly promoted. A curriculum document from 1986 noted that students "must be aware of the blessings of *Jihad*, and must create yearning for *Jihad*."[18] With such a clear promotion of *Jihad* against the 'enemy', especially as one of the highest levels of service to the nation, anti-India sentiment has been clearly cemented in the school-going youth of Pakistan over the past several decades.

Pakistan's perception of India is also tied to the Kashmir dispute. In a way, it is the Kashmir dispute which prevents Pakistan, and to an extent India, to move beyond 1947. The 'unfinished' business of 1947 keeps Pakistan's *raisond'être* alive in the minds of the government and people and prevents positive perception of India. As several scholars have pointed out, Pakistan has time and again used the Kashmir issue to forge national unity. In a country bereft with internal tensions between provinces, classes, etc., for decades, it was the Kashmir issue which brought all shades of opinion together in the country. Therefore, it was a very useful tool to create a sense of common cause against a 'tyrant' (India) which had been oppressing the Muslim majority region of Kashmir since 1947. Also, since the Kashmir dispute was tied to the events of independence in August 1947, the massacres of the time—mainly blamed on the Hindus and Sikhs in Pakistan—were a continuous memory. While the Sikhs were largely redeemed in the Pakistani mindset after Operation Bluestar, the bulk of the responsibility for the 1947-48 massacres then fell on the Hindus, who of course inhabited 'Hindu India'.

For a long time, the virulent anti-India stance of the Pakistani media has also fuelled the negative perception of Pakistan. For decades, the state-run Pakistan Television Network—till early 2000s the main news and entertainment channel in Pakistan—aired a programme on prime time focusing on Indian 'atrocities' in Indian Kashmir. This emotive programme was full of patriotic songs and gory scenes of torture, murder and pillage which kept the memory of antagonism against

India alive. Even though Pakistan had not fought a war with India over Kashmir since 1965, these scenes, repeatedly shown every day reinforced the notion that 'Hindu' India still persecuted Muslims and therefore one should be thankful that Pakistan was created to save Muslims from the fate currently suffered by the their hapless Kashmiri Muslim brethren. The print media in Pakistan has also been largely anti-India. The Urdu daily, *Nawa-i-Waqt*, founded by Hameed Nizami in 1941, declared itself to be the 'custodian of the Ideology of Pakistan,' which is the 'Two Nation Theory'. The reinforcement of this mantra especially on the anniversary of the Lahore Resolution (March 23), Independence Day (August 14) and Jinnah's birth and death anniversary (December 25 and September 11, respectively), among other days, has kept the memory of the Two Nation theory alive.

Like conjoined, but estranged twins, Pakistan and India have also been tied together by an eternal comparison—more so in Pakistan than in India perhaps. Since Pakistan was the newer nation, it had to be more successful than India in order to prove its existence. When Pakistan performed better economically (e.g., in the 1960s), a number of Pakistanis saw it as 'proof' of the success of the Pakistani experiment. Writer Kamila Shamsie noted in *The Guardian* article: "At the start of the 90s when I was, bafflingly, taking A-level economics in Karachi, our teacher taught us all we needed to know about India's protectionist economy with the sentence: 'The only part of Indian cars which doesn't make a noise is the horn'."[19] That India was economically worse off than Pakistan reflected well on Pakistan and gave its people confidence that the separation they achieved was worthwhile. However, the downturn in the Pakistani economy in the 2000s and the rapid development in India has given something to think about to Pakistanis. As successful entrepreneur and Managing Director of Oxford University Press in Pakistan, Ameena Saiyid, told Kamila Shamsie, Pakistanis envy Indians for refusing to allow "its cows and elephants and other religious symbols and beliefs to impede their march to economic growth while we have got totally entangled in our burqas and beards."[20] Again, what Pakistan thinks of India is critically tied to what it thinks of itself and what is happening in the country.

The Change in Perception

Recently, the perception of India has begun to undergo a change in Pakistan. It is still too early to gauge to what extent it has changed, but there are clear signs of a different air. A lot has to do with the changed circumstances within Pakistan. The increasing tide of militancy and extremism in Pakistan has made the country more introvert, and India—though still enemy number one for a large percentage—has begun to fare differently. Pakistan's more flexible attitude towards Kashmir—especially since the Musharraf formula of 2006-07 which articulated a four-point solution of the dispute including demilitarisation, self-governance, open borders and joint management of the territory—has further changed the environment. This was the first time when Pakistan presented a solution outside its traditional stance of the implementation of the UN resolutions regarding plebiscite in the region.

Lately, anti-India trend in the media is being countered by a cross current of proponents of peace on both sides. The joint initiative of *The Times of India* and the *Jang Group* of Pakistan (which runs the Urdu daily, *Jang*, the English daily, *The News*, and the *GEO* media enterprise), *Aman ki Asha* (Hope for Peace), is testament of a change in direction. This initiative, launched on January 01, 2010, aims to "create an enabling environment to facilitate dialogue between the governments, encourage people-to-people contacts and thus contribute to bringing about peace between India and Pakistan."[21] The mere existence of this endeavour (despite the recent crackdown on the *Jang* media group) speaks volumes. A few decades ago, something like this could not have even been contemplated let alone initiated. The fact that the largest media groups on both sides of the border are spearheading the move clearly shows that it will not lose them revenue and will also promote peace and development in the region. Through this initiative, in addition to promoting people-to-people contact and initiating an open debate, both the media groups also committed themselves to "using their print and electronic media to aggressively promote the benefits of peace in terms of economic development, uniting families, tourism, developing trade, and removing the obstacles to peace."[22] This is clearly about using their media clout towards creating a more conducive environment for a peaceful resolution of contentious issues and mutual co-existence and development. This project is only a few years old, and therefore it is hard to assess its implications fully. However, their various endeavours, like the Indo-Pak Business meets, the *Milne Do* initiative, and simply connecting people from various walks of life across the border through their media networks, have begun to make a difference. From my own perspective, the relative ease with which I can now go to India, and even take students, has enabled me, and more importantly my students, to understand the 'other side'. *Aman ki Asha* will not transform perceptions overnight or even in a decade perhaps—long held beliefs will take more time—but the dent has already been made.

In the last decade or so, Pakistan's attitude towards Kashmir has been changing. Interestingly, among the first to amend his opinion on the Kashmir issue has been the so-called *Mujahid-e-Awal* or the 'first fighter', Sardar Abdul Qayyum Khan, who was one of the main leaders of the Kashmiri revolt against Maharaja Hari Singh in October 1947, and was both president and prime minister of Pakistani Kashmir several times. Showing flexibility, Sardar Abdul Qayyum Khan has several times pointed out that 'all' options for the solution of the Kashmir dispute should be discussed. In 2002, even while denying that Sardar Abdul Qayyum had called for the conversion of the Line of Control into a permanent border (as reported in several Pakistani and Indian newspapers), his spokesman said that his "viewpoint is clear that instead of putting forward new proposals, we should analyse the suggestions coming from responsible quarters."[23] However, even in this denial, there was an acknowledgement that proposals other than a plebiscite—which used to be a *sina qua non* for Kashmiri and Pakistani leaders—could be considered. Coming from the 'first fighter,' this was a significant move. In more recent years, Sardar Abdul Qayyum has even offered support for the Musharraf formula, plainly exhibiting his support for a settlement not based on the old plebiscite model. In 2005, he clearly indicated that he was supportive of creating a 'United States of Kashmir'. He was, according to *Dawn*, "in favour of the proposal of creating what he called the 'United States of Kashmir (USK)' which, he said, was the extension of President Pervez Musharraf's proposal about dividing the entire Jammu and Kashmir territory into seven regions." The *Dawn* further reported, "[He] suggested that there should be separate legislative assemblies, for both the parts of Jammu and Kashmir, emerging through free and fair elections. The two assemblies should then form a third assembly for the whole territory to be called the United States of Kashmir. Sardar Qayyum was of the view that the election for the purpose could either be held either under the joint supervision of Pakistan and India or the United Nations."[24] Such flexibility from Kashmiri leaders in Pakistan is indeed a firm indication of their softening stance on the issue, which obviously had an effect on the public at large.

That said, the existence of organisations such as the Lashkar-e-Toiba, Harkat-ul-Mujahidin and the Defence of Pakistan Council still keeps the flame of Kashmir and anti-India sentiment alive in Pakistan. They have taken out rallies in the past (though recently there has been no such rallies), and a large part of their rhetoric is anti-India. However, what is also apparent is that the rallies are largely anti-American too. Further, despite posters like '*Bharat se rishta kya, dushmani ka inteqaam ka*' ('what is our relation to India, it is of revenge and of them being the enemy') being splashed throughout the city, the number of people at these rallies has steadily declined. There has also been a perceptible decline in the number of donation boxes for 'Jihad in Kashmir' which used to be omnipresent in Pakistan a decade ago. This lack of interest and support for the *Jihad* in Kashmir is clearly supported by evidence of fewer Jihadis trying to cross over into India. *The Times of India* recently reported, "According to statistics until July 31 [2014], this year has witnessed the lowest number of militants successfully infiltrating into India from Pakistan side...The drop in infiltration is keeping in line with the pattern that has emerged over the recent years, when Kashmir has been witnessing an overall drop in enthusiasm for armed militancy."[25] With increasing insecurity in the country itself, Pakistanis are more concerned about their day-to-day survival and security than harbouring hopes of incorporating Kashmir into Pakistan.

In 2012, in an article I wrote in a leading Pakistani newspaper, entitled, "Maybe We Have Forgotten Kashmir?",[26] I have used anecdotal evidence from a university event on Kashmir where hardly anyone was interested in the Kashmir dispute, to posit the theory that perhaps the younger generation of Pakistanis is not that attached to the issue as the older generation was. Not being part of the generation that saw the horrors of 1947, and being more embroiled in the security situation after attacks on Pakistan by the Taliban and al Qaida in the 2000s, the younger generation is concerned mainly with problems at home. In these changed circumstances, even the right-wing Maulana Fazlur Rahman, chief of his faction of the Jamiat-e-Ulema-e-Islam, had to state: "Obviously, we are in favour of a political solution.... Things have changed so much. Now the concept of wining Kashmir has taken a back seat to the urgency of saving Pakistan."[27]

Where Next?

While Pakistan's perception of India might be improving in terms of a decline in the number and influence of militant organisations, flexibility on the Kashmir issue and the promotion of better relations with India at least in a section of the media, Pakistan's perception of India will not dramatically improve unless it develops a more confident image of itself. As long as Pakistan continues to find its rationale for existence in the Two Nation Theory (especially after the secession of Bangladesh in 1971), and keeps viewing the world in terms of 'Muslim' countries, 'Hindu' countries and 'Christian' countries (e.g., Christians in Pakistan bear the brunt of anti-Americanism since America is supposed to be a 'Christian' nation), its perception of India will not improve.

Pakistan's perception of India is tied to its identity crisis, and unless Pakistan becomes a stable and secure country, the perception will not improve. Where India can help Pakistan is in making Pakistan feel confident that the 1947 partition is a fact of history and that India has no designs of changing that reality. This would entail focusing on what could bring both the countries together now rather than talking about what happened in the past. India should also promote stability in Pakistan, since a more integrated and stable Pakistan would be able to engage with India without the baggage of the past.

Pakistan has a long way to go in solving its identity crisis. However, starting with accepting the fact that there are two other South Asian countries—India and Bangladesh—which have as many Muslims as it has could be a first step. Pakistan needs to incorporate the Muslim communities of these two countries in its textbooks and be comfortable talking about them as another dimension of South Asian Islam. Pakistan also needs to restart teaching ancient India (abandoned in 1961) in its school curriculum so that students in the country are also aware of the rich non-Muslim heritage of the subcontinent. Further, Pakistan needs to develop a more nuanced view of India when it is discussed within the contexts of conflicts. While the wars of the past are a reality, making 'Hindus' and 'Enemy' synonymous with 'India' should change. Pakistan also needs to begin teaching the history and politics of post-independence India—hitherto seldom taught in Pakistani universities. The more Pakistanis will know about how independent India has developed over the past more than six decades and how complicated it has been, the more nuanced their view will be of the country. Pakistan and India have a long and shared history and there is much that brings both countries together. Both countries, while keeping their sovereignty and separate identities, can certainly work together for a better South Asia.

ENDNOTES

1. Indian Independence Act 1947, 10 & 11 GEO 6, Chapter 30.
2. "Presidential Address at the Session of the All India Muslim League, Lahore, March 1940," in Jamil-ud-Din Ahmed (ed.), *Speeches and Writings of Mr. Jinnah*, Vol. 1, Sheikh Muhammad Ashraf, Lahore, 1968, p. 169.
3. "Speech of Sris Chandra Chatopadhyaya, March 12, 1949," *Constituent Assembly of Pakistan Debates*, V (5), p. 93.
4. "Address delivered at the All-Pakistan Educational Conference held at Karachi, 27 November, 1947," in Fazlur Rahman, *New Education in the Making in Pakistan: Its Ideology and basic Problems*, Cassell & Company, London, 1953, p. 3.
5. Ibid. See "Speech at the Opening of the Second Annual Session of the advisory Board of Education for Pakistan held at Peshawar from February 7-9 1949," p. 20.
6. For one of the best assessments of biases in Pakistani textbooks, see A.H. Nayyer and Ahmed Salim (eds.), *The Subtle Subversion: The State of Curricula and Textbooks in Pakistan*, Sustainable Development Policy Institute, Islamabad, 2002. Also, see Ashok K. Behuria and Mohammad Shehzad, "Partition of History in Textbooks in Pakistan: Implications of Selective Memory and Forgetting," *Strategic Analysis*, Routledge, 37 (3), 2013, pp. 353-365.
7. *Muasherati Ulum for Class IV*, Punjab Textbook Board, Lahore, 1995, p.81.
8. *Urdu Class V*, Punjab Textbook Board, Lahore, 2002, p. 108.
9. *Social Studies Class VIII*, 2002, p. 94.
10. Ibid., pp. 94-5.
11. *Social Studies Class VIII*, Punjab Textbook Board, Lahore, 2014, p. 74.
12. Ibid., p. 75.
13. Rubina Saigol, "Textbooks: An Education in Demonology," *India Today*, August 11, 2012, at http://indiatoday.intoday.in/story/rubina-saigol-pakistani-textbooks-divisive-ideology-muslims-are-always-heroic-and-hindus-invariably-diabolical/1/212833.html.
14. *Social Studies (in Urdu) Class-V*, Punjab Textbook Board, Lahore, p. 112.
15. One only has to look at the comments section of any article on Indian Muslims in Pakistan to ascertain this.
16. *Curriculum Document, Primary Education, Class K-V, Urdu Curriculum, Class IV-V*, 1999, p. 41.
17. *Urdu Curriculum (First language) for Classes IV and V*, National Bureau of Curriculum and Textbooks, Ministry of Education, Islamabad, 2002, p. 3, as cited in A.H. Nayyer and Ahmed Salim, no. 6, pp. 38-39.
18. *Urdu Curriculum (first and second language) for classes VI-VIII*, National Bureau of Curriculum

and Textbooks, Ministry of Education, Islamabad, 1986, p. 13, as cited in A.H. Nayyer and Ahmed Salim, no. 6, p. 44.

19. Kamila Shamsie, "How Pakistanis See India," *The Guardian*, August 14, 2007, at http://www.theguardian.com/world/2007/aug/14/india.features116
20. Ibid.
21. *Aman ki Asha*, at http://amankiasha.com/faqs.asp
22. Ibid.
23. "Qayyum Not for Conversion of LOC into Border," *Dawn*, December 30, 2002, at http://www.dawn.com/news/75184/qayyum-not-for-conversion-of-loc-into-border
24. "Sardar Qayyum Wants LOC Points Used for Trade," *Dawn*, December 10, 2005, at http://www.dawn.com/news/169273/sardar-qayyum-wants-loc-points-used-for-trade
25. "Valley Paradox: Infiltration Down, But Violence on the Rise," *The Times of India*, August 20, 2014, at http://timesofindia.indiatimes.com/india/Valley-paradox-Infiltration-down-but-violence-on-the-rise/articleshow/40454647.cms
26. Yaqoob Khan Bangash, "Maybe We Have Forgotten Kashmir?," *The Express Tribune*, December 10, 2012, at http://tribune.com.pk/story/477777/maybe-we-have-forgotten-kashmir
27. Yaqoob Khan Bangash, "Time to Forget Kashmir," *The Express Tribune*, July 04, 2011, at http://tribune.com.pk/story/202209/time-to-forget-kashmir

3

Changing Relations between Bangladesh and India: Perceptions in Bangladesh

M. Humayun Kabir

Perception formation is essentially an exercise in social construction. In most cases, it is shaped by the interplay of complex set of social, political, economic and psychological factors. Geographical location and historical experiences along with public discourse and policy orientations of other nations can also deeply affect the formation of collective perception of a nation. Beyond these factors, what is equally important is the way available information is arranged and interpreted to generate a meaningful picture or image about events and developments, and how these interpretations are absorbed and used by the people and the policymakers.[1] This process could either be rational or biased depending on their orientations.

Needless to say that such a process is incredibly complex in South Asia. It grows out of the proximity of nations, their shared history, cultural affinities and their search for distinctive national identity in contemporary times.[2] Regardless of what the South Asian nations think of their national identity, fact is that the process is still evolving. For some, it is a process of developing and consolidating a particular kind of national identity, while for others, it is a question of updating the existing sense of identity in the context of evolving realities.[3] This nuanced and complicated process often demands rigorous analysis and sympathetic understanding.

It is a challenge to articulate a composite picture about perceptions a nation holds about other nations, as the process is often fragmented and highly nuanced. Different segments of people in a society can also have different perceptions about a neighbouring country, depending on their personal experience, or their receptivity to general discourse or even their interaction with various social and political institutions, such as the media, political parties, civil society organisations and even the government.

Self Perception in Bangladesh

Self perception is a key element in developing perceptions about others, including other nations. In Bangladesh, perceptions of the people about the outside world, including the neighbourhood, have been shaped by their past collective experience, which was often tumultuous, and their aspirations for the present and the future. Two related processes may have worked closely to create a deep impact on the collective psyche of the people of Bangladesh. First, historically, the people of Bangladesh have suffered from a deep sense of deprivation and victimisation, which was caused first by the oppression carried out by the Hindu *zamindars* and then by the British and Pakistani rulers.[4] They also suffered from a deliberate process of putting them into a social and political stereotype. As result, they developed a strong negative view about the hierarchical power structure. Second, the people in this part of the South Asian landmass generally responded to the above in two ways. One was to harness their intrinsic strength. In this context, social mobilisation, organisational creativity and resilience were used as tools to overcome the perceived sense of deprivation. The second method was to mobilise support from outside. In this pursuit, depending on the situation, they formed temporary alliances with different social and political forces, including the external ones, to fight out the adversity. In the process, they developed skills in the art of public mobilisation and flexibility in choosing friends for protecting and promoting their collective goals, which essentially culminated in the creation of Bangladesh as a nation state through the glorious war of liberation in 1971.

A socially-driven, egalitarian and enterprising nation was thus born in Bangladesh, which is fiercely independent in its outlook and attaches high value to individual entrepreneurship, social creativity and collaborative connectivity to its neighbourhood. As Bangladesh aspires to become a middle income nation,[5] it will dig deep into the collective insights generated from its historical experiences and the interplay of factors in the present day reality. Perhaps, motivated by this aspiration, Bangladesh has consciously tried to stay away from the binary outlook based on realist approach in South Asia and advocated utilisation of collaborative approach for improving political understanding,[6] strengthening economic cooperation as well as promoting open social interactions to engender a climate of trust and understanding among the nations in the region and beyond.[7]

Perception Parameters between Bangladesh and India

Several factors frame or condition the perceptions about India in Bangladesh. Some of the following are noteworthy:

- *Geography:* India sits at the centre of the South Asian landmass and all South Asian nations including Bangladesh share borders, cultures and ethnic affiliations with India. Bangladesh shares more than 4,000 km of land borders along with a sizeable portion of maritime boundary with India and shares huge number of followers of major religions with India. These factors have had a complex impact on its identity formation, evolution of self-image, shaping of collective outlook and its policy options vis-à-vis India.[8] Indeed, proximity has created both opportunities and challenges for Bangladesh and India. The Indian High Commissioner to Bangladesh Pankaj Saran articulated it rather appropriately when he said, "India and Bangladesh are neighbours. It is a fact of life. But how we become good neighbours, [*sic*] that is a challenge for us."[9]
- *Identity process:* Bangladesh has the unique distinction of achieving its independence through an armed struggle, which no South Asian nation had done before in that scale and intensity. War, being a great mobiliser and leveller, made a deep impact on the self-image of the people of Bangladesh and their sense of national identity. Learning from historical experiences, the people of Bangladesh have a strong belief in their own strength of determination and their ability to stand up for protecting their vital collective interests.[10]

  History has endowed Bangladesh with two mutually reinforcing pillars of identity—culture and religion. Over the centuries, these two elements have blended seamlessly to give the people of Bangladesh a unique sense of strength, flexibility and diversity. Bangladeshi scholars have articulated this phenomenon of duality in identity in this way: "The justification for Bangladesh's political independence from Pakistan and (earlier) India...was to be found in the identity of the nation-state as both Bengali and Muslim."[11] There was, thus, this 'duality of heritage'[12] that, among other things, contributed to shaping the external behaviour of Bangladesh. Historically then, what is now the Bangladesh nation evolved through its having to deal with the West Bengali Hindu community, now a part of India, and their fellow Muslims in the rest of South Asia, most of the latter eventually assuming the form of Pakistan.[13]

  Contrary to prevailing perceptions in certain quarters in India,[14] Bangladesh has remained a functionally secular polity. National priorities and past electoral outcomes and recent polls on possible preferences of the voters in the elections of 2014 would reconfirm this understanding.

Nonetheless, there is no denying that the continued governance deficits perpetuated by the successive governments in Bangladesh have somehow eroded the public trust on the liberal and secular values and practices. Marginal forces are trying to capitalise on this governance gap.[15] It is possible that these developments have generated some images in India to reinforce the stereotyped mindset about Bangladesh.[16] What would be helpful is to appreciate, show some respect and reinforce, the delicate balance which exists between these two pillars of Bangladeshi identity.

- *Power setting:* Power setting in South Asia is asymmetric in nature. For Bangladesh, it is far more complex than many other nations in South Asia. India was the closest ally of Bangladesh both during its war of liberation in 1971 and its aftermath as Bangladesh began its journey as a nation.[17] This period in a way saw the continuation of the solid social compact, which was formed among the people and government of Bangladesh and those in India based on shared values and sacrifice made during the war of liberation.[18] However, this process of understanding and trust somehow weakened as a statist approach started to define the relations between Bangladesh and India.[19] Differences in aspirations became apparent as India pursued its strategic objectives, while Bangladesh pursued its self exploration as an independent nation. Even today, the narrative on the war in 1971 on both sides of the border is nuanced and sometimes one-sided.[20] Unfortunately, this gap still persists and continues to shape the nature of our relationship. [21]
- *Policy initiatives:* Unique location, size and history, particularly the recent history, has endowed India with certain advantages. Based on them, India has conceptualised its role in the region and developed its strategic objectives and tools to advance its interests. Generally, India has relied on hard approaches under different doctrines and models to achieve its objectives.[22] Although relations between Bangladesh and India have remained largely stable during the last 42 years, a few bumps have appeared along the way. As against the bilateral approach pursued by India in South Asia and its emphasis on security issues, Bangladesh has always advocated a concept of collaboration and cooperation on larger scale among the South Asian nations, the basic framework of which was laid out under the South Asian Association for Regional Cooperation (SAARC) process.[23] Having fought hard for establishing its own identity and dignity, Bangladesh is keen to pursue a creative and sustainable model of relationship with India, instead of investing energy on dated models of engagement, which generally stoke fears rather than friendship.
- *India as an economic power:* The rise of India as an economic power has created a new environment in South Asia. It has influenced the way people

think about India and how they shape their responses to this new phenomenon. For Bangladesh, India has remained a close economic partner since 1971 and currently stands second to China as its largest import source.[24] India is also a partner in informal trade transactions, which is either equivalent or more in size to formal one.[25] In theory, Bangladesh enjoys duty-free access to Indian market for almost 98 per cent of its products since the end of 2011. Overall, Bangladesh considers the rise of India as an economic power as a positive development and looks at India as a major partner in economic progress and prosperity. Indeed, the potential of economic cooperation is huge given the complementary nature of their national aspirations and objectives.

Recent Developments

The interplay of these factors has produced several consequences in terms of perception formation in Bangladesh. A few noteworthy trends will be discussed below, with particular focus on some of the recent initiatives:

First, over the last 42 years, relations between Bangladesh and India have moved through an uneven trajectory. However, since 2009, Bangladesh and India have decided to introduce new energy into their bilateral relations and proactively explored the areas of convergence between them. Accordingly, the government of Bangladesh under Prime Minister Sheikh Hasina unilaterally took several policy initiatives. One of them was to extend key strategic concession to India by allowing it to use various facilities in Bangladesh for getting access to the north-eastern Indian states.[26] Second, Bangladesh firmly dealt with the extremist elements, which had a significant impact both on the domestic environment and on bilateral relations with India.[27] This policy strengthened the process of security collaboration with India particularly on counter terrorism and also supported India's larger regional and global aspirations.[28] On its part, India responded with a strong support for the Bangladesh Government and signed a protocol to implement the Land Boundary Agreement (LBA), extended a credit line of $1 billion, agreed on utilisation of common resources, including waters of common rivers under a basin wise concept, opened its market for duty-free entry of products from Bangladesh under the bilateral and regional trade framework, and relaxed visa procedures to improve people-to-people contacts, among others.[29] During this period, political relations were also consolidated through series of high-level visits in both directions.[30]

These policy initiatives had a positive influence on the public perception in Bangladesh; they were viewed as necessary steps to jump start the relationship with India in the positive direction. Most of the political parties supported these initiatives of the government; local think tanks, research organisations, business leaders, media and members of civil society also endorsed these initiatives.[31] On the other side, in India, favourable public opinion also endorsed these initiatives for improvement in bilateral relations.[32] It looked like that after many years of benign neglect at the best and adversarial orientation at the worst,[33] Bangladesh received an objective review in India for its proactive policy initiatives.[34] To a large measure, the governments in both countries were indeed responding to public aspirations with their initiatives.[35] However, the initial burst of optimism soon lost momentum exposing the fragile nature of changing perceptions. It also raised the critical question about the overall sustainability of public support for the new initiatives.[36]

Challenges

The big question is why this happened? Let us explore some of the underlying challenges:

Conceptual confusion: Despite claims by a former Indian foreign minister to make the relations between Bangladesh and India as a new model of relationship in South Asia,[37] Indian policy line on Bangladesh lacked creativity and consistency.[38] Bangladesh made several dramatic concessions to India, which had transformed the regional strategic scenario, but the response from India was laggard. It became apparent that India was largely unprepared to meet the new game changing demands of the hour in terms of building a new model of relationship with Bangladesh.[39]

Consequently, a perception gained ground in Bangladesh that instead of forming a partnership for utilising the new openings in bilateral relations, India was pursuing its traditional realist agenda to consolidate its own national gains. Several instances contributed to reinforce such an impression. On the transit issue, for example, the Indian approach was widely seen as being insensitive to the expectations in Bangladesh although public mood was generally supportive of granting this arrangement to India. India fell short on several counts.

First, as the deal on transit issue fell through during the visit of the then Indian Prime Minister Manmohan Singh in September 2011, India appeared to have acted sneakily to advance its objectives by utilising the revised bilateral Inland Water Trade and Transit Protocol of 1972 and that again was done in great haste.[40] The people of Bangladesh in general did not view this attempt kindly.[41]

India also came slow on fulfilling its commitments to develop the Ashuganj river port for facilitating movement of its cargo, including oversized ones, to its north eastern region. India also completely disregarded the environmental concerns while transporting its oversized cargo along Ashuganj-Akhaura land route.[42] Again, the controversy created over the payment of service charges for utilising the port facilities and other services was read as an effort to manipulate the system in India's favour.[43] Such an effort irritated even the most ardent proponents of providing transit facilities to India. One of them termed the Indian behaviour on this issue as 'trickery' and warned that this kind of attitude would not help in building trust between Bangladesh and India. He indeed echoed general sentiment prevailing in Bangladesh.[44] Recent effort by India to secure access to road infrastructure in Bangladesh, pending finalisation of a regional road network under the SAARC framework, represents another instance of hasty move by India on a purely unilateral motive.

Second, the recent decision to establish a coal-fired 1320 MW joint venture power plant in Ramphal in Bangladesh also came under strong public criticism for not putting up adequate protection to safeguard the environmental issues in the Sunderbans in Bangladesh.[45] Media and civil society actors have been raising public consciousness on this issue since the idea was first floated. Regardless, the prime ministers of both Bangladesh and India laid the foundation stone for the project on October 05, 2013. Consequently, while the people in general welcomed the joint venture project with India, they could not find the justification for insisting on the controversial venue.[46] It seemed that neither the government of India nor that of Bangladesh could read the sentiments of the common people in Bangladesh, and in the process contributed to reinforcing the negative trend of public perception, which could have been easily avoided.

Likewise, on the security and political issues, India seems to be stuck in the past mindset rather than looking forward. Three subtexts could be noted in this context. First, Indian political approach in Bangladesh seems to be fragmented and short-sighted. While Bangladesh Government showed leadership and took a high-risk firm position against security threats emanating from the extremist elements, which served the strategic objectives both of Bangladesh and India, the Indian response was at best half-hearted. It could not also muster enough domestic support to deliver on the formal commitments made to Bangladesh. Second, Indian outreach to various stakeholders in Bangladesh also sent mixed signals. While the people of Bangladesh appreciated the even-handed approach taken by the Indian leadership, particularly by the Indian President Pranab Mukherjee and the then Prime Minister Manmohan Singh with regard to reaching out to major political parties in Bangladesh during their visits to Dhaka, many other Indian initiatives associated India too close with the present government of Bangladesh, which suffers from a questionable reputation due to its pronounced failures on many governance issues. Open partisan positions taken on some of the internal developments in Bangladesh also did not help India's public image in Bangladesh.[47]

Third, the Indian propensity to look at its relationship with Bangladesh through the prism of Indo-Pakistan rivalry is not generally appreciated in Bangladesh. There is a widespread impression in Bangladesh that India has not been able to lift itself above the India-Pakistan binary approach even after Bangladesh has taken some bold initiatives to address major security concerns of India and delivered steadfastly on some of the long standing challenges in this area.[48] Many Bangladeshis view the Indian approach as too static and feel frustrated with India having not suitably capitalised on the new collaborative security framework offered by Bangladesh.[49]

The concept of regional cooperation, as embodied in the SAARC, fits well into the foreign policy vision of Bangladesh and as such enjoys high degree of respect in Bangladesh. Recent Indian interest and activism in SAARC is seen as a positive development. However, there is a feeling in Bangladesh that India is still unsure about its relationship with SAARC, may be still reluctant to empower the SAARC process and is still hesitant to allow SAARC process to drive the regional collaboration. Against the backdrop of lacklustre performance of SAARC, an experiment has been launched during the last few years to energise the concept of sub-regional cooperation among Bangladesh, India, Nepal and Bhutan to deal with issues of common concern and interest. Bangladesh and India have been particularly advocating sub-regional collaboration for exploring connectivity, developing infrastructure and energy network, and preserving environment, among others.

Yet, the public perception in Bangladesh remains unclear about the modalities for implementing the identified agenda under the sub-regional cooperation. In fact, public perception is largely divided on this issue. One group of people considers this idea as a means to validate the Indo-centric foreign policy agenda of the present government in Bangladesh, and as such they are confused about the possible destination of this process. The other group views it as a deliberate effort to create a sub-group, which would be dominated by India and used to reduce the capacity of SAARC as a vehicle for regional cooperation. Regardless, the idea of sub-regional cooperation in general enjoys a positive review in Bangladesh.

Skewed information flow: Free flow of information is a critically important element in shaping the perceptions of common people. Yet, this has been either in short supply or available only in unidirectional manner in the case of Bangladesh-India relations. Despite a great deal of activism in recent years, neither the government of Bangladesh nor that of India has been able to sufficiently explain its objectives and agenda to the people through an effective communications strategy.[50] Piecemeal availability of information obviously led to confusion about various initiatives undertaken in bilateral relations. This was particularly noticeable in Bangladesh, where different policy versions were offered by the ministers and advisers on issues of vital public interest, which only complicated the understanding on issues of national priority.

A larger issue revolves around the skewed nature of flow of information between Bangladesh and India.[51] While Bangladesh has allowed around 30 Indian private television channels to regularly telecast their programmes in Bangladesh, many of which have huge audience, only few private television channels from Bangladesh have been allowed to reach out to the Indian audience and that too in limited number of places.[52] Even after a formal agreement was signed between India and Bangladesh during the visit of Indian Prime Minister to Bangladesh in 2011[53] for exchange of programmes between *Doordarshan* and *Bangladesh Television* (BTV), the process is yet to commence. Again, serious questions have been raised about the kind of exposure the Indian audience will get through BTV programmes, which are widely considered as extremely partisan in nature, and hence, rated poorly even in Bangladesh.

Obviously, the reluctance to allow free flow of information between these two neighbourly states neither helps to shape the public perceptions in an objective way nor improves understanding about each other's objectives and priorities. Despite citing commercial arguments by the Indian side, there is a widespread impression in Bangladesh that Indian authorities have not been active enough to allow free flow of information between Bangladesh and India. Consequently, despite the widespread attraction for Indian TV programmes in Bangladesh, India does not have enough traction in terms of favourable public perception as a friendly neighbour.

Socialisation gaps: The socialisation process conditions public perception in a significant way. Family, academic institutions, professional organisations, media and social networks play their roles in this process. Due to historical reasons, national narratives in South Asian nations have a strong dose of local perspectives, often casting others in a negative stereotype. What is striking is the fact that neither Bangladesh nor India has made any serious effort to make enough objective information available to their citizens to allow them to understand the priorities of the other side in the correct context. Gossip, innuendoes and often negative stories making headlines in the newspaper therefore fill this gap and frame the public discourse accordingly. The result is that what we know about a particular event in India may not be true or give complete picture, and vice versa. Mixed with domestic cultural orientation, distorted stories may indeed frame public perception.

Domestic challenges: As relations between Bangladesh and India took a visible upswing, particularly during the last five years, the Indian leadership was obviously keen to project it as a success story of Indian diplomacy in the region. It looked that way after the visit of Bangladesh Prime Minister to India in January 2010. However, the mixed outcome of the Indian Prime Minister's visit to Dhaka in September 2011, followed by a series of unsuccessful efforts to secure ratification of LBA and reaching an agreement on the sharing of Teesta water exposed the internal governance challenges faced by the Indian Government. Inability of the government to deliver on its commitments diminished the reputation of India as a responsible nation, with corresponding impact on its image as an emerging power.[54] Even many Indian experts acknowledged that the mismatch between what was promised to Bangladesh and what could be delivered had negatively affected the image of India in Bangladesh and in the region.[55]

Again, the lack of coordination between the commitments of the political leadership and the capacity of bureaucracy to deliver also affected public perception about India in Bangladesh. Unworkable provisions in the contract and the delay in disbursement of $1 billion credit to Bangladesh were not seen positively.[56] Likewise, the continued killing of Bangladeshi nationals on the borders produced two types of strong public reactions in Bangladesh. First, it demonstrated the lack of coordination between the commitments made by the political leadership of India and actions taken by law enforcing machinery on the ground, which in the process exposed a serious weakness of the system. Second, continued killing of Bangladesh nationals at the borders by the Border Security Force (BSF) created a hugely negative backlash on the collective mindset in Bangladesh. Most people in Bangladesh perceive India as an insensitive neighbour motivated by the objective of promoting only its own interests.[57] Erection of border fences around Bangladesh also does not transmit a friendly message, and people in Bangladesh widely resent such an 'unfriendly' act.[58]

Given the fact that social forces exert considerable influence on public perceptions and policy process in Bangladesh, any initiative with India evokes considerable degree of questions and passions. In addition to the Indian behaviour, the reputation of the government in Bangladesh has also affected the outcome. While the present government can deserve credit for taking a number of forward-looking initiatives with India, many of these initiatives somehow lost their intrinsic value as the government could not sufficiently explain its position and policy to the people. Consequently, a widespread impression grew that the government had conceded more than what they could get from India. Again, as the popularity of the government plummeted, so did the reputation of India.[59] With the sharpening of public consciousness and interest in policy matters, it is possible that policy initiatives will remain under constant public scrutiny both in Bangladesh and India in the coming days. India being the larger neighbour perhaps needs to demonstrate more maturity, insight and fairness in dealing with its neighbours, including Bangladesh.

Way Forward

The relations between Bangladesh and India are unique and at the same time complex from several points of view. Bangladesh began its journey as an independent nation with an extremely close partnership with India. Moreover, Bangladesh and India share similar democratic values and aspirations, pursue similar economic goals, offer economic opportunities to each other and face similar challenges.[60] Bangladesh is surrounded on three sides by India, while Bangladesh encircles a large part of the North eastern states of India, which makes it integrally linked to the future development of this region.[61] Both Bangladesh and India also share maritime boundaries and have many common regional and inter-regional interests to advance the mutually supportive objectives.

Despite all these compulsions and attractions, the level of public trust between Bangladesh and India is still rather thin and the conceptual confusions have added further complexity to this relationship. India's continuing preference for bilateralism in advancing its national interests, and the propensity of some key stakeholders in India to interpret events in Bangladesh in their own image, do not fit into the dynamic trajectory of relationship.[62] In order to lift the bilateral relationship to a new level, it is time that India takes the lead in developing a collaborative, creative and forward-looking framework for conducting relations in the neighbourhood, and Bangladesh could be a useful model for this purpose.

A growing tail wind could assist this process to mature. Over the last few years, a favourable public opinion has been created both in Bangladesh and India over the growing convergence of interest in some key areas. It is encouraging to note that the people on both sides have developed shared expectations in the following areas, among others: mutual desire for continued domestic and regional stability and strengthening of democratic governance, shared aspiration for upholding the liberal values and practices, delivering on the promise of good governance and intensifying cooperation against any possible rise of extremism, mutual aspiration for consolidating the economic partnership, resolution of outstanding bilateral issues through dialogue and in a mutually beneficial manner and exploring opportunities on bilateral, sub-regional, regional and inter-regional basis. Given their deep significance in the lives of common people, even if there is a change in political set up in India and Bangladesh, these elements would perhaps continue to provide solid building blocks to construct a collaborative and creative partnership between Bangladesh and India.

While the relationship between Bangladesh and India has witnessed a considerable degree of movement in recent years, the structure for high-level consultation is still weak. Existing bilateral consultation mechanisms at the bureaucratic level seem to play a largely inconsequential role in terms of influencing public perception and outcome. In view of this, it would be good if the visibility of relations could be lifted through institutionalising a high-level mechanism for holding regular consultations between the leaders of the two countries. If possible, multiple stakeholders, including the Opposition, could be brought into the loop of such high-level consultations. This would definitely widen and deepen the traction for creative and sustainable initiatives.

In recent years, India has been toying with the idea of creating new partnerships with its neighbours based on economic priorities and linkages.[63] This model could get a lively face in Bangladesh given the fact that Bangladesh and India share common economic goals and enjoy complementarities in their endowments. India could engage Bangladesh with a robust economic agenda and expand cooperation in trade, investment, technology transfer and connectivity on bilateral, sub regional, regional and inter-regional basis. Bangladesh, on its part, could offer peace, stability, connectivity, economic progress and a secure regional environment for India. If this process succeeds, it would definitely have a beneficial impact on public perceptions and create a new set of stakeholders with a positive outlook.

Despite considerable movement of people in both directions, social connectivity between Bangladesh and India has remained relatively modest. Given the deep impact of social interactions on public perceptions, it is imperative to energise the process of building people-to-people contacts in both directions. Facilitating easy movement of people, promoting cultural, educational and scientific exchange at official and civil society levels could serve this purpose. Updating the bilateral agreements and utilising the regional institutional arrangements deserve serious attention in this respect. Needless to say, high visibility of social interaction is likely to exercise a positive influence on public perceptions about the bilateral relations.

Parallel to this, special attention need to be given to free flow of information between Bangladesh and India. In this context, it is important to allow private TV channels from Bangladesh to telecast their programmes in India without any further delay. Government and private sector could work together to facilitate this process. Research has shown that TV and radio communication can deeply influence public perception and given the existing gap in this area urgent efforts should be made to improve the communication flow both ways.

In addition to the general framework of relationship, a roadmap could be worked out to resolve the outstanding issues between Bangladesh and India. Otherwise, these issues will continue to cast a negative shadow on public perception. In the short term, the ratification process of LBA could be completed and the agreement on sharing of waters of the Teesta River should be signed. Urgent steps could also be initiated to remove non-tariff and para-tariff barriers and encourage investment in Bangladesh to facilitate more trade between

Bangladesh and India. Visa regime could be further updated to facilitate easy movement of people in both directions.

In the medium and long-term, efforts could be undertaken to develop common projects based on utilisation of shared resources such as water, energy and environment in line with the Framework Agreement on Cooperation for Development signed in 2011,[64] and leverage on the opportunities in such areas as regional and inter-regional connectivity and communication. The demarcation of maritime boundary, maritime security, counter terrorism, economic integration and investment, disaster management and climate-related issues, among others, could also come under this category.

Conclusion

Relationship between Bangladesh and India is unique in many respects and they need each other for advancing their own interests. India was a partner during the birth of Bangladesh and steadfastly stood behind it during early years of its journey as a nation. This was possible due to the social compact, which grew during the trying times of the war of liberation in 1971. But, as India started pursuing its statist objectives, the social compact collapsed. Bangladesh responded with a similar outlook. Relationship between the two nations thereafter meandered through many ups and downs.

The current government in Bangladesh has undertaken a number of bold and in some cases unilateral initiatives to address some of the major concerns and interests of India. On its part, India has also responded with its own agenda. Despite initial optimism of a breakthrough, the process is yet to gain a desirable level of traction in public perception as both the governments fell short in explaining their objectives to their people. Indian efforts to pursue its own objectives without showing much regard to the expectations of the people of Bangladesh and its inability to deliver on its commitments, largely due to its domestic challenges, has cast a shadow on public perception in Bangladesh about India.

Perception is a complex social phenomenon having deep roots in the cultural edifice of a society; therefore, it is important for both India and Bangladesh to understand each other's priorities, concerns and constraints, and then design their policy responses accordingly. Incomplete and partial understanding of the nature of public perceptions may lead to unanticipated policy handicaps and mistakes, as has been seen on many occasions. Given the strong complementarities in their relationship and having many common aspirations and goals, it would be better for India and Bangladesh to build up on the converging trends in their relationship. In this pursuit, they could design a new model of relationship keeping in view the outlook, orientation and aspirations of the people of Bangladesh for a better future under a collaborative, mutually beneficial and sustainable partnership with India.

ENDNOTES

1. Robert Jervis, *Perception and Misperception in International Politics*, Princeton University Press, Princeton, 1976, p. 35.
2. S.L. Sharma and T.K. Oommen, *Nation and National Identity in South Asia*, Orient Longman Limited, New Delhi, 2000.
3. Muchkund Dubey, *India's Foreign Policy: Coping with the Changing World*, Pearson Education, Delhi, 2014, pp. 43-52.
4. Habib Siddiqui, "Letter from America: Bengal under the English Rule (1757-1905) – Part 1," *Asian Tribune*, December 08, 2013.
5. "Bangladesh Overview," *The World Bank*, at http://www.worldbank.org/en/country/bangladesh/overview
6. Cody M. Poplin, "India-Bangladesh Relations: A Review of Bilateral Opportunities and Constraints," *Background Paper No. 1*, India Development Cooperation Research (IDCR) Project, February 2013.
7. Kamal Uddin Ahmed, *Bangladesh and Its Neighbours*, Asiatic Society of Bangladesh, Dhaka, 2008.
8. Bayezid Ismail Choudhury and Peter Armstrong, "Monument and Architecture in Shaping Bangladeshi National Identity," *Global Built Environment Review* (*GBER*), 8 (3), 2012, pp. 45-67.
9. "Youths Can Build Bridges," *bdnews24.com*, Dhaka, October 20, 2013.
10. Bayezid Ismail Choudhury and Peter Armstrong, no. 8.
11. Naureen Chowdhury Fink, "On the Borderlines: Politics, Religion and Violence in Bangladesh," *International Peace Academy*, New York, 2009, as mentioned in Iftekhar Ahmed Chowdhury, "The Roots of Bangladeshi National Identity: Their Impact on State Behaviour," *Working Paper No.63*, Institute of South Asian Studies, National University of Singapore, June 10, 2009, p. 17.
12. Ali Riaz, "'God Willing': The Politics and Ideology of Islamism in Bangladesh," *Comparative Studies of South Asia, Africa, and the Middle East*, 23 (1 & 2), Project Muse, Chicago, 2003, p. 2.
13. Iftekhar Ahmed Chowdhury, no. 11.
14. For an analysis of the remarks made by the Indian Prime Minister Manmohan Singh on Bangladesh on June 29, 2011 based on the reported intelligence inputs, see Tom Wright, "Singh Steps In It Again," *The Wall Street Journal*, July 06, 2011.
15. M. Mukhlesur Rahman Chowdhury, "Good Governance in Bangladesh: A Quest for Democracy," January 19, 2014, at http://www.countercurrents.org/chowdhury190114.htm.
16. "US to Intensify Talks with India on Bangladesh," *bdnews24.com*, Dhaka, November 08, 2013.
17. Muchkund Dubey, no. 3, pp. 77-100.
18. Ibid.
19. J.N. Dixit, *India's Foreign Policy and Its Neighbours*, Gyan Publishing House, New Delhi, 2001.
20. Afsan Chowdhury, "1971: Why India and Bangladesh Should be Mutually Grateful," *bdnews24.com*. Dhaka, December 15, 2010.
21. For an excellent study on this subject, see Smruti S. Pattanaik, "Internal Political Dynamics and Bangladesh's Foreign Policy towards India," *Strategic Analysis*, 29 (3), July-September 2005, pp. 395-426.
22. Muchkund Dubey, no. 3, pp. 46-48. For an interesting perspective, see Smruti S. Pattanaik, "India's Neighbourhood Policy: Perceptions from Bangladesh," *Strategic Analysis*, 35 (1), 2010, pp. 71-87.

23. Bangladesh initiated the process through consultation among the South Asian nations in early 1981, and then the entire process culminated in the creation of SAARC as a regional organisation in December 1985 in Dhaka.
24. In fiscal year 2012-13, Bangladesh imported goods worth US$ 6.3 billion from China and exported only $485 million; and imported Indian goods worth US$ 4.2 billion, while exporting to India goods worth US$ 563 million during the same period. For more details, see Talha bin Habib, "Business Brass to Urge China to Ramp up BD Garment Import," *The Financial Express*, Dhaka, June 05, 2014.
25. "India-Bangladesh Bilateral Trade and Potential Free Trade Agreement," *Paper No. 13, Bangladesh Development Series*, The World Bank, 2006.
26. Joint Communiqué, Government of India, Ministry of External Affairs, New Delhi, January 13, 2010.
27. Bruce Vaughn, "Bangladesh: Political and Strategic Developments and U.S. Interests," *Congressional Research Service*, April 01, 2010.
28. Rajeev Ranjan Chaturvedy and David M. Malone, "Re-engaging with Bangladesh: Active Economic and Security Co-operation Can Help India Reinvigorate Ties with Bangladesh," *The Business Standard*, New Delhi, July 15, 2011.
29. Cody M. Poplin, "India-Bangladesh Relations: A Review of Bilateral Opportunities and Constraints," *Background Paper No. 1*, India Development Cooperation Research (IDCR) Project, February 20, 2013.
30. Syed Tashfin Chowdhury, "Bangladesh Lauds Sonia Gandhi Visit," *The Asia Times*, Hong Kong, July 29, 2011; Harsh V. Pant, "A Tale of Two Visits," *The Telegraph*, Kolkata, March 09, 2013.
31. Anisur Rahman, "B'Desh Media Welcomes Inking of 'Historic Treaties' with India," *The Business Standard*, New Delhi, January 12, 2010.
32. Harsh V. Pant, "Why India Must Pay Attention to Bangladesh?," *Rediffnews*, New Delhi, March 08, 2013; and M. Serajul Islam, "Indo-Bangladesh Relations: The Importance of Perception," *The Daily Star*, Dhaka, October 09, 2010.
33. Muchkund Dubey, no. 3, pp. 54-55.
34. Indrani Bagchi, "With Pranab Visit, India Signals Changed Approach to Bangladesh," *The Times of India*, New Delhi, August 06, 2010.
35. "Embraceable You: Growing Geo Political Interest Push India to Seek Better Relations Nearer Home," *The Economist*, July 30, 2011.
36. For an excellent analysis on this subject, see Mahfuz Anam, "Bangladesh: A Fine Bilateral Balance," in *Neighbourhood Views of India*, South Asia Studies, Gateway House Research Paper No. 7, Mumbai, 2012, pp. 16-31.
37. Remarks of the Indian Minister for External Affairs S.M. Krishna at Bangladesh Institute of International and Strategic Studies (BIISS), Dhaka, July 08, 2011.
38. M. Serajul Islam, "New Era of Bangladesh-India Relations Based on Development-Democracy-Demography," *The Daily Sun*, Dhaka, July 17, 2011.
39. "Bangla Miffed over Teesta Hurdle: Dhaka Terms 'Very Frustrating' India's Last-Minute Decision Not to Ink the 'Crucial' Deal," *The Telegraph*, Kolkata, September 07, 2011; "No Water, No Transit," *The Samakal (Bangla)*, Dhaka, September 07, 2011; "PM's Bangladesh Visit: A Non-Starter," *The Shillong Times*, Shillong, September 09, 2011; and "Indian Media blamed Mamata," *The Samakal*, Dhaka, December 07, 2011. For an Indian perspective, see Devadeep Purohit, "PM's Teesta Dismay Flows," *The Telegraph*, Kolkata, September 08, 2011.
40. Sarath Kumara and Wimal Perera, "Indian Prime Minister Visits Bangladesh," September 10, 2011, at http://www.wsws.org/en/articles/2011/09/indi-s10.html
41. Adverse public opinion led to the halt of trial run of overland transportation of Indian

cargo through Ashugunj-Akhaura route during September–October 2011. For details, see "No Transit without Preparation," *Prothom Alo (Bangla)*, Dhaka, October 27, 2011.

42. Ishak Mia, "India-Bangladesh Land Transit: An Environmental Perspective," *International Policy Digest*, August 11, 2012. Also, see Asjadul Kibria, "Rush for a Transit Deal," *The Daily Star*, Dhaka, June 30, 2011.
43. M. Emdadul Haq, "Integrity Pact for Indo-Bangladesh Relations," *The Daily Star*, Dhaka, June 21, 2013.
44. Moinul Islam, "India Will Lose If It Cheats on Transit Issue," *Prothom Alo (Bangla)*, Dhaka, November 06, 2011.
45. Khalilur Rahman, "Controversy over Ramphal Power Plant Site," *The Financial Express*, Dhaka, April 21, 2013; "Disastrous for the Sunderbans: Eminent Citizens for Site Change," *The Daily Star*, Dhaka, October 07, 2013; Mohammad Badrul Ahsan, "Railroading Ramphal Power Plant," *The Daily Star*, Dhaka, October 04, 2013; "Government Unmoved by Environmentalists Concerns: Ramphal Foundation Stoke Laying on Oct 22," *The Daily Star*, Dhaka, September 25, 2013; and Anu Muhammad, "Ramphal Power Plant: A Project of Deception and Mass Destructions," *bdnews24.com*, Dhaka, September 19, 2013.
46. Hasan Jahid Tusher and Amanur Aman, "Ramphal Get Rolling," *The Daily Star*, Dhaka, October 06, 2013; and "PM Asks Not to Create Confusion over Ramphal Power Plant," *The Daily Star*, Dhaka, November 13, 2013.
47. Sheikh Shahriar Zaman, "India: Elections Must Be Held on Time," *The Dhaka Tribune*, Dhaka, December 05, 2013; Manik Miazee and Abu Baker Siddique, "JP's Resignation Drama Lingers," *The Dhaka Tribune*, Dhaka, December 09, 2013; M. Serajul Islam, "A Diplomat's Disappointing Visit," *The Financial Express*, Dhaka, December 09, 2013; Harun Ur Rashid, "Indian Foreign Secretary's Visit to Dhaka: What does it mean?," *PriyoAustralia.com*, Canberra, December 05, 2013; Suhasini Haider, "Back Bangladesh, Not Hasina or Zia,"*CNN-IBN Blog*, New Delhi, January 11, 2014; Jayanth Jacob, "Bangladesh on Boil, India Part of the Cauldron," *The Hindustan Times*, New Delhi, December 17, 2013; Sudha Ramachandran, "Bangladesh Elections: Was India Right?," Gateway House, Mumbai, January 16, 2014; and "Indian Responsibilities," Editorial, *Anandabazar Patrika*, Kolkata, January 10, 2014.
48. Bangladesh Government took several initiatives against the local militants and alleged Indian insurgents in Bangladesh just after the assumption of power in January 2009. For details, see "Bangla: Leader of Indian Terror Group Arrested," *Rediffnews*, New Delhi, July 17, 2009; "Indian Militant Arrested in Bangladesh," *Rediffnews*, New Delhi, October 01, 2009; and "Blow to ULFA, NLFT: Top Leaders Held in B'Desh," *Rediffnews*, New Delhi, December 02, 2009. For an interesting analysis of the positive fallout of the Bangladesh Government's strong stand against extremism, see Anand Kumar, "Crackdown on Northeastern Insurgents: Dhaka Prepares for Hasina's India Visit," *Institute for Defence Studies and Analyses*, New Delhi, November 18, 2009; and Jyoti Malhotra, "Looking East via the North-East," *The Business Standard*, New Delhi, March 01, 2010.
49. Hasnat Abdul Hye, "India Disappointing?,"*The Daily Sun*, Dhaka, February 17, 2011.
50. M. Humayun Kabir, "Bangladesh-India Relations in the Age of Globalization: Post Prime Ministerial Summit Conference: Track-I Diplomacy," Paper presented in a seminar at the University of Dhaka, Dhaka, September 11, 2011.
51. "Pankaj for Reducing Dhaka-Delhi Info Gap," *The Morning News 24*, Dhaka, March 29, 2014.
52. Omar Khasru, "Refusal of Indian Access to Bangladeshi TV Channels," *The New Age*, Dhaka, July 01, 2012.
53. Information available on the website of High Commission of India, Dhaka, Bangladesh.
54. Sadeq Khan, "Discordant Indian Sound Waves Sours Indo-Bangladesh Amity," *The Holiday*,

Dhaka, July 04, 2013; Abdul Hanna, "A Raw deal, from a friendly neighbour," *The Holiday*, Dhaka, August 15, 2013; "Delhi Again Fails to Introduce LBA bill," *Bdnews24.com*, Dhaka, August 19, 2013; and Kamal Davar, "Let's Not Miss the Big Picture,"*South Asia Monitor*, September 05, 2013.

55. Jyoti Malhotra, "Where did India-Bangladesh Talks Go Wrong?," *Wall Street Journal*, New York, September 14, 2011.

56. For an assessment on the progress on the implementation of projects under $1 billion loan from India, see Jagaran Chakma, "India to Give 85 pc Raw Materials; Tough Strings Tie Five India-Funded Projects," *The Independent*, Dhaka, December 08, 2011.

57. For a glimpse of perilous life along Indo-Bangladesh borders, see Maher Sattar, "Bangladesh-India Border: 'Wall of Death,'" *The Global Post*, January 04, 2012. Bangladesh had to issue a protest note to the Indian authorities following the killing of four Bangladeshi nationals along the border in late December 2011.

58. Brad Adams, "India's Shoot-to-Kill Policy on the Bangladesh Border," *The Guardian*, January 23, 2011.

59. Mizanur Rahman Shelly, "Bangladesh Politics: The Indian connection," *The New Age*, Dhaka, November 24, 2013; "Embraceable You: Growing Geo Political Interest Push India to Seek Better Relations Nearer Home," *The Economist*, July 30, 2011; Haroon Habib, "Resistance to Jan 5 Polls Continues," *The Hindu*, Chennai, January 04, 2014; and Pratyush, "Indian President Visit a Tumultuous Bangladesh," *The Diplomat*, March 08, 2013.

60. For civil society perspective on Bangladesh-India relations, see Rehman Sobhan, "Restoring Commonsense into Indo-Bangladesh Relations: Graduating Diplomacy and Politics into the 21st century," *The Daily Star*, Dhaka, September 05-06, 2011; M. Humayun Kabir, "Bangladesh-India Relations: Confidence Building Initiatives," Paper presented at a seminar hosted by the Rashtrabiggan Samity (Political Science Association) at the Press Club, Dhaka, September 04, 2011; and Mamun Rashid, "Manmohan's Upcoming Visit," *The Financial Express*, Dhaka, September 04, 2011.

61. Pranay Sharma, "East Indiaman Afloat," *Outlook*, September 12, 2011; "Mission to Bangladesh," *The Shillong Times*, September 03, 2011; and "Manmohan Singh's Bangladesh Visit to Transform Ties," *The Gulf News*, Dubai, September 05, 2011.

62. Shah Husain Imam, "A Glimpse of the Indian Mind," *The Daily Star*, Dhaka, September 30, 2013; Sandeep Dikshit, "Prime Minister's Comment on Bangladesh Raises Eyebrows," *The Hindu*, Chennai, July 01, 2011; and Harun Ur Rashid, "Manmohan's Incredible Remarks," *The Daily Star*, Dhaka, July 06, 2011. For a recent perspective, see Kanwal Sibal, "India Has to Take a Long Hard Look at Its Foreign Policy," *Indian Defence Review*, New Delhi, June 02, 2014.

63. For an overview of this policy line, see Christian Wagner, "From Hard Power to Soft Power: Ideas, Interaction, Institutions, and Images in India's South Asia Policy," *Working Paper No. 26*, South Asia Institute, University of Heidelberg, March 2005.

64. "Framework Agreement on Cooperation for Development between India and Bangladesh," *Ministry of External Affairs, Government of India*, New Delhi, September 06, 2011, at http:/ /mea.gov.in/bilateral-documents.htm?dtl/5218/Framework+Agreement+on+Cooperation+ for+ Development+ between+India+and+Bangladesh

4

The Geo-Strategic Matrix and Existential Dimension of Sri Lanka's Conflict, Post-War Crisis and External Relations

Dayan Jayatilleka

I think geopolitics has been underestimated; perhaps overestimated earlier, then there was a reaction, and the pendulum swung too far in the other direction. I am not a geopolitical determinist. I do not believe that geography is destiny. If we look at the case of Cuba, for instance, it is very clearly a dramatic rupture from any notion of geopolitical determinism. However, if we have a notion of long-term history as recommended by Fernand Braudel, Marc Bloch and Lucien Febvre, then we understand the importance of place. We are materially and psychologically constituted at least in part by where we are. Though I would not say that who we are is determined in a monocausal sense by where we are, it is certainly one of the decisive and perhaps one of the determinant factors.

Sri Lanka, as most of us know, is an island. This is a constitutive factor because Sri Lanka is shaped by the fact that it is embedded in the sea. It has no land borders, and this is important.

Geopolitical Component

In the tourist books and the journal articles, Sri Lanka is often identified as the island off the tip of India. It is the most obvious introduction, the shortest introduction to Sri Lanka. However, it is a fundamental factor in a geopolitical sense, in understanding the history and the trajectory of Sri Lanka. Sri Lanka has been defined by India, but it has also defined itself, demarcated itself, as against India. Thus, it is this dialectical relationship with India that has been the single most important geopolitical component in Sri Lanka's evolution.

Usually, we tend to forget the specificities, the concreteness, of a society or a nation, and put them in categories—which is necessary—but without due reference to their concrete specificities. However, there is also the other and opposite phenomenon, and this is true not only for Sri Lanka but also for the United States (US). Specificities are often confused for, or give rise to, notions of exceptionalism and of manifest destinies.

If we consider the notion of the long-term blocks of several thousand years of history, which historians like William McNeill and theorists like Gunder Frank, Giovanni Arrighi and Immanuel Wallerstein have been using, then to understand Sri Lanka today we, perhaps, would have to go back to an early version of the struggle between Catholicism and Protestantism and between Hinduism—the Brahminic concept—and Buddhism, which unlike in the case of the Protestant reformation did not result in a major clash of arms as such. But there was a Counter-Reformation. I use the term Counter-Reformation because Buddhism had not only no notion of caste, the sociological hierarchy into which one is born, which the Brahminic or Hindu faith placed great emphasis on, but even critiqued its very notion. In India, after the zenith of the Emperor Ashoka, who was a Buddhist, there was a counter-reformation, and Buddhism itself was pushed back, downwards to the South. It also migrated to the North and the East, that is, Nepal, Tibet, China, the Far East and Japan. In the South, there was only one place that it could go, and that was Lanka, or Sri Lanka.

Sociological Colouration of Pre-existing Society

The successful counter-reformation or counter-revolution—ideological, sociological, and, interestingly, non-violent in terms of the well-known great wars—pushed Buddhism to this little island to the South of India. Moreover, there this philosophy was retained, one might even say contained, because unlike to the North of the subcontinent where there was the Silk Route, this was an island. Buddhism either converged or became an over-lay, on the ethnic community, the Sinhalese, who may have auto-centrically evolved or come from India, the latter view is open to debate.

The Sinhalese constituted the arithmetical majority of the island, roughly two-thirds, living in two-thirds of the island. Three factors converged: ethnicity, language (which is Sinhala) and the religion of Buddhism. Moreover, Buddhism appraised itself as a philosophy rather than a religion. However, when it was absorbed and retained by this island, it naturally took the sociological colouration and configuration of the pre-existing society. And one might even say that it shifted from a cerebral philosophy to a religion. Further, Sri Lanka was an island with only one neighbour, the Maldives, and nothing to its south. The next constellation of Buddhism was far away, in what is known as Indo-China, the Far East—Laos, Cambodia and Myanmar. Thus, there was a strong amalgam of a religion which no longer dominated, was almost non-existent and had no co-religionists in the vast landmass of the Indian Subcontinent; and an ethno-linguistic community which had no co-ethnics or co-religionists and a language which had some affinities with one or two other languages in the area but was not spoken by a large collective anywhere else in the world. Though for a language that was isolated in the island, it developed considerably. It did not remain an underdeveloped language, and it is said that at least one of the texts is among the oldest pieces of history writing: the *Mahavamsa*.

Sri Lanka has been constituted by its relationship with India in terms of migration, religious diffusion/transmission, as well as military interference and power play, incursion and resistance. Sri Lanka is also defined by the dialectics of its relationship with India.

India inheres in the very fabric of the island; or to change the metaphor, Sri Lanka is an inverted and miniaturised mirror of India: the belief system of the majority in the Southern two-thirds of the island is derived from the teachings of, and is identified with the greatest son and sage of India, Gautam the Buddha, while the minority in the Northern third of the island shares the same language and ethnicity as those in the South of the Indian Subcontinent. In this strange inversion, the domestic geopolitics of the island of Sri Lanka is the reverse, a *camera obscura*, an upside down image of its giant neighbour India. In India, the southernmost part contains Tamil Nadu: 70 million people, who speak the Tamil language, consider themselves of the Tamil ethnicity and are for the most part Hindu. On the island of Sri Lanka, which is separated from India by a very thin strip of water, it is exactly the opposite. It is not the Southern tip but the Northern tip that is pre-eminently Tamil. So, one-third, the top, of the island, is predominantly Tamil, the southern two-thirds is predominantly Sinhala.

Interpretation of Facts

This domestic geopolitical configuration has given rise to a certain narrative. (I would not call it a history because I do not know whether we are talking about objective facts all the time.) From Nietzsche we know that interpretation is as important, and perhaps more important, than fact—though that itself is an interpretation. The interpretation or the pre-eminent narrative, the hegemonic narrative of the history of the island has been one of a southward push from South India by the Tamil kings invading the island and leaving behind a residue from ancient times: of constant waves pushing southward and the Sinhalese pushing back northwards and attempting to rule the entire island. Therefore, this is partly a story of dual power, of shifting balances in a bipolar situation and much longer periods of unipolar hegemony. We can see how the geopolitical configuration gives rise to a kind of a domestic geo-strategic narrative of competing centres and bipolarity: one pole in the North attempts to be auto-centric, and the other in the South, which considers that it has no strategic 'defence in depth' because it is a small island, attempts to constantly prevail, re-impose itself in a project of unification or reunification, reconquista.

In this context, the aforementioned concepts of specificity and exceptionalism become relevant. There are more than two major communities in Sri Lanka. In terms of religion, there are Buddhists, Hindus, Christians—the only religious community comprising both Sinhalese and Tamils (about 7 per cent)—and Muslims. So, there are four religious communities, and two major ethno-lingual communities. Each of these two ethno-linguistic communities has a specific, distinctive kind of a collective psyche where both the Tamils and the Sinhalese consider themselves at one and the same time a minority and a majority. The Tamils feel that they are a minority on the island and therefore discriminated against, and so oppose that discrimination, but at the same time they see themselves as a majority because there are 70 million co-ethnics across the water and of course another million in the diaspora including in the West. This is possibly why the Tamil armed movements and even the unarmed Tamil nationalist parliamentary parties will not accept the kind of solution that Northern Ireland's Catholics, including the Sinn Fein, have accepted. This strange duality is true also for the Sinhalese. The Sinhalese feel that they are the majority on the island, and therefore, they deserve a certain special status, but this is reinforced by the sense of being a minority in the sub-region and in the larger region and in the global space. Thus, there is a striving to assert as a majority but also to defend as a minority. And the fact that Buddhism in what is considered in a pure or more rigorous form (Theravada) is the most predominant faith among the Sinhalese gives them a sense of exceptionalism. They are defending, protecting Buddhism in the area in which Buddhism hardly exists, and a Buddhism which they feel is purer than the variant of the doctrine found in Japan or China. If you look at it in terms of the history of Christianity, the parallel is the kind of Catholicism that prevailed on the Iberian Peninsula in Portugal and Spain until a few decades ago, a somewhat rigid orthodoxy. This is part of the matrix of conflict.

Contemporary Violence

I would embed the contemporary violence and history in this aforementioned matrix of conflict. It is in this matrix that the war took place, the war of 30 years.

Sri Lanka has been an independent state for 64 years, and a little under half of this has been in a situation of war. Interestingly, these wars have not only been between North and South or the two power centres which are preponderantly Sinhalese and Tamils. There have also been wars, anti-systemic wars, waged by an ultra-left insurgent movement, two insurrections in the South of Sri Lanka. Even in the North, while the secessionist war was going on, there was a struggle between the left of the Tamil movement which was drastically weakened and the ultra-nationalist right of the Tamil movement represented by the Liberation Tigers of Tamil Eelam (LTTE). Now we have testimonies from former founder members of the Tigers, testimonies which say that at the beginning of the movement, the leader of the Tigers, Velupillai Prabhakaran, was already an admirer of Adolf Hitler, that *Mein Kampf* had been translated and that even the LTTE's salute was the fascist salute. (As a political scientist, I note that in the 1920s and 30s, in some parts of Central and Eastern Europe, there were movements that were ethno-nationalist but also of a fascist character.)

The two power centres on the island, almost naturally, instinctively, tried to play the larger geopolitics of reaching out to allies, in the region and outside the region, over the past 30 years. These attempts of alliance and of blocs of power balancing underwent drastic, radical recomposition. It was not the same set of alliances that prevailed during the period of 30 years. Most dramatic is the role of India, which, because of Tamil Nadu, was originally supportive not of the project of an independent Tamil country but of the armed movement as a kind of counterweight to the central government in Sri Lanka, the power centre in Colombo. For one phase of the war, from the late 1970s through the 1980s, Delhi was dragged in by Tamil Nadu. The role that Tamil Nadu played and still plays is rather like the role of Miami in the US, in relation to Cuba.

There was a dramatic turning point, when the grandson of Jawaharlal Nehru, the then Prime Minister Rajiv Gandhi, used coercive diplomacy but played a kind of Bonapartist balancing role and got the Sinhalese Government to sign a peace accord which provided provincial autonomy to the Tamil majority areas and sent a peace keeping force of 70,000 Indian troops to police this ceasefire. Now, dramatic as that was, what was more dramatic and illustrative of the specificities of the Tamil ultra-nationalist movement and of the Tamil Tigers was that the Tigers far from supporting this reform and making it work, and perhaps playing a longer term game of greater autonomy, instead fought a war against the Indian peace-keeping force. Moreover, after the peace-keeping forces were withdrawn, not least because of the Tamil Nadu politics, they assassinated Rajiv Gandhi using a suicide bomber on the soil of Tamil Nadu. That caused a dramatic shift in all these alliances, and from that point on, it was not that there was a convergence or an open alliance between Colombo and Delhi but there was a steady rapprochement. When the decisive stage of the war arrived three years ago, the enormous—and now, stronger than ever—geopolitical weight of India was on the side of the Sri Lankan State in determining the final outcome.

Element of Competition between China and India

From the point of view of geopolitics, it is also interesting that not only India but also China supported the Sri Lankan State in the final phases of the war. It is interesting because the relationship between India and China is not devoid of an element of competition though there is great economic cooperation as well. Why did India and China put aside their competition and support the Sri Lankan State in the end game of the war? In this context, the term "Eastphalia" is relevant. Even Henry Kissinger in his new book on China has made a point—made by others as well—that the classic Westaphalian notion of state sovereignty which is no longer observed strictly in the West, certainly in Europe, has migrated to Asia. Why? I would reason that perhaps Asia is at that particular historical stage of state-building—which had been superseded by Europe—where national/state sovereignty becomes of paramount importance.

Thus, it is the convergence of a particular historical moment and particular geopolitical balances on the island, in the region and beyond, between the East and the West, one may even say the global North and the South, which jointly determined the outcome of the Sri Lankan conflict.

Certainly, the story is not over yet. It is still being played out, in the aftermath of the war, in the debate and struggle on the kind of peace. While Sri Lanka has won the war, could it lose the peace? We have seen this happen in the Middle East in the decades after the 1967 Arab-Israeli War which Israel so brilliantly won.

While domestic dynamics and dialectics led to the Sri Lankan war and its outcome, we may, borrowing a term from Lacan and Althusser, say that geopolitics played a role of "over-determination".

Geo-strategic Imperatives of Co-existence

Sri Lanka views India from a Southern or Southernist perspective. In international politics, a perspective from the south is quite distinctive. The third-worldist perspective, later known as the perspective of the global south of global dynamics, is well known. Moreover, a southern perspective is quite specific in terms of the narrative, the causal relationship, and things look differently when viewed from the south whether it is the tri-continental world looking at the global north or whether it is a neighbour looking up at a great landmass. So, I would like to draw attention to the southern vantage point, a rather legitimate notion in the study of politics. (Interestingly, Antonio Gramsci, the great Italian political thinker, often referred to the southern question within Italy too.)

Furthermore, Sri Lanka's is a perspective from the periphery of India. One may think that these two perspectives are co-terminus, but of course they are not because India has a periphery that is not to its south, but Sri Lanka exists at the southern periphery of India, and its relationship with India is, going by Sri Lankan perceptions, mediated by the complex relationship between itself and India's own inner periphery, that of Tamil Nadu. So, it is a story of two or perhaps even three intersecting peripheries: Tamil Nadu being the inner periphery of the Indian State, northern Sri Lanka having co-ethnics from Tamil Nadu or Tamil Nadu being the northern periphery of Sri Lanka, and the relationship between Sri Lanka and India being perceived as filtered through and mediated by the relationship between these two peripheries. In other words, Sri Lanka is on the periphery of India, the north of Sri Lanka is Sri Lanka's northern periphery, Tamil Nadu is the inner periphery, or the southern periphery of India, and Sri Lanka is on India's outer periphery with the point of contact, or the interface being Tamil Nadu and Sri Lanka's north. It may be argued that this is a distortion and an exaggeration, but once again I wish to remind that we are talking about the view from the south, the way things look from the south and from a complex concatenation of peripheries internal and external.

Sri Lanka's relation to India is almost unique. There are no neighbours to the south of Sri Lanka or around it except for the Maldives, and only the Indian Ocean surrounds it right down to Antarctica. There is, as I have mentioned earlier, no other landmass in which Sinhala is spoken by a community. Buddhism, especially Theravada Buddhism, is not practiced in any adjacent land area, the closest being Myanmar, Thailand and Indo-China. Thus, in geographic and cultural terms, Sri Lanka stands alone, next to the giant India.

Even if the Tamil factor did not exist, Sri Lanka's relationship with India would be its most vital external relationship. However, in as much as the Northern part of Sri Lanka ethnically mirrors the Southern part of India and is separated only by a narrow strip of water, or in so far as there exists a demonstrable and felt ethnic kinship between the Tamils of Northern Sri Lanka and those of the Tamil Nadu state of India, the relationship with India is a vital constituent of its management of the internal ethnic relationships, just as its relationship with its own Tamil minority is intrinsic to the management of the larger and essential relationship with its sole and giant neighbour India.

Given the demographic reality of an ethnic group that cross cuts the borders of India and Sri Lanka, Sri Lanka's Tamil issue is not only a domestic problem for Sri Lanka, it is a domestic problem for India as well. For Sri Lanka, it is an internal problem with an external dimension, while for India it is an external problem with an internal (Tamil Nadu) dimension.

An unresolved problem with Sri Lanka's Tamils can and probably will jeopardise Sri Lanka's relations with India. At the same time, a bad relationship with India will deprive Sri Lanka of one of the instruments which can help safely regulate its relations with the Tamil minority.

Given its aloneness on India's doorstep, Sri Lanka cannot afford to sustain a negative strategic relationship with India. For this reason too, it has to resolve the problem with its own Tamil minority.

Similarly, given the fact that the Tamils and Sinhalese have to live together on a small island, Sri Lanka has to resolve its problems, and for this it needs India's leverage; therefore, it needs good relations with India.

There is thus an existential imperative of dual co-existence: Sri Lanka's co-existence with India and Sinhala co-existence with the Tamils. Co-existence would be unsustainable and impossible if it were to be purely on the terms of one or the other—India or Sri Lanka, Tamils or Sinhalese.

India's is an ethnically multi-polar mosaic, which is safely accommodated by a federal framework. Sri Lanka's is an ethnically bipolar model, the bipolarity of which must not be aggravated—especially given the pull factor of the adjacent Tamil Nadu—by a federal system. The Sinhalese majority will resist this, as it has for half-a-century and as it fought secessionism for a quarter. Conversely, a unitary system with no serious devolution of power, in a state that is non-secular and gives a privileged place to one language and one religion, cannot be imposed on the Tamil minority. The minority, let us recall, is not a minority in the sub-region. It has leverage upon New Delhi through Chennai and on Washington DC through the Tamil diaspora.

India cannot afford recrudescent Tamil Nadu separatism, which thrives on the charge that New Delhi is insensitive to Tamil Nadu's feelings for their ethnic kin in Northern Sri Lanka. Tamil is an important and influential component of the Indian Union; when push comes to shove, it could carry more weight than Sri Lanka and the Sinhalese in New Delhi, Washington, Moscow and Beijing. If faced with a serious crunch in domestic geo-politics, Delhi will choose Chennai over Colombo. It is up to Sri Lanka to prevent matters coming to that.

Sri Lanka needs to countervail and neutralise the anti-Sinhala extremists in Tamil Nadu and the Tamil diaspora. It can do so only by satisfying at least the anti-Tiger Sri Lankan Tamils and the no less anti-Tiger Tamil Nadu elite fraction of the all-India power-bloc (visibly represented by *The Hindu* newspaper grouping).

A bitter ethnic polarisation and socio-economically ruinous protracted occupation is unavoidable unless sufficient political space is opened up at the periphery and Colombo has Tamil allies/partners who are truly empowered. Tamil (sub) nationalism cannot be contained by the status quo of the unitary, un-devolved, non-secular Sri Lankan state structure and concomitant centralist political culture.

The balanced solution of fullest autonomy within a unitary framework may be opposed by smaller extremist and fundamentalist forces among the Sinhala majority in the island. The grim reality though is that even at their most disruptive and violent, these forces can do much less harm to the Sri Lankan State than a potential decision by India, under mounting Tamil Nadu pressure, to tilt against or simply stop tilting towards Sri Lanka, and a corresponding decision by India's strategic partner, the US, to mount economic pressure through multilateral institutions and agencies. Under the unlamented George Bush Administration, there was daylight between the positions of the US and the European Union (EU). Under the incumbent and universally welcomed Barack Obama Administration, there may be convergence between the positions of the US, EU and India on Sri Lanka.

Dilemmas of Post-war Devolution

Devolution of power to a province which is a 'frontier' or 'buffer,' is a sensitive affair, especially when the prospective administration may not be allies. Maintaining a sufficiently strong but 'smart' (not 'heavy') military presence in the province, on its perimeter and embedded in small deployments within the community (as recommended by David Petraeus' COIN doctrine), could allay Colombo's security concerns. While the degree of devolution cannot be excessive, a dilution and delay of devolution could have even worse consequences of a hostile populace in a sensitively located province. Attempts to tamper with the demographics of the area will only cause disaffection to deepen—which would undermine stability and security. The dominant Tamil nationalist party, the Tamil National Alliance's (TNA) recent election manifesto citing self-determination (without even the qualification of "internal") has further complicated its relationship with the state and the Sinhala south in general which may perceive its reluctance to drop the slogan as inflexibility on the part of a party which until the defeat of the Tamil Tigers a year ago was a strident proxy of the LTTE.

What are the consequences for the Sinhalese and Tamils if the path of mutual moderation and convergence is not taken or deferred? With the Southern/Sinhala equivalent of the 'Sangh Parivar' trying to compensate for the erosion of its electoral representation, manifestations of Tamil civil disobedience could be met, as in the past, with violent counter-measures. Both communities will pay heavily. The Sinhalese will find that any use of coercion against unarmed Tamil federalists meets globally and regionally with a reception entirely unlike cracking down on armed

Tamil secessionists (who murdered former Prime Minister Rajiv Gandhi). A restive Tamil Nadu will cause worries for Delhi again. If Sri Lanka begins to lose the 'legitimacy war' (Emeritus Professor Richard Falk's phrase), it will find itself becoming an easier target for a combination of international players (far and near) who see it as a pawn in the 'grand strategic' power struggle (especially maritime) in and for an emerging Asia. Sri Lanka's most consistent friend, China, is too far away to project power and in any case does not allow itself to be provoked into conflicts, which will disturb the great harmony it requires in its external relations for its overarching economic purpose.

Reading a spate of recent reports highly (and less than fairly) critical of Sri Lanka, such as those of the International Crisis Group (ICG), Amnesty International (AI), and Human Rights Watch (HRW), it is clear that a crucial variable in the successful conclusion of the war against the LTTE was the conduct of India, much to the dismay of the 'international humanitarian intervention' lobby and some in Western capitals. In the face of serious and targeted external pressure, failure to fulfil Sri Lanka's solemn and reiterated bilateral commitments with India with respect to devolution will only leave it with a vital regional umbrella furled.

Referring to the continued US presence in Asia, and the rise of China, Singapore's Minister Mentor Lee Kuan Yew spoke to the editor of Japan's *Asahi Shimbun*, 'seeking to enjoy the shade' in the spot beneath where the branches of those 'two great trees' intertwine. It is in the interest of Sri Lanka to adopt the same perspective with regard to India and China. The latter is too far away to project power to its environs, while the former has demonstrated the clear ability to do so during the tsunami, even up to Indonesia. So of course has the US, much more impressively and far further. Speedily settling the Tamil issue in the spirit bilaterally agreed upon with its great neighbour India is a security and strategic imperative, which would enable Sri Lanka to pre-empt or contain the threat of the 'near enemy'—the hostile elements in Tamil Nadu—and balance against the 'far enemy,' the pro-Tamil Eelam secessionist strand of the Tamil diaspora and its sympathisers in the West.

PART II

Mutual Perceptions and Expectations

5

Perceptions and Memories: Making Sense of Bangladesh's India Outlook

Partha S. Ghosh

The argument that the Bangladeshi society is divided between the 'Bengali nationalists' and the 'Bangladeshi nationalists', is not completely valid. There is a fairly large cusp zone between the two, otherwise the Awami League (AL) and the Bangladesh Nationalist Party (BNP) would not have alternated in power. At the core of the recent controversy over the issue of dealing with the criminals of the 1971 liberation war is the question of punishment and forgiveness. Did Bangladesh forgive the war criminals all these years, and suddenly it has woken up to punish them? Though efforts were made in the initial stages to punish those who collaborated with the Pakistani military junta to suppress the Bengali freedom struggle, nothing happened in the post-Mujib era to bring them to book.

Evidences, however, suggest that at the subcutaneous level the traumatic memory of 1971 remained in public consciousness though Jamaat-i-Islami and BNP did succeed in obfuscating the discourse by injecting into it the controversy over secularism at the expense of Islam. In the same context, questions arose as to what extent India too mattered in the collective memory of Bangladesh. Has the political divide between 'Muslim Bengal' and 'Hindu Bengal', which had its first expression in the Partition of Bengal of 1905, been a matter of the past? Or, has it remained as a constant fixture in the politics of East Bengal which neither the Partition of India in 1947 nor the creation of Bangladesh in 1971 in which India had a substantive and positive role to play could do away with? In what way would Bangladesh be able to reconcile itself to the baggage of this multifaceted memory and how would the process shape its India outlook? This paper tries to understand precisely these issues.

Introduction

Historically, Bangladesh, or for that matter undivided Bengal, is a mix of Hindu-Muslim harmony and discord. If one looks at the way East Bengal was peopled, which historian Richard Eaton has discussed,[1] or the way 'one social community' was in the process of being constructed there during the same period based on the 'sahajiya' (meaning, easy-going) philosophy, which social anthropologist Ramakrishna Mukherjee has explained,[2] one would argue that had the British intervention not taken place, probably, Bengalis would have emerged as one composite nationality allowing neither Islam nor Hinduism to leave their divisive marks. The divide started in the latter half of 19th century, in the aftermath of the 1857 revolt, which witnessed both Hindu and Muslim revivalism. Against this background, on the one hand, Bengali Hindu historians started rewriting Indian history to prove that the decline of India was a consequence of Muslim conquest of India, meaning thereby that Muslims were aliens whose presence was detrimental to India's interests, and on the other, Islam started getting more rigidified which found its expression in the Persianisation drive of the Bengali language, expunging Sanskrit words and substituting them by Persian words, a subject that Sufia Uddin has explained in detail.[3]

This emerging social dichotomy was reflected in the ways Hindus and Muslims started viewing their opposition to the British rule. Thus, while the Partition of Bengal in 1905 was seen by Bengali Hindus as a British ploy to strike at the roots of Bengali nationalism (which was then in the forefront of Indian nationalism), it was not viewed that way by Bengali Muslims. One can get a sense of this divide in the officially sponsored *Banglapedia,* which has a chapter on the event. It subscribes to the British logic that the 1905 Partition of Bengal was an administrative decision to streamline the administration of Bengal. The Partition of India in 1947 marked the culmination of the process. It was championed by both Hindu and Muslim Bengalis, more so by the latter who went to the extent of even trying to make Calcutta (former name, until 2000, for Kolkata) the capital of East Bengal. It is not surprising, therefore, that this dichotomy would remain in the postcolonial period. The difference is that while the assertion of secularism in India's constitution together with the Nehruvian emphasis on democracy and socialism coupled with the rise of Leftism in West Bengal prevented Hindu nationalism from raising its head to the critical level in those formative years, the emphasis on Islam in Pakistan and the dominance of *Muhajirs* in the then politics of the country allowed the pro-Islamist forces to thrive in Pakistan, including East Pakistan/Bengal. How the introduction of Urdu as the national language drove a wedge in Pakistan's Islamic unity is another story.[4]

Three Influences, Three Events

The history of the Indian Subcontinent during the last 150 years has seen three social trends vying for pre-eminence in South Asian politics—Hindu nationalism, Muslim nationalism and the composite Hindu-Muslim nationalism. In the development of Bengal politics too, all these three trends have been equally relevant but with a difference. In West Bengal, there is an added dimension of a Leftist trend. To understand the respective influences of these trends on Bangladesh politics vis-à-vis India and West Bengal, we would refer to three events, namely, the Partition of Bengal in 1905, the Partition of India in 1947, and the creation of Bangladesh in 1971. The first event (1905) can be explained through an analysis of the second and third trends, the second (1947) can be explained through an analysis of all the three trends and the third (1971) by the second and third trends. In these three analyses are contained the germs of present Bangladesh's dichotomy of Bengali versus Bangladeshi nationalisms and their impact on the country's split image of India.

It is commonplace to understand Bangladesh politics in binary terms: as a contest between the forces of Bengali nationalism and those of Bangladeshi nationalism, the first representing the composite Muslim-Hindu social ethos of the nation, while the second the Islamic ethos at the cost of minority (Hindu) interests. This kind of analysis does not hold water because between the two elements there is a huge cusp zone which floats between the two depending upon political and social circumstances which can be empirically tested. The alternation in power of AL, the so-called Bengali nationalists, and BNP, the so-called Bangladeshi nationalists, vindicates the point. The important point to note is that in Bangladesh society there are strong pro-Islamic forces as well as strong pro-secularist forces that vie for power, and their respective rise and fall depend on their record of governance in which the role played by the international community, most notably India and Saudi Arabia, matter a lot on account of geographical, economic and cultural connections.

The Flashpoint Shahbag

The controversy over the Shahbag agitation of February 2013 hovered around three questions—punishment, justification and pardon. Who did what during the liberation war of Bangladesh and why not those responsible for suppressing the freedom struggle in collaboration with the Pakistani military junta be brought to book? While AL argued that such criminal elements which organised the massacres of 1971 should be punished, the forces supporting the Islamists, most notably the BNP and the Jamaat-i-Islami, tried to whitewash their crimes as most of them formed the core of these parties. Since the politics of Bangladesh is polarised, arguably, between secularists and Islamists, the issue assumed political colour. In the late 1980s, too, it was a big issue when Jahanara Imam had become a household name in the country for her forceful tirade against some of the war criminals of 1971.[5]

Let us recapitulate some important developments prior to the Shahbag agitation. After coming to power, following its victory in the elections held in December 2008, the AL Government started the proceedings to try the pro-Pakistan Islamist elements which had committed war crimes in 1971. In 2009, the International Crimes Tribunal was set up, and in January 2010, Bangabandhu Mujibur Rahman's killers were executed. In July, the same year, a number of Jamaat leaders were arrested. In the next few months, the Fifth and the Seventh Amendments to the Constitution were annulled. These amendments had indemnified the assassins of the Bangabandhu and had legitimised the military regimes, including that of H.M. Ershad. This opened the gates for all those who had been victimised by the military regimes to seek justice in the courts of law. Simultaneously, the AL Government also restored the secular character of the country. The war crimes tribunal announced several verdicts, the most important being the one in February 2013 about the Assistant Secretary of Jamaat-i-Islami, Abdul Quader Molla. He was first given life imprisonment, but the pro-Liberation forces wanted more stringent punishment, which meant the death sentence. The social media went viral in making such a demand which eventually led to the Shahbag agitation. Subsequently, the verdict was converted into capital punishment, which was endorsed by the Appellate Division of the Supreme Court.

The opposition to the Shahbag agitation came both from Jamaat and BNP, but in their respective political positioning, a subtle difference was noticeable. For Jamaat, the argument was that the agitationists were anti-Islamic in the garb of secularists who must be taught a lesson for their heresy. True to their ideological commitment, they brutally killed Ahmed Rajib Haider, a pro-Shahbag blogger, on March 02, 2013 just outside his house. The BNP, however, took a political route to decry the agitation. Unlike Jamaat's violent rant, BNP's opposition was tempered by a mixture of antagonism and moderation, for after all it was a leading political party which had a significant presence in the aforementioned cusp zone. Thus, while the BNP initially expressed its support for the Jamaat, it soon cautiously welcomed the Shahbag protest. It, however, warned the government not to succumb to street agitations demanding capital punishment for war criminals. It questioned the legality of the court proceedings and launched a 60-hour general strike starting from October 27, 2013. When the death sentence of Molla was carried out on December 12, 2013, the party argued that as per the constitution of Bangladesh the ruling AL Government had no legitimate authority to go on with the proceedings of the International Crimes Tribunal. According to the constitution, the ruling party must step down three months ahead of the national elections (scheduled for

January 2014) to make room for a free and fair election. Expectedly, the party boycotted the election held on January 05, 2014 along with other opposition parties resulting in a massive victory for the ruling AL.

Elections of 2014

In the absence of any electoral challenge, the election was a walkover for the AL. Of the 300 elected seats, AL won 154 seats uncontested. In the remaining seats, the contests were between AL and its rebel leaders or between AL and some friendly parties. Overall, AL won 232 seats, which meant more than a two-third majority. The percentage of voting was as low as less than 30 per cent compared to 2001 and 2008, when it was 74.37 per cent and 85.93 per cent, respectively. In the election violence, at least 20 people lost their lives. Hindus in several places were on the receiving end for their alleged support for the ruling party.[6] Internationally, Sheikh Hasina Wajed as the AL leader earned a bad name for failing the democracy in the country. India's approach was conciliatory to AL. India said that the election was a 'constitutional requirement' which should be left to the people of Bangladesh and that the democratic processes 'must be allowed to take their own course'.[7]

Memory as Collective Memory

In the current scenario of Bangladesh, the discourse is how much of vengeance the tormented souls can think of perpetrating on the tormentors of 1971, how much they can collectively remember of those traumatic events, what kind of punishment they want to give to those responsible and, last but not the least, should one forget and forgive and move ahead to build a new Bangladesh. How long can Bangladesh nurture a split personality where even a consensus on who is the father of the nation has not yet been built? From a long-term perspective, was 1971 the starting point, or, behind that was another set of memories of a Hindu-Muslim divide going back to the days of the second phase of the British rule? One must not forget that had the verdict of the 1970 Pakistan general election been honoured by the Pakistan military authorities, history would have taken a different course. One must not as well forget that the Bangabandhu himself was a failure as a democratic ruler. Therefore, even if AL seems to be in command now, forces opposed to it are no less powerful and the situation can change overnight. It is thus a clash of memories, 1905 and 1947 on the one hand and 1947 and 1971 on the other. Does international literature on memory research give us any clue to make sense of these puzzles?

Evolution of Memory Research

Even in ancient times, many Greek social thinkers had preoccupied themselves with the discourse on memory. However, it was only in the late 19th and early 20th century that a distinctly social perspective on memory emerged. The first explicit use of the term was by Hugo von Hofmannsthal in 1902. He referred to "the damned up force of our mysterious ancestors within us." Still, no clear sociological theory of memory was in place, and it was largely "piled up layers of accumulated collective memory"—a poetic allusion. Hofmannsthal distinguished between 'autobiographical memory' and 'historical memory,' the former representing the events in one's own life experienced directly while the latter constituting the residues—"events by virtue of which groups claim a continuous identity through time." Olick writes: "The individual's memory is shaped by personal recollections. But no one is alone with his or her memories. In fact, each human being is influenced by events in the distant past—by a grandmother's stories as well as by traditional rites, history lessons at school, films at the cinema.... Without such a collective perspective, after all, it is difficult to provide good explanations of mythology, tradition, and heritage, among other long-term symbolic patterns."[8] It was, however, in 1925 that the exact phrase 'collective memory' was coined by the French sociologist Maurice Halbwachs: "Entire peoples—just like religious or ethnic communities or families—are capable of maintaining a 'collective memory'." In recent times, Aleida Assmann in collaboration with her Egyptologist husband, Jan Assmann, has greatly contributed to the further development of the notion. She is "considered a pioneer of the young subject Memory Studies, which in contrast to history, does not focus on the past as such, but the forms in which this past is upheld in present consciousness." According to her, "Each 'I' is connected with a 'we', from which it draws fundamentals of its identity."[9]

Principles of Collective Memory

There are three principles for the analysis of collective memory. Firstly, collective memory of an entire society is hardly monolithic though there is a tendency amongst politicians, commentators and academics to invoke it that way. Collective remembering is a complex phenomenon that involves numerous individuals, practices, materials and themes. No society has one collective memory, and no one is certain what kind of public memories would be produced. Olick writes, "It is important to remember the different demands on participants in different discursive fields, such as politics or journalism, religion or the arts, and to appreciate subtleties of context and inflection. Doing so, of course, makes it difficult to judge a whole epoch or a whole society."[10] Secondly, since history and mythmaking go side by side, collective memory is seldom authentic. It is often the case that history is invented to suit the requirements of the power elites. As Barry Schwartz puts it, "Sharp opposition between history and collective memory has been our Achilles Heel, causing us to assert unwillingly, and often despite ourselves, that what is not historical must be 'invented' or 'constructed'—which transforms collective memory study into a kind of cynical muckraking."[11] Thirdly, "collective memory is something—or rather many things—we *do*, and not something—or rather many things—we *have*. We therefore need analytical tools sensitive to its varieties, contradictions, and dynamism. How are representations of and activities concerning the past organized [*sic*] socially and culturally? When and why do they change? How can we begin to untangle the diverse processes, procedures, and practices through which societies confront and represent aspects of their pasts?"[12]

Memory and Reconciliation

The memory discourse has close connection with the idea of social capital, which is generated by connections among individuals and groups—social networks and the norms of reciprocity and trustworthiness that arise from them. When social cohesion weakens, social capital loses its effectiveness. Boundaries separating the '*other*' are created and norms of mutual respect and tolerance are threatened. Objects, events and histories are re-presented to rationalise suspicion and distrust. From the normative sense, one is forced to ask what political and institutional instruments would help in the expansion of social capital and in the making of mature democracies. In the same context, one should show greater interest not in the origins of *memory* but more in its effects in the present. William Gladstone famously said that "the cause of the problem in Ireland is that the Irish will never forget and the British will never remember."[13]

Since the days of the Holocaust, there has been a growing literature on these issues. The Rwandan and Bosnian massacres have given further fillip to the discourse. The following is a 2005 statement of M. Subasdic, President of the Association of Citizens 'Mothers of Srebrenica and Zepa Enclaves':

> The word 'forgiveness' insults me. It makes me victim again. I have never been in [a] fight with anybody hence there is no need to forgive the other. Nobody has the right to demand from the victim to forgive or to reconcile with the offender. We want neither forgiveness nor reconciliation. All we want is that each perpetrator gets its name and surname, hence to be punished. It is a *shame* to talk about forgiveness while the main perpetrators who have killed our children and husbands still have not faced legal prosecutions.[14]

Martha Minow writes: "To seek a path between vengeance and forgiveness is also to seek a route between too much memory and too much forgetting. Too much memory is a disease, comments Michael Roth.... In his afterword to *Death and the Maiden*, the chilling play of post-terror revenge and justice, Ariel Dorfman writes, 'How do we keep the past alive without becoming its prisoner? How do we forget it without risking its repetition in the future?'"[15] She narrates the joint efforts of Mona Weissmark, whose parents survived Nazi concentration camps, and Ilona Kuphal, whose father was a Nazi SS officer, in organising a get-together of the children of Nazis and those of the Holocaust with the intent of rebuilding the future through explorations into their sense of guilt, anger and resentment piled up in their memories.[16] Nelson Mandela's Truth and Reconciliation Commission was a testimony as to how to put the idea into practice. The meeting between Priyanka Gandhi, daughter of Rajiv Gandhi, and Nalini Sriharan, one of the killers of Rajiv Gandhi, on April 15, 2008 in the Vellore jail (Tamil Nadu) was yet another example of reconciliation of a dreadful past though it was at a very personal level. Priyanka Gandhi reportedly said on her return to Delhi that "It was my way of coming to peace with the violence and loss that I have experienced."

The Bangladesh Context

Did Bangladesh forgive its war criminals and has suddenly woken up? The answer is: No. Even the country's first Prime Minister Bangabandhu Sheikh Mujib-ur Rahman had banned the Jamaat and passed ordinances such as the Collaborators Order and the International Crimes (Tribunals) Act. But his assassination in August 1975 and his growing loss of popularity before his death came in the way of reaching these goals. The subsequent coming to power of his detractors reversed the situation though many activists under the leadership of Jahanara Imam kept the torch burning, particularly in the 1980s and 1990s.[17]

Indeed at the subcutaneous level, the painful memory of 1971 remained in the public consciousness through literature such as *Ekatturer Dinguli* (Those Days of 1971), *Ami Birangana Bolchi* (I, the Brave, Speaking) and *Narir Ekattur* (1971, As Experienced by Women). The contribution of documentaries and cinema in this regard was even more forceful. Some of these productions were *Muktir Gaan* (The Song of Liberation), *Shei Raater Kotha Boltey Eshechi* (Came to narrate the stories of those nights), *The War Crimes Files* and *Itihash Konya* (The Daughter of History). It was not actually collective memory but collective remembrance—memory is "the act of gathering bits and pieces of the past, joining them together in public... [but] it is the palpable messy activity which produces collective remembrance."[18] The Shahbag agitation, however, proved that the Jamaat and the BNP have been successful in obfuscating the discourse by injecting the virus of secularism versus Islam—Shahbag demonstrators are "atheists, secular-fundamentalists, Hindus and India's agents."

Bangladesh's India Outlook

From the perspective of memory-policy interface, Bangladesh faces two challenges—how to work out its Pakistan outlook on the one hand and how to define its India outlook on the other. So far as the first is concerned, let us paraphrase Gladstone's statement mentioned above: The cause of the problem is that the Bangladeshis would never forget and the Pakistanis would never remember. Any reconciliation between Bangladesh and Pakistan which the Pakistan Government would accept, given South Asia's complicated strategic reality, must start with an apology from Pakistan for what it did in 1971. Hamid Mir, the Chief of *Geo TV* of Pakistan, had suggested exactly that:

> I am sure that Pakistan is changing fast. A day will come very soon when the government of Pakistan will officially say sorry to Bengalis and March 26th will become an apology day for patriotic Pakistanis. I want this apology because Bengalis created Pakistan. I want this apology because Bengalis supported the sister of Jinnah against General Ayub Khan. I want this apology because I want to make a new relationship with the people of Bangladesh. I don't want to live with my dirty past. I want to live in a neat and clean future. I want a bright future not only for Pakistan but also for Bangladesh. I want this apology because I love Pakistan and I love Bangladesh. Happy Independence Day to my Bangladeshi brothers and sisters.[19]

But Mir's advice has no takers in Pakistan.[20] The execution of Mollah has been protested at the highest political level, that is, in Pakistan's National Assembly which passed a resolution condemning the act. The Bangladesh Government equally retaliated at this interference in its domestic affairs. Sheikh Hasina said it was clear that "Pakistan has proved that it never accepted the victory of Bangladesh in the Liberation War of 1971, and they still have allies in Bangladesh."[21]

As long as Bangladesh's Pakistan outlook remains blurred, its India outlook cannot be any clearer. The ghosts of 1947 and 1971 would keep haunting all the three countries in three different ways. India would love to do away with Partition, but Pakistan would love to cling to it; Pakistan would love to do away with its dismemberment in 1971, but Bangladesh would love to cling to it. For both Pakistan and Bangladesh, 1947 and 1971 are their umbilical cords. Flashbacking this story to 1905, Bangladesh would have to handle its memory discourse at two levels: one, Hindu *zamindari* oppression during the pre-Partition days which justified the partitions of 1905 and 1947, and two, the indispensable Indian help in its liberation struggle of 1971 but for which Bangladesh would not have been created. While the former has its constituency in the pro-Islamic forces, the latter in the secularist forces of the country which owe their origin essentially to the days of the liberation movement. It is this dichotomy that gets epitomised in the Bengali and Bangladeshi nationalisms. The way the Shahbag agitation gathered momentum and then the way it was challenged prove the persistence of this social divide. India's split image in Bangladesh, therefore, is foreordained.

Conclusion

Perceptions and memories of Bangladesh about India are contradictory. The country suffers from its collective memory of Hindu oppression during the colonial times and at the same time from a sense of inferiority for it was India that was its real liberator. The cleavage gets perpetuated because of lack of appreciation of each other's ways of thinking. Most Indians have no clues to the realities of Bangladesh which is simply a potential den of future Taliban. Bangladesh's ignorance about India is no less. Whenever I speak in Bengali in Bangladesh, a common man on the street is surprised that I can speak Bengali. He is virtually unaware that an almost equal number of Bengali speakers live in India. Both the countries must be exposed to each other much more than what it is now to get to know each other better. Jean Dreze and Amartya Sen's 2013 book is an eye opener to the world to know how that 'basket case' (Henry Kissinger's phrase) Bangladesh is now ahead of India in terms of several social indicators.[22]

ENDNOTES

1. Richard M. Eaton, *The Rise of Islam and the Bengal Frontier, 1204-1760*, Oxford University Press, Delhi, 1994.
2. Ramakrishna Mukherjee, "Nation-building in Bangladesh," in Rajni Kothari (ed.), *State and Nation Building*, Allied Publishers, Bombay, 1976.
3. Sufia M. Uddin, *Constructing Bangladesh: Religion, Ethnicity and Language in an Islamic Nation*, Vistaar, New Delhi, 2006.
4. For more on this point, see Partha S. Ghosh, *Cooperation and Conflict in South Asia*, Manohar, New Delhi, 1989, pp. 20-22.
5. Partha S. Ghosh, "Bangladesh at the Crossroads: Religion and Politics," *Asian Survey*, 32 (7), July 1993, pp. 697-710.
6. Garga Chatterjee, "Bengali Hindus in Muslim-majority Bangladesh," *The Hindu*, New Delhi, January 16, 2014 and Pranay Sharma, "Half-Tone Country," *Outlook*, New Delhi, January 20, 2014, pp. 24-26.
7. Haroon Habib, "Election amid Anarchy," *Frontline*, Chennai, February 07, 2014, p. 47.
8. Jefferey K. Olick, "From Collective Memory to the Sociology of Mnemonic Practices and Products," in Astrid Eril and Ansgar Nuenning (eds.), *Cultural Memory Studies: An Interdisciplinary Handbook*, Walter de Gruyter, Berlin, 2008, pp. 156-57.
9. Quoted in Christina Berndt, "Constructing Memory," *Humboldt Kosmos*, Bonn, No. 94, 2009, p. 45.
10. Jefferey K. Olick, no. 8, pp. 158-59.
11. Ibid., p. 159.
12. Ibid.
13. Martha Minow, *Between Vengeance and Forgiveness: Facing History after Genocide and Mass Violence*, Beacon Press, Boston, p. 119.
14. Nadine Murshid, "The Shabag Uprising: War Crimes and Forgiveness," *Economic and Political Weekly*, Mumbai, March 09, 2013, p. 14.

15. Martha Minow, no. 13, pp. 118-19.
16. Ibid., p. 119.
17. For details, see Partha S. Ghosh, "Conservative Ascendancy in Bangladesh," *South Asian Survey*, 12 (2), New Delhi, July-December 2005, pp. 247-265.
18. Bina D'Costa, "War Crimes, Justice and the Politics of Memory," *Economic and Political Weekly*, Mumbai, March 23, 2013, p. 43. It may be noted that any genocide is always an important element of remembrance, but its quantification can sometimes be politicised as it has happened in Bangladesh. The statement of Mujibur Rehman after his release from the Pakistani jail to triumphantly return to the newly created nation of Bangladesh in 1972 as its leader was one of that kind. He said that three million Bengalis had perished in the hands of the Pakistani military junta, a figure which has assumed iconic sanctity ever since particularly among the forces supportive of the liberation struggle. Though several estimates in subsequent years have shown that that it was not more than 300,000 to 500,000, still it is virtually a blasphemy in Awami League circles to question this figure. In early 2014, this was dramatically demonstrated when the on-going War Crimes Tribunal initiated contempt proceedings against a Bangladesh-based British journalist, David Bergman, for questioning the death toll during the liberation war. In an article published in an Indian newspaper, the journalist convincingly proved that the three-million-figure was not a well-founded one. See David Bergman, "Questioning an Iconic Number," *The Hindu*, New Delhi, April 24, 2014.
19. Hamid Mir, "Apology Day for Pakistanis," *Point Counterpoint*, March 30, 2010.
20. Hamid Mir was recently violently attacked, ostensibly for his these kinds of sentiments which were not what an important section of the Pakistani ruling establishment would like to hear. See Hamid Mir, "The Truth will Set us Free," *Hindustan Times*, New Delhi, May 10, 2014.
21. *Strategic Digest*, New Delhi, January 2014, p. 46.
22. Jean Dreze and Amartya Sen, *An Uncertain Glory: India and its Contradictions*, Allen Lane, New Delhi, 2013.

6

Changing Dynamics in Nepal-India Relations

Dinesh Bhattarai

Nepal-India relations are multidimensional, unique in character and scope. The relations recognise the complete sovereignty, territorial integrity, and independence of each other. Nepal shares borders with India (south, east, and west) and China (north), and enjoys with them historic and friendly relations, which have acquired new dimensions and dynamics over the years. While relations with the two neighbouring countries are the lynchpin of Nepal's international relations, the geopolitical realities and wide-ranging relations with India make it an indispensable neighbour. Probably no other neighbours in the world share so many similarities and comprehensively interact on a daily basis both at the government and people's level. The bilateral relations are deep-rooted and interdependent, yet they have reoccurring irritants, constraints and complexities born out of misperceptions and conflicting narratives of the emerging dynamics. The gap between fact and fiction has blurred the necessary debate on core issues in Nepal-India relations, and has added new complexities. Since 2006, Nepal has been undergoing historic democratic transformation after over a decade-long armed conflict (1996-2006) and struggling to institutionalise democracy. A rare second Constituent Assembly (CA) election was held on November 19, 2013 as the first CA failed to deliver a constitution.

While the prolonged political stalemate continues within Nepal, emerging dynamics at both domestic and external fronts are causing shifts in areas of security, political and economic power and social values. The global power shift to the Asia-Pacific region based on the economic growth of China and India has brought

Nepal's neighbours—India and China—into prominence in global affairs. Their rise puts Nepal on the geo-strategic spotlight without it being a beneficiary of their rapid economic transformation. The recent 'pivoting' to Asia in American foreign policy further adds to the significance of Nepal. Reviewing facts from emerging dynamics, this paper seeks to present an overview of historical perceptions, political mindsets, values, and attitudes towards these dynamics. It intends to look at how the emerging dynamics are shaping Nepal-India relations and how they can be adjusted to make the best and most from the existing opportunities.

Background

Nepal's relations with India are intimate, complex, multifaceted and unique in character and scope. The relations between the two countries have acquired new dimensions and dynamics over the years. Nepal shares its borders with both India and China and enjoys with them historic and friendly relations that are "under more scrutiny than usual."[1] While relations with both the neighbours takethe highest priority, the geographical reality and historical, socio-economic and cultural affinities make ties with India, operating on a daily basis both at the people's and government's level, crucially important.

The international relations being "the realm of great power politics",[2] added by the recent power shift to Asia based on the growth of India and China, have heightened "geopolitical interests" on Nepal, historically termed as a "yam between the two big boulders." The 'simultaneous and cooperative rise' of China and India, which together have 40 per cent of the world's people, has brought the gravity of geopolitics and geo-economics to the region. They have emerged as the two fastest growing economic powers and emerging markets from the shadows of Europe, Japan and the US that dominated world affairs during most of the 19th and 20th centuries.[3] The speed, scale and reach of China's rise are without precedent in modern history. Within just 30 years, China's economy has grown from smaller than that of the Netherlands to larger than those of all other countries except the US. If China soon becomes the largest economy, it will be the first time since George III that a non-English speaking, non-Western and non-democratic country would be leading the global economy.[4]

The ongoing fundamental transformation of the economy of India and China has brought in an unprecedented range of opportunities and challenges at Nepal's doorsteps. Nepal can find a better place in the emerging world order by reprising its historical role as a 'vibrant bridge' between India and China.[5] It needs to work wisely amidst its interminable political transition, to benefit from its proximities to these economic powerhouses, and contribute to the construction of a shared peaceful, stable, democratic and prosperous order.

The current deadlock in international discussions on trade and climate change, energy, food security and conflicts over water can be attributed to "the big geopolitical transformation that accompanies the rise of emerging countries in the world economy." The politics of resources for development has been one of the commanding factors shaping global politics today. China and India as planetary powers are shaping the global biosphere, and are therefore central to whether the world succeeds in building a healthy, prosperous and environmentally sustainable future for the next generation.[6]

History testifies to the fact that political and strategic power has followed economic power. The increased global attention on the region is not without considerable significance for Nepal. Chinese power in Tibet is no less of an issue today.[7] Nepal's proximity and affinity to Tibet has made it a meeting point of overlapping and intersecting interests of various kinds for multiple power centres including that of the European Union and the US. The recent pivot or rebalancing strategy in American foreign policy focusing on 'strategic significance of Asia' as 'a counter balance to the Chinese giant', is being watched with great interest "not because China is perceived as a threat but because governments in Asia are uncertain what a China dominated region would mean."[8]

Under the new circumstances, gone are the days of Nepal's parroting the past policy and "tacking northward or southward as the occasion demanded" and "as a tactic rather than a policy with severe limitations on its utility."[9] This places the conduct of Nepal's relations with its immediate neighbours on highest priority at a time when it is passing through the most critical phase in its history and remains "one of the poorest and most politically turbulent countries in Asia."

As stated earlier, no other neighbours in the world probably share so many similarities and interact as comprehensively and regularly as Nepal and India do. They continue "to be dominated more by historical antecedents than by the demand of time and context."[10] Personalities, traditional institutions and their political cultures have influenced their domestic policies and external relations. It has been aptly stated that "There is much that binds and little that divides our two countries except the fact that, politically, the two are separate and distinct entities."[11] The deeply interdependent relations, however, often exhibit reoccurring irritants that emanate from misperceptions and conflicting narratives of emerging dynamics. It seems the structure of parties' elites and their game of political survival is not fundamentally different from their predecessors, regardless of the change of political system and the composition of the elites. Thus, an elite approach to Indo-Nepal relations is as much significant today as the determinants of bilateralism.[12]

The dynamics of India-Nepal relations have been inextricably linked with that of domestic political developments in the two countries.[13] This makes the mutual interests on either side immediate and wider. Unlike Nepal's relations with other countries, Nepal-India relations tend to be easily politicised due to the domestication of relations. There has been a tendency to link each domestic issue with India, as if India has all the leverage against Nepal.[14] It is argued that political culture created and nurtured during the underground movement is not sacrosanct for the constitutional processes. The movement parties that dramatically transformed themselves into the new evolutionary roles in the post-movement phase still need to follow a modest democratic culture.[15] Parties often carry on with their own standard of political culture, which sometimes appeared to be more parochial than opting for shared gains.

The blind jingoism of some political parties often hurts bilateral relationships. When nationalism is equated to anti-Indianism by some left or left-leaning parties, especially, while in opposition, bilateral relationship between Nepal and India remain unclear when such parties come into power. In a scathing criticism of the 'narrow and blind' nationalism that afflicts sections of Nepal's political class particularly the left, including his own party, a senior communist leader underlined the need for the country to shed its 'suspicion' of Indian actions.[16] Such double standards often create confusion, turning Nepali official position unclear and vague.[17]

Nepal matters to India for all sorts of deep historical, cultural and economic ties. Moreover, with Nepal "forming a key part of the sacred geography of Hinduism, the large southern population of relatively recent Indian origin or with close ties to India; a degree of competition with China for influence in the South Asian region; and more recent concerns over India's vulnerability to a terrorist attack mounted through Nepal,"[18] the country is bound to be particularly important to India.Since no part of national life remains untouched in the spectrum of Nepal-India relations, several lenses are used to observe them. The gap between perception and reality has blurred the necessary debate on core issues in Nepal-India relations, and has added to the complexity in bilateral ties. With great discrepancy between perceptions and realities, the results to a country's foreign policy may be disastrous.[19] For a clear and better understanding of the perceptions of both the countries and creating a congenial environment for cooperative partnership, it is necessary to have discourses in the complexity of geo-politics and emerging dynamics in bilateral relationship.

Political scientists have identified a host of areas of divergent security perceptions, conventional approach to Indo-Nepal relations, external factors, either perceived or real that generate conflict and lack of understanding of Indo-Nepal relations.[20] Some political parties and policymakers are said to have three negative perceptions about India: First, a weak Nepal is in India's interest; second, India always tries to extract maximum concessions from a falling regime and ends up supporting the emerging ruler, and third, it extends hospitality to rebel political personalities or organisations to use them as a leverage with the Nepali regime of the day.[21]

The problems between Nepal and India also emanate from open borders, the 1950 Treaty of Peace and Friendship, human trafficking, Gurkha recruitment, cross-border criminal activities, movement of terrorists across the border, growth of religious fundamentalism, Nepal's ballooning trade deficit, delayed implementation of agreed projects, politicisation of the utilisation of water resources, economic offences includingfake currency, presence of extra regional powers in Nepal, anti-India feelings in Nepal and anti-Nepal activities in India, mistreatment of Nepali workers and concerns of Indian business houses in Nepal. Covering all these issues is beyond the scope of this article. This paper will focus on pressing issues in Nepal-India relations and recent developments including the dynamics of the peace process. The engagement of the West including that of the United Nations (UN) in the peace process and India's approach to these issues will be discussed here. This paper will also look at the role of the emerging dynamics in Nepal-India relations and how it can be adjusted to create conducive environment for both the countries.

Changing Dynamics: Rise and Revolt of Maoists

Ever since Nepal was unified in 1769, Nepali politics and external relations have witnessed sea changes, new dimensions and dynamics. There has been rise and fall of ruling families in Nepali politics. History is full of internecine conflicts and conspiratorial politics within the ruling families for power struggle taking the forms of coups, counter coups, plots and counter plots against each other. This struggle for power within the ruling establishment paved the way for outsiders to influence the evolution of internal politics and weaken the country's external freedom of manoeuvres. Rana family that ruled Nepal for 104 years (1847-1951) with an iron hand sought British support to perpetuate its autocratic rule, and kept the country in isolation from the rest of the world. The regime was, however, able to maintain country's independence and sovereignty.

The popular revolution of 1950-51 led by the Nepali Congress (NC) party overthrew the Rana regime. The monarchy that was captive during the Rana period came into prominence following the Nepali freedom movement, which had its origin in the Indian soil, and to a large extent the Indian nationalist movement served as a model and inspiration to the Nepalese.[22] Prime Minister Jawaharlal Nehru of India brokered an agreement in February 1951, popularly known as the Delhi Agreement, and supported gradual transition to democracy in Nepal.[23] Nepal had diplomatic relations with just four countries until 1950 that included the United Kingdom (1815), the US (1947), India (1947) and France (1949). The diversification of diplomatic relations after 1950 (the number now stands at 138) has introduced new dimensions and dynamics in Nepal's international relations.

Post 1950s, incessant internal conflicts among the political parties gave political space to the king to manoeuvre, manipulate and prevail in the day-to-day governance. The king dissolved the first democratic constitution of the country, abolished an elected parliament and imprisoned the first democratically-elected Prime Minister B.P. Koirala and his cabinet colleagues without any charges when they were just 18 months (1959-1960) into office, thereby throttling the parliamentary system of democracy. India expressed regret over the end of 'democratic experiment' and called it a 'setback' to democracy.[24] NC launched a movement against king's moves but was neutralised following Sino-Indian War of 1962. The king introduced a partyless panchayat system, which continued until the restoration of the parliamentary system of democracy in 1990.

The use of foreign policy issues in the domestic power play is a glaring dynamics in Nepal's relations with India. Nepali politicians have long invited Indian involvement by turning to the Indian Government for support against their rivals.[25] However, the difference is noted during the B.P. Koirala-led government that did not feel the need to use foreign policy as a means of strengthening its political position.[26] In the years that followed, the king started to appease the political parties who opposed NC, and permitted them to function despite the fact that political parties were banned in Nepal. The leftist parties were even encouraged at times[27] and awarded key positions in the state structures to counter the democratic forces. The king and the communists worked hand in glove and overtly adopted an anti-India posture under the cover of nationalism, farsightedness and progressivism, and termed NC as an anti-nationalist party.

The Sino-Indian war in October 1962 changed the regional power balance and led India to "pay more attention to its security concerns in the Nepalese sector of the Himalayas than to the establishment of parliamentary government in Nepal."[28] NC suspended its movement against the royal rule. India appeared to be "more accommodating toward the royal regime than toward the struggle of the NC."[29] In subsequent years, India maintained a façade of sympathy for the opposition forces by allowing the opposition democratic forces and leftist forces to reside in India. Such sympathy was often overshadowed by India's desire to appease the monarchy as a means to ensure stability in the Himalayan region.[30] Restrictions were placed on political activities of Nepal's democratic forces in India. Against the unfolding strategic developments in South Asia and the "growing tendency to look to foreign hands" in Nepal, B.P. Koirala felt that national crisis was taking a turn for the worst, "endangering" the "very existence" of Nepal.[31] He called democracy as a prerequisite for country's survival and returned home from exile to work for his policy of national unity and reconciliation.

Following Koirala's return, the tight political climate gradually eased out, with the declaration of the national referendum that put question on the partyless Panchayat system for the first time. Panchayat system through manipulated referendum results continued with more contradictions amidst internal repression. Sharp disagreements surfaced in the late 1980s between India and Nepal on economic and security matters particularly over Nepal's purchase of weapons from China in May 1988 and non-renewal of trade and transit treaties between the two countries. People's Movement of 1990 highlighted the total failure of the system to respect people's democratic rights, provide economic security to them and maintain the best of relations with neighbouring countries particularly India. When the movement was at its peak, an Indian delegation led by Foreign Secretary S.K. Singh reached Kathmandu with a proposal to conclude a new treaty. It seemed to the Nepali people that the Government of India was eager to strike an advantageous deal with a tottering establishment in Nepal, regardless of the popular sentiments[32] and amidst voices in Indian political circles which was of the view that "we do not want a relationship with one person only. It was the people to people relationship that mattered."[33] The popular movement, however, succeeded in restoring the parliamentary system of democracy. The ensuing transition faced intense struggle between traditional and democratic forces for the primacy of priority and place in the new democratic set up.

Though a new constitution, considered a unique role model by its creators, was promulgated in 1990 with provision for a parliamentary democratic system and a constitutional monarchy, but barely six years into the practice, democracy came under sharp attack from the Communist Party of Nepal (Maoist).[34] Maoists called for the revision of discriminatory treaties with India and strict regulation of the open border. They repeatedly claimed that "Indian expansionist designs" were the most crucial factor in the underdevelopment of Nepal.[35]

Amidst the ongoing armed revolt by the Maoists, King Birendra, Queen Aishwarya and all members of their family were decimated under mysterious circumstances on June 01, 2001. The blame for this carnage was placed on severely inebriated Crown Prince Dipendra who shot himself to death. Prince Gyanendra, brother of the late king, was thereafter crowned as the King of Nepal on June 04, 2001. The new king took unconstitutional and arbitrary steps in the name of removing difficulties under Article 127 of the 1990 constitution. The three-way power struggle between an assertive king who wanted to be seen in action; parliamentary political parties devoid of capacity, vision and leadership to push for political and economic reforms; and the rebel Maoists who identified the issues without the required capacity to address them, intensified in the following years.[36]

Though the Maoist revolt appeared to be a product of internal social, political and economic dynamics, it was not without external linkages. Owing to Nepal's open border with India, the Maoists successfully used the Indian territory as safe haven and "its base from which to plan operations,"[37] and built a robust support network supplying trained manpower, weapons and finances into Midwestern Nepal.[38] The Maoists were reported to be creating bases of their own in the inaccessible areas of north Bihar region to target security forces in Nepal.[39] Whereas India declared Maoists as terrorists long before Nepal did, and though New Delhi promised Nepal its increased support in denying the Maoists sanctuary in the Indian territory, "yet the main international support base of the Maoists was primarily in neighbouring India."[40] Maoist leaders in June 2002 assured the Indian leaders in writing that they wanted the best of relations with India and would not do anything to harm its critical interests.[41] Some communist politicians in Nepal see this as a threat of Indian expansionism in Nepal, and consider that India has been using Unified Communist Party of Nepal (Maoist) to serve its interests in Nepal."[42]

Maoists maintained links with the People's War Group (PWG) and Coordination Committee of Maoist Parties and Organisations in South Asia (COMPOSA)—which are active in some Indian states such as Andhra Pradesh, Madhya Pradesh, Jharkhand and Bihar. Their coming together was said to be for strengthening functional unity among the ultra-left parties and to further heighten the People's War being launched in South Asia. The Maoists also established ties with the United Liberation Front of Assam (ULFA) and other insurgent groups in India's northeast. It is also believed that the Maoists had ties with the Liberation Tigers of Tamil Eelam (LTTE) of Sri Lanka.[43] Maoist chief had termed Sri Lanka's Tamil Tigers as an "organisation of the brave."

Despite adopting the ideology of Mao Zedong, there is no evidence that the Maoists received any support from China.[44] China viewed Nepal's Maoists as "anti-government outfits," who were misusing the name of the great Chinese helmsman, and "can serve as an excuse for the international anti-China forces to create troubles."[45] Though China termed the absolute takeover by the king in 2005 an internal matter, it later noted the change of politics in Nepal and felt the need for all parties in Nepal to narrow down their differences. It was a clear signal to the palace.[46] This was a perceptible shift in China's Nepal policy since March 2006 when State Councillor Tang Jiaxuan met political leaders and urged the king to "reach out to the political parties to restore democracy and peace in the country."[47] Since the start of the peace process, China has been playing a proactive role to determine the future shape of Nepali politics. The Chinese leadership believes that any political instability in Nepal has a bearing on China's Tibet Autonomous Region (TAR).[48] This has enhanced the significance of Nepal as the next-door neighbour to Tibet.

End of Armed Conflict with India's Help

There are three rather different poles to international engagement with Nepal. India and China each has its own distinctive interests in Nepal. Then there is what is commonly called the 'donor community'. This includes the UN, represented by some 20 different agencies, and the major bilateral development partners: the UK, the EU, Japan, Denmark, Norway, Finland, Germany, the Netherlands, the US, Australia and Canada.[49]

India's role in Nepal's transformation has been predominant. The 12-point understanding between the agitating political parties and the armed Maoist rebels which concluded in 2005 in Delhi played a very important role in the political evolution of Nepal, clearing the way for the Maoists to join the political mainstream.[50] It underlined the need for implementing the concept of full democracy through a forward-looking restructuring of the state to resolve the problems related to all sectors including class, caste, gender, region, political, economic, and social and cultural by bringing the autocratic monarchy to an end and establishing full democracy.[51] After the success of *Jana Andolan* (People's Movement) in 2006, the king issued a proclamation, which was virtually dictated by G.P. Koirala in consultation with other Seven Party Alliance (SPA) members and the Indian Embassy.[52] The proclamation restored the parliament, which through its May 18, 2006 resolution stripped the king of all his executive powers, moved towards the abolition of the autocratic monarchy and the establishment of full-fledged democracy by "safeguarding the achievements of the 1990 People's Movement and institutionalising the achievements of the present People's Movement" It also declared that "Nepal shall be a secular state"[53] though it was not a part of the 12-point understanding and demands of the movement.

India's role was recognised by the UN Secretary General (UNSG) Ban Ki-moon, who "thanked India for her engagement in Nepal and said that itsrole is important for the successful transition of Nepal to democracy and stability."[54] However, various publications talked of "secrets of India's heavy influence" on Nepal's political activities. These publications perceived that India trying to 'micromanage' Nepal would be detrimental to it and hamper its relationship with Nepal.[55] To the larger world, including China, the Maoist leadership works more closely with India. This is also reflected in China not inviting Baburam Bhattarai during nearly two years of his premiership, apparently because of that suspicion;[56] however, Bhattarai was invited to a week-long private visit to China beginning on May 07, 2014 at the expense of the Chinese Government.

Peace Process and the UN

Ever since the then Secretary General of the UN, Kofi Annan, publicly offered to use his good offices in 2003 to seek an end to an increasingly bloody armed conflict between the Maoist insurgents and the state in Nepal, the UN engaged itself with various actors in support of Nepal's peace process. The UN in-country involvement with the conflict deepened when, in April 2005, the government of King Gyanendra sought to defuse international condemnation of both conflict-related abuses and its violations of democratic rights by accepting the establishment of the Office of the High Commissioner for Human Rights in Nepal (OHCHR-Nepal). Later, parliamentary parties, the Maoist leadership and civil society, all lobbied for the presence of UN in Nepal to assist in the peace process.[57] The engagement further deepened after the Government of Nepal and the rebels formally wrote to the UN on August 09, 2006 inviting it to:

- continue its human rights monitoring through OHCHR-Nepal;
- assist the monitoring of the Code of Conduct during the Ceasefire;
- seek UN assistance in "the management of arms and armed personnel of both the sides";
- deploy qualified civilian personnel to monitor and verify the confinement of CPN-M combatants and their weapons within designated cantonment areas;
- monitor Nepal Army to ensure that it remains in its barracks and its weapons are not used for or against any side; and
- provide election observation facility during the election of the CA.[58]

The mandate was incorporated in the Comprehensive Peace Agreement (CPA) signed on November 22, 2006. The CPA formally ended the armed conflict and turned the ceasefire into the peace process. Over 19,602 Maoist combatants were sheltered in various cantonments throughout the country after UN verification. CPA provided the much-needed ground towards institutionalising the democratic gains made by the movement. Subsequent months saw the adoption of Interim Constitution—a consensus document among the political parties and establishment of the Interim Parliament with a significant number of representatives from the Maoist Party through nomination. This made the Maoist party one of the major actors in the transformation process.

The UN Mission in Nepal (UNMIN) was established in 2007 with the mandate "to monitor the management of arms and armed personnel of both sides, to assist in the monitoring of ceasefire arrangements, and to provide technical support for the planning, preparation and conduct of the election of a Constituent Assembly in a free and fair atmosphere, in consultation with the parties."[59] India reluctantly accepted the need for any UN role, and initially hoped that Nepal could be kept away from the Security Council. Delhi certainly did not want to see a UN peacekeeping force in a neighbouring country with which it has an open border.[60] India was feeling increasingly uncomfortable about the UN presence in Nepal.[61] It was mainly Nepal's deference to Indian wishes that precluded a request for the UN technical assistance to resolving security sector issues in the mandate and staffing of the mission.[62]

The CA elections on April 10, 2008 produced an Assembly with the Maoists as the largest political party, winning 38 percent of seats (30 per cent of the vote). The post-election phase witnessed the most serious breakdown in power sharing and consensual decision-making. The shock saw the end of cooperation among the major parties, which could not be achieved either by a Maoist-led coalition or by a coalition without the Maoist which replaced it.[63]

The UNMIN sought extension of the original mandate. But deference in views of Nepali political leaders and of Security Council members to Indian opposition to a larger UN role stood in the way.[64] The UNMIN though initially came on a high note, its acts were publicly criticised for not monitoring Maoists' movement, and letting the Maoists get away with not registering weapons. It also did not care about the consequent tensions in the cantonments and barracks. Further, the UNMIN was criticised for accepting thousands of combatants who had never been part of the Maoists' army in the verification process, thus making them potentially eligible for integration into the state security forces. It also failed in the task of supervising the Maoists in cantonments.[65] Its chief was said not to have acted as a referee, but as the 'Cultural Tsar' of the West consolidating its strategic and cultural interest.[66] India remained extremely sensitive about international meddling in what it considered to be its sphere of influence. It was concerned that the UN would "use the Madhesi card" to steadily expand its mandate and term to stay on and treat Nepal as its protectorate.[67] The UNMIN term ended in January 2011 without resolving the management of the Maoist combatants. India was blamed for being instrumental in pushing the Mission out of its backyard; the reason supposedly was that the presence of the UN had thwarted India's desire to control the political process in Nepal.[68] With the UNMIN's departure, it seemed inevitable that India would have "to step up to more of a leadership role."[69] The OHCHR also left the country in 2012 as the government refused to grant further extension.

Open Border between Nepal and India

Nepal and India share an open border; people on either side cross the border daily in hundreds of thousands for socio-cultural and economic purposes. Activities related to human, arms and drug trafficking, and kidnapping and economic offences, are also reported from across the border. It is often highlighted that Indian security personnel cross into Nepal to carry out their searches and arrests without informing Nepali authorities. Politicians and scholars alike often take up border issues to flare up nationalism. After having resigned as prime minister on the issue of dismissing the army chief in 2009, Pushpa Kamal Dahal found it convenient to use the term 'foreign lord'—meaning India—behind the reasons for his resignation, raised the issue of civilian supremacy, stirred up Nepali nationalism of Panchayat-era, strongly marked by anti-India rhetoric, and took 'flag marches' to border areas in the South. Scholars in Nepal say that the border was encroached at 53 places 10 years back, and it has reached 71 places to-date.[70]

A leading Nepali weekly editorialised that after having arrested two terrorists and taken them to India without the knowledge of Nepal police, Indian security forces repeated their high handedness in carrying out a raid in a private house in Gulariya of Bardia District of Western Nepal in search of criminals, who fled India after committing crimes there. The editorial termed it as unfortunate for a democratic country to have openly encroached another sovereign country.[71] Some are of the view that India deals with Nepal "in an undignified manner, as if Nepal was nothing but its wagging tail."[72] The Nepali elites overwhelmingly feel that repetition of the Gulariya chapter could stoke the issue of self-dignity[73] and sovereignty. One of the early reactions to the raid came from former prime minister and senior Unified Communist Party of Nepal (Maoist) leader Baburam Bhattarai in his tweet, "Incursion of Indian police in Bardia is a gross violation of Nepali sovereignty."[74] This exposes the high vulnerability of the open border to misuse to each other's detriment. The management of open border calls for close cooperation and increased intelligence sharing between the intelligence and security agencies of two countries.[75]

Treaty of Peace and Friendship 1950

The 1950 Treaty of Peace and Friendship between Nepal and India and the Letters of Exchange (LoE) attached to the treaty on July 31, 1950 are indicative of the depth of Nepal-India friendship and also perceived as a source of problems. The Treaty along with the LoE and the 1965 Agreement on Arms appeared to have been carefully designed to insulate the Chinese influence from the south of Himalayas. The 1965 Agreement remained secret until revealed by a newspaper in March 1989. India considers Nepali Himalayas as a common defence to be protected by both Nepal and India. Two overriding factors remained instrumental in formulating the 1950 Treaty. These include clear assertion of the Chinese sovereignty in Tibet and increasing probability of 'an armed revolution' in Nepal,[76] affecting the Gangetic belt, the heartland of India. India thought any violent upheavals in Nepal could create anarchy and chaos and lead to communist takeover.

The Treaty is a pointer to India's intention to keep Nepal within its sphere of influence.[77] The LoE, interpreted as 'penalty clauses' imposed by a big power over a small one,[78] were made public in 1959 and contained far more important provisions than the treaty itself. They contained clauses requiring the two governments to consult each other and devise effective counter measures, which required seeking the *assistance and agreement* of India for the import of arms and ammunition or warlike materials. They also mentioned that both the governments agreed not to employ any foreigners whose activities may be prejudicial to the security of the other.[79] An aide memoire handed over to Nepal by the Government of India in July 1958 demanded among others that Nepal consult the Government of India to any matters relating to foreign policy or relations with foreign powers, with a view to coordinate policy, in particular in matters relating to the relations with Tibet and China.[80] The review of the 1950 Treaty is, therefore, one of the major issues in Nepal-India relations. Political parties in Nepal feel that many of treaty clauses are an affront to the dignity of Nepal.

From Monarchy to Republic

The CA on May 28, 2008 declared Nepal a "federal, democratic, republic state by legally ending the monarchy."[81] It was an important day for Nepal to fulfil the long held aspirations of its people for sustained peace, stability, development, economic and social progress, rule of law, human rights and fundamental freedoms. It was also hoped that a democratic constitution will be drafted through people's representatives. The Assembly served an ultimatum on the king to vacate the palace by June 15. On June 11, the last king of the Shah Dynasty left the Narayanhity Royal Palace after holding a press conference. He said that he wanted to be a facilitator for the implementation of people's decision at the CA. With the abolition of monarchy, India's policy on Nepal that was based on constitutional monarchy and multiparty democracy as twin pillars of peace and stability too changed.

People-to-People Relations

The people of Nepal and India have enjoyed unique harmony, tolerance and mutual understanding since time immemorial. People-to-people relations reached their height when Nepali leaders joined the Civil Disobedience and Quit India Movement at the call of Mahatma Gandhi for Indian Independence. Leaders of that generation, who were educated in India and had cultivated deep friendship with Indian leaders, benefitted from their direct contacts with Mahatma Gandhi. However, with the older generation of leaders gone, a new class of people with Western education, thinking and much wider exposure of the world has since emerged in Nepal.

Such emotional bonding, cordiality and closeness derived from informal people-to-people relationship created positive atmosphere for decision making at the governmental level and thus made a significant contribution in bringing the two countries closer. Many organisations operating at the regional and local level have also facilitated people-to-people relationship between Nepal and India.

India disburses pension worth NRs. 22 billion annually to the army pensioners in Nepal.[82] People who have taken up jobs in India have been a very important factor in lobbying and influencing the policymaking process at home. They are being engaged in various spheres of national life, and have a positive perspective on traditional relationship between Nepal and India. Though India remained the primary destination for Nepali jobseekers almost until recently, lately over three million Nepali people have taken up jobs in third countries. The dynamics of such a young and dynamic population exposed to Western ideas and way of life and proliferating domestic media need to be factored not only in the discourse of Nepal-India relations but also on the development of Nepal.

Water Resources

Nepal is a least developed and a landlocked country. Despite its abundant water resources, the nation endures 16 hours of blackouts on an almost daily basis. Its total power generation at present does not exceed 700 MW, whereas its projected potential stands at 120,000 MW. Nepal exemplifies 'a resource curse'. This curse has come without exploiting its resources reserves, let alone making exports.[83]

Water resources in Nepal have been highly politicised. Misinformation, guesswork bordering on suspicion, misperception and press reports based on ignorance or illicit influence is frequently at the root of hydro politics. Many of the issues can be resolved if hydro harmony is allowed precedence over hydro politics.[84] Nepal's immediate neighbours could benefit from the utilisation of Nepal's immense water resources. However, India is viewed to be always aiming at monopolising Nepal's water resources according to its needs and binding the Nepalis into signing agreements including a clause like prior use.[85] Often floods and landslides cause heavy losses of life and property every year. The worst such incident occurred in 2013 when flood and mud slides in the Uttarakhand State of India killed hundreds of people, mainly pilgrims. There are recurring problems of natural disaster and inundation along the Nepal-India border. This demands that Nepal and India work together and adopt a joint approach to make diverse uses of shared rivers including flood control.

Aid and Trade

Nepal receives resources from foreign countries in the form of aid, loans, grants and investments. India has been its long-standing development partner. India is Nepal's largest trading partner. It is a country best placed to invest in Nepal. With a view to offer assurances and incentives to attract significant investment from India, Nepal and India concluded a Bilateral Investment Promotion and Protection Agreement (BIPPA) in 2011. Though yet to be ratified, the agreement is considered to have introduced a new trend in practice with regard to the conclusion of bilateral investment treaties.[86]

The development partnership includes a multilayered programme comprising 477 ongoing and completed projects at the cost of over NRs. 65 billion in almost all key economic sectors.[87] However, around 23 per cent of the foreign aid is still off the government budget. Nepal faces a daunting challenge to bring foreign aid under budgetary system to enhance transparency and accountability on spending in Nepal.[88]

Two-thirds of Nepal's foreign trade (66 per cent) is with India. Nepal's imports stand at 87.09 per cent while exports are mere 12.01 per cent. Despite years of trade diversification measures, there has been no shift in the direction, structure, and composition of Nepal's foreign trade. India accounted 65.09 per cent of Nepal's total imports, while its exports to India alone constituted 66.03 per cent. Ratio of exports to imports with India is 13.09 per cent. Trade experts opine that concentration of trade with a single country has increased the vulnerability of Nepal's economy.[89] Nepal's escalating trade deficit is a matter of serious concern. While Nepal needs to undertake rigorous restructuring of its economy, India will continue to remain a major market for Nepali products in the foreseeable future.

Recent Developments

The historic CA-I that was the symbol of inclusiveness and proportionality and legitimate instrument of social transformation failed to deliver a constitution. It is hoped that the second CA that was elected on November 19, 2013 will complete the remaining task of constitution writing within the stipulated time, that is, by January 22, 2015. In the CA II election, Maoist Party was downsized from the first to third position. Now in the opposition, Maoists often use nationalism card strongly backed by anti-India rhetoric. However, at certain point, after realising the follies and futility of double standards, Prachanda-led Maoist faction often drops its anti-India rhetoric and proposes for reconciling with the neighbouring giant. The souring of relations between Nepal's major political parties and New Delhi often gets locked in a war of attrition.[90] It appears that most political leaders in Nepal have diverted "all their energy to appease Indian establishment so that the southern neighbour could put them into power. Such a mindset of Nepali political elites is not shaped by their understanding of the emergent geopolitical dynamics; rather, they are driven by their own desire and complex."[91]

India places its relations with Nepal as "a matter of the highest priority."[92] It has provided support for CA-II election, peace process, and institutionalisation of democracy and socio-economic development of Nepal. For example, India provided 764 vehicles (48 vehicles to the Election Commission and 716 vehicles to the Nepal Police) and other support to CA II elections. It also agreed to resume the supply of defence hardware to the Nepal Army as identified in the Bilateral Consultative Group on Security Issues.

India considers federalism to be a thorny issue and though has stated that it has no federal model to offer, but wants voices of all communities to be heard and reflected in the law. In the Indian perception, "Nepal is attempting an unprecedented transformation, and everyone is uncertain about their future. No external power has any magic wand to resolve the concerns of little over 27 million Nepalis. India's role was to 'offer support', not specify prescriptions."[93] Further, according to the then Indian Foreign Secretary Ranjan Mathai, "Whatever decision Nepali people take on future federal setup has to be sustainable decision.That decision can be sustainable only if political parties have consensus on it."[94] It is perceived that "India desires the Terai politically stronger than the hills."[95]

The psychology that India is an important factor when it comes to staying in power seems to have moderated the position of politicians in the country vis-à-vis India. So, India is always a major preoccupation with Nepali politicians, though the veracity of such thinking needs to be established.[96] India holds that it has no favourites in Nepal and that it would maintain relations with all political parties. It is said that "India's influence is much the greater, and its spies have been active in splitting parties it dislikes, and in ferrying favoured leaders to Delhi to shop and be flattered by bigwigs."[97]

Conclusion

The mainstreaming of the armed Maoists into the democratic process and peaceful transformation of Nepal from an authoritarian monarchical to a democratic republican order, presents a rare example in contemporary history. However, high expectations and hopes generated by this transformation have been shattered by prolonged political transition and failure of the first CA to deliver a constitution. Peace process stays on hold amidst mounting social, political and economic challenges and ethnicisation of politics. Political parties remain locked in power politics. Though engaged in mutual dialogues and negotiations, political parties continue to be plagued by a cycle of distrust and confusion. Leaders have repeatedly failed to deliver on democracy and development promises. As a result, the nation suffers from political gridlock, underdevelopment, poverty, inequality, and lack of job opportunities for young people entering into the job market. The middle class that provides the backbone to sustaining the democratic transformation process remains disillusioned. This pushes the country into a volatile mix of political instability, social decay and economic stagnation, each reinforcing the other.

Though the peace process is labelled as home-grown, a deeper analysis of conflict reveals a set of causes deeply rooted in uneasy geopolitics.[98] What appeared to be internal in the beginning became a complex synthesis of several micro and macro factors. With continued lack of necessary democratic institutions in place to sustain the change and institutionalise the democratic transformation after it turned into a republic, Nepal risks becoming a proxy state to outside forces, a laboratory for them to test their theories, exploit its weaknesses and reap strategic benefits.

Nepal's highest national priority is to have a democratic constitution promulgated by the CA to create a supportive environment to manage the historic democratic transformation, and institutionalise the fundamentals of a republican state. This is possible only with the goodwill, support and assistance from neighbours and friends in the international community. India and China have greater roles to play in Nepal's political and economic development. Extensive social, economic, cultural and political ties give India a bigger role. China recognises this hard fact and reality, and is of the view that it would be "better and fruitful for Nepal to maintain good relations with India."[99]

Nepalis do not need to be anti-Indian to be patriotic. The era of equating Nepali nationalism with anti-Indianism by left parties in Nepal should be over now. Nepal's assertion of its independence and sovereignty should not be taken as its being against the interests of India. Nepal is never ignorant and insensitive to India's legitimate concerns. At the same time, Kathmandu wants New Delhi to understand that as an emerging global power, already the second largest economy and trading superpower in the world, China is just on the other side of border, and Nepal has to live with it. India, being China's immediate neighbour with extensive ties, is no stranger to its increasing assertiveness on various issues. Further, it should be appreciated that Nepal is walking a tightrope from a very sensitive geopolitical position. Nepal's concern for its integrity and independence should be appreciated by both of its neighbours as much as Nepal appreciates their security concerns.

Nepal lives in paradox-pervasive poverty in the midst of abundance of human and natural resources which have liberating capabilities from growing scarcities. It has suffered from a decade-long Maoist insurgency and has witnessed "many lost opportunities, costly misjudgements and avoidable misunderstandings." Moreover, successive governments in Nepal and India have rather comprehensively failed to establish a stable, mature relationship based on mutual trust and a long-term vision of cooperation.[100] Given the continuation of the present state of affairs, there is real danger of radicalisation of political life in Nepal, conflict residues that remain unmonitored threatening to reignite, and massive outflow of Nepal's young and dynamic population in search of job opportunities abroad leading to disruption of families and rural communities in the country. This generates the biggest threat from within.

Continued stalemate and absence of stable and rule-based institutions will deprive the country of the much promised democracy and development, and encourage those who talk of seizing the state amidst chaos and instability. A communist takeover in Nepal would have grave implications for the country and the region. For India, a Maoist Nepal would mean moral and military support to insurgencies in its northeast and other radical groups that aim to destabilise the government in New Delhi. India might be pressured to intervene if such a scenario arises. China would view a possible control of Nepal by India as a serious security threat, and both nuclear rivals would be pushed to the brink of conflict.[101] This would only please those forces who want India and China to remain at loggerheads and make Nepal a playing ground for their narrow self-interests.

In an increasingly interdependent and interconnected world, things have gone from "local and linear" to "global and exponential." The traditional concept of security has undergone change and is extended to include economic, societal, identity, demographic, cultural and environmental dimensions. Whatever 'happens over here' impacts 'over there'. This makes challenges common to all and demands common solutions in a comprehensive manner.

We cannot remain oblivious to the unleashing of people's aspirations and the winds of change sweeping across the region and the globe. It is time for leaders of both the countries to call a spade a spade in bilateral relations, discuss comprehensively the entire gamut of relations and work towards reorienting them to the changing dynamics. It is said that an Indian 'initiative' could alone "set a positive tone for better ties in the future."[102] Nepali leaders should end double talks, assure India in no uncertain terms that they are sensitive towards its legitimate concerns, and express ardent desire to maintain the best of relations within the framework of an independent, sovereignand a democratic nation. The recent contacts at the highest political level are highly inspiring. This has opened up avenues to uplift Nepal-India relations to a newer level, paving way for building trust and confidence at the political level, transforming the quality of relationship constructively and creating a win-win situation for improving the quality of life of the people.

ENDNOTES

1. "Nepal and Its Neighbours: Yam Yesterday, Yam Today," *The Economist*, January 18, 2012, at http://www.economist.com/blogs/banyan/2012/01/nepal-and-its-neighbours?zid=306&ah

=1b164dbd43b0cb27ba0d4c3b12a5e227.

2. Kenneth N. Waltz, *Theory of International Politics*, Addison-Wesley, Reading, 1979, pp. 72-73.
3. Christopher Flavin and Gary Gardner, "China, India and the New World Order," in *The State of the World: A Worldwatch Institute Report on Progress Toward a Sustainable Society*, W.W. Norton & Company, New York, 2006, p. 3.
4. Kevin Rudd, "Beyond the Pivot: A New Road Map for US-Chinese Relations," *Foreign Affairs*, March/April, 2013, p. 9.
5. *The Economist*, no.1.
6. Christopher Flavin and Gary Gardner, no.3, p. 3.
7. *The Economist*, no.1.
8. Kevin Rudd, no. 4, p. 10.
9. Leo E. Rose, *Nepal: Strategy for Survival*, University of California Press, Berkeley, 1971, p. 287.
10. Lok Raj Baral, "Political System and the Elite Behaviour in the Context of India-Nepal Relations," in Kalim Bahadur and Mahendra P. Lama (eds.), *New Perspectives on India-Nepal Relations*, Har-Anand Publications, New Delhi, 1995, p. 66.
11. Arvinda Ramchandra Deo, "India-Nepal: Few Steps, Giant Strides,'" in *India-Nepal Relations: The Challenge Ahead*, Rupa& Co., in association with Observer Research Foundation,New Delhi, 2004, p. 44.
12. Lok Raj *Baral*, no.10, p. 28.
13. S.D. Muni, *India and Nepal: A Changing Relationship*, Konark Publishers, Delhi, 1992, p. 27.
14. Lok Raj Baral, "Democracy and Indo-Nepal Relations," in *India-Nepal Relations: The Challenge Ahead*, Rupa &Co., in association with Observer Research Foundation, New Delhi, 2004, p. 79.
15. Lok Raj Baral, no. 10, p. 33.
16. Prashant Jha, "Former Nepal Premier criticises his country's 'blind nationalism,'" *The Hindu*, July 25, 2013, at http://www.thehindu.com/todays-paper/tp-international/former-nepal-premier-criticises-his-countrys-blind-nationalism/article4950651.ece. Former Nepali Prime Minister and senior leader of the Communist Party of Nepal (Unified Marxist Leninist), Madhav Kumar Nepal, said that it was time his country shed its suspicions of India's actions, and also that India should empathise with the insecurities of its smaller neighbour.
17. Lok Raj Baral, no. 14, p. 77.
18. Andrew Hall, "Nepal: An Incomplete Peace,"*Asian Affairs*, XLII (III), November 2011, p. 413. Hall is former British Ambassador to Nepal.
19. K.J. Holsti, *International Politics: A Framework for Analysis*, Prentice Hall, New Jersey, 1992, pp.119-120.
20. Lok Raj Baral, no. 14, p. 79.
21. Yubraj Ghimire, *Nepal: Dignifying interdependence: Neighbourhood Views of India,* The Gateway House, Indian Council on World Affairs, Mumbai, 2012, p. 60.
22. Rishikesh Shaha, *Nepal and the World*, 1955, p. 38, as quoted in Jayant Kumar Ray, *India's Foreign Relations, 1947-2007,* Routledge, New Delhi, 2011, p. 415.
23. Ramjee P. Parajulee, *The Democratic Transition in Nepal,* Rowman & Littlefield Publishers Inc., New York, 2000, p. 179.
24. A.S. Bhasin (ed.), *Documents on Nepal's relations with India and China 1949-66*, Academic Books Ltd.,New Delhi, 1970, p. 51.
25. *The Economist,* no. 1.
26. Bhuwan Lal Joshi and Leo E. Rose,*Democratic Innovations in Nepal: A Case Study of Political Acculturation*, University of California Press, Berkeley, 1966, p. 364.

27. Leo E. Rose, as quoted in Dinesh Bhattarai and Pradip Khatiwada, *Nepal-India: Democracy in the Making of Mutual Trust,* Nirala Publications, Jaipur, 1993, pp. 170-179. Prof. Rose shared this view with the *Independent Weekly* in Kathmandu on May 22, 1991.
28. Frederick H. Gaige, *Regionalism and National Unity in Nepal,* University of California Press, Berkeley, 1975, p. 91.
29. S.D. Muni, no. 13, p. 194.
30. Ramjee P. Parajulee, no. 23, p. 179.
31. B.P. Koirala, "Appeal to the Countrymen Issued on the Eve of Returning Home in December 30, 1976 after 8 years of Exile in India," in Sushil Koirala (ed.), *Democracy Indispensable for Development,* Sandaju Publications, Varanasi, 1982, pp. 137-140.
32. Dinesh Bhattarai and Pradip Khatiwada, *Nepal-India: Democracy in the Making of Mutual Trust,* Nirala Publications, Jaipur, 1993, p. 140.
33. *The Times of India,* New Delhi, February 23, 1990, as quoted in Dinesh Bhattarai and Pradip Khatiwada, no. 32, p. 121. Janata Dal leader Chandra Shekhar said this at a meeting in New Delhi organised by the CPM in support of the Nepalese movement on February 22, 1990.
34. On February 04, 1996, Chairman of the United People's Front, Nepal, Baburam Bhattarai, submitted a 40-point demand to Prime Minister Sher Bahadur Deuba of the Nepali Congress and gave an ultimatum to fulfil the demands within two weeks. Nine of these demands related to nationality starting from the abrogation of many treaties considered to be discriminatory including the 1950 Nepal-India Treaty of Peace and Friendship, banning of all vehicles with Indian license plates from Nepal and strictly regulating the open border between Nepal and India. Baburam Bhattarai did nothing when he became the Prime Minister to address his own demands, instead received a 70-point demand from the splinter group of the Communist Party of Nepal (Maoist) led by his former senior party colleague, Mohan Baidya.
35. Ali Riaz and Subho Basu, *Paradise Lost: State Failure in Nepal,* Lexington Books, Maryland, 2007, p. 133.
36. For details, see Dev Raj Dahal, "Nepal: Supporting Peace Process through a Systemic Approach,"*Berghof Foundation for Peace Support*, Berlin, October 03, 2005, at http://www.berghof-foundation.org/fileadmin/redaktion/Publications/Other_Resources/NEP_Supporting_Peace_Processes_Through_a_Systemic_Approach.pdf
37. M.A.Thomas, "Nepal: Political Uncertainty amid the Maoist Threat," in William M. Carpenter and David Wiencek (eds.), *Asian Security Handbook: Terrorism and the New Security Environment*, M.E. Sharpe, New York, 2005, p.196.
38. Ibid., p. 198.
39. Pranava K. Chaudhary, "Maoists' bases in N Bihar likely," *The Times of India*, New Delhi, October 15, 2003, at http://timesofindia.indiatimes.com/city/patna/Maoists-bases-in-N-Bihar-likely/articleshow/233956.cms
40. M.A. Thomas, no. 37, pp. 196-199.
41. S.D. Muni, "Bringing the Maoists down from the Hills: India's Role," in Sebastian von Einsiedel, David M. Malone and Suman Pradhan (eds.), *Nepal in Transition: From People's War to Fragile Peace,* Cambridge University Press, New Delhi, 2012, p. 321.
42. *My República*, May 12, 2013. General Secretary of CPN-Masal Mohan Bikram Singh was reported talking to the media.
43. M.A. Thomas, no. 37, p. 198.
44. Ibid.
45. Statement by Ambassador Wu Congyong at the launching of the Chinese Embassy website in Kathmandu on May 10, 2002. Chinese Ambassador Yang Houlan on October 16, 2011 claimed to have authentic information that "our oldest and nearest friend Nepal is turning

into a playground for anti-Chinese activities. Some international and domestic forces are coordinating their activities against China." He repeated them in his remarks made at the Nepal Council of World Affairs in Kathmandu on September 13, 2012.

46. Prashant Jha, "A Nepali Perspective on International Involvement in Nepal," in Sebastian von Einsiedel, David M. Malone and Suman Pradhan (eds.), *Nepal in Transition: From People's War to Fragile Peace,* Cambridge University Press, New Delhi, 2012, p. 353.
47. Yubaraj Ghimire, "Nepal: China Wants King, Parties Patch up," *Indian Express*, March 18, 2006, at http://www.indianexpress.com/news/nepalchina-wants-king-parties-patchup/619.
48. Abanti Bhattacharya, "China and its Peripheries: Strategic Significance of Tibet," *Issue Brief 220,* Institute of Peace and Conflict Studies, May 2013, at http://www.ipcs.org/issue-brief/china/china-and-its-peripheries-strategic-significance-of-tibet-220.html
49. Andrew Hall, no. 18, p. 413.
50. For Shyam Saran's interview to *The Kathmandu Post,* see "India isn't constantly trying to subvert Nepali politics," January 14, 2013, at http://www.ekantipur.com/2013/01/14/top-story/india-isnt-constantly-trying-to-subvert-nepali-politics/365586.html
51. See "12-Point Understanding Concluded between the Seven Political Parties and the Communist Party of Nepal (Maoist)," in *Peace Agreements 2005-10:From Conflict to Peace in Nepal,* Asian Study Center for Peace and Conflict Transformation, Kathmandu, 2011, pp. 1-4.
52. S.D. Muni, no. 41, pp. 329-330.
53. For details, see "May 18, 2006 Proclamation of the House of Representatives", in *Peace Agreements 2005-10: From Conflict to Peace in Nepal,* Asian Study Center for Peace and Conflict Transformation, Kathmandu, 2011, pp. 8-11.
54. "India's role in peace process crucial: Ban," April 28, 2012, at http://www.ekantipur.com/2012/04/28/top-story/indias-role-in-peace-process-crucial-ban/353087.html. According to the Spokesperson of the Indian Ministry of External Affairs Syed Akbaruddin, as quoted by Mahesh Acharya in *The Kathmandu Post,* the United Nations Secretary General (UNSG) Ban Ki-moon mentioned that India's role in Nepal's peace process will be more useful as the United Nations, which used to be deeply involved in the process, has now just a small team in Nepal.
55. *The Kathmandu Post*, September 24, 2013. Maoist leader Pushpa Kamal Dahal made these remarks at a book release function: "*Prayogshala: Nepali Sankramankalma Delhi, Darbar ra Maobadi"* (Laboratory: Delhi, Palace and Maoists in Nepal's transition) authored by *Kantipur Daily* (Nepali) Editor-in-Chief Sudheer Sharma. Dahal called on the Indian leadership to desist from instigating Nepali political parties. He rather emphasised on holding direct talks to address common concerns between both the countries, including economy, security, and sovereignty, at the political level. The Maoist leader admitted that his party made diplomatic agreements with national and international powers, as mentioned in Sharma's book, but he claimed that all those accords were not against the interests of the Nepali people.
56. Yubaraj Ghimire, "China in Nepal," *The Indian Express*, April 22, 2013, at http://indianexpress.com/article/opinion/columns/china-in-nepal/99/
57. Ian Martin, "All Peace Operations Are Political: A Case for Designer Missions and the Next UN Reform," in *Review of Political 2010 Missions: A project of the Center on International Cooperation*, New York University, 2010, p. 9.
58. "Peace Agreements 2005-10:From Conflict to Peace in Nepal," *Asian Study Center for Peace and Conflict Transformation*, Kathmandu, 2011, pp. 39-40.
59. "Security Council Establishes United Nations Political Mission in Nepal, Unanimously Adopting Resolution 1740 (2007)," *United Nations*, January 23, 2007, at http://www.un.org/press/en/2007/sc8942.doc.htm
60. Ian Martin, no. 57, p. 9.

61. Bhojraj Pokharel and Shrishti Rana, *Nepal Votes for Peace*, Foundation Books, Delhi, 2013, p. 101.
62. Ian Martin, no. 57, p. 10.
63. Ibid., p. 11.
64. Ibid., p. 10.
65. Prashant Jha, no. 46, p. 349.
66. Tarun Vijay, "India Must Speak Out,"*The Times of India*, April 17, 2008, at http://timesofindia.indiatimes.com/tarun-vijay/the-right-view/India-must-speak-out/articleshow/2960238.cms
67. Prashant Jha, no. 46, p. 351.
68. Bhojraj Pokharel and Shrishti Rana, no. 61, p. 185.
69. Andrew Hall, no. 18, p. 414.
70. A leading surveyor and expert on border issues, Buddhi Narayan Shrestha, shared the details with the media in *The Kathmandu Post*. See "India has encroached border at 71 places: Scholars," April 05, 2013, at http://www.ekantipur.com/2013/04/05/top-story/india-has-encroached-border-at-71-places-scholars/369536.html
71. "Michaha Prabriti" (Encroachment Trends), *Kantipur Daily* (Nepali), September 20, 2013 (Ashwin 04, 2070).
72. Kirti Nidhi Bista, "Neighbourly Help,"*My República*, Kathmandu, October 02, 2013. Bista is former Prime Minister of Nepal.
73. Surya Nath Upadhyay, "Kina dohorinchha Gulariya prakaran?" ("Why Gulariya Chapter Gets Repeated?"), *Kantipur*, Kathmandu, September 30, 2013 (Ashwin 14, 2070).
74. Utpal Parashar, "Not kept in loop, Nepal irked by Indian police incursion," *The Hindustan Times*, September 20, 2013, at http://www.hindustantimes.com/world-news/not-kept-in-loop-nepal-irked-by-indian-police-incursion/article1-1124574.aspx
75. *Asian Age*, September 24, 2013.
76. Prem R. Uprety, "Nepal and South Asian Regional Security,"*Contributions to Nepalese Studies*, 18 (1), CNAS,Tribhuvan University, January 1991, p. 24.
77. Kirti Nidhi Bista, no. 72.
78. Prem R. Uprety, no. 76, p. 22.
79. See detailed text of the Treaty of Peace and Friendship between the Government of India and the Government of Nepal and Letter Exchanged with the Treaty dated the 31st July 1950 in S.D. Muni, *India and Nepal: A Changing Relationship*, Konark Publishers, Delhi, 1992, pp. 188-192.
80. *Jhyali*, July 08, 1958, p. 2, as quoted in Prem R. Uprety, no. 76. The aide memoire was handed over to Dr. Dilli Raman Regmi in New Delhi.
81. *The Interim Constitution of Nepal 2063 (2007) as amended by the First to Sixth Amendments.* The amendment was inserted on 2065 Jestha 15 (May 28, 2008) by the Interim Constitution of Nepal (Fourth Amendment) Act, 2065.
82. *My República*, August 15, 2013.
83. Brahma Chellaney, *Water: Asia: New Battleground*, Georgetown University Press, Washington D.C., 2011.
84. Jayant Kumar Ray, *India's Foreign Relations, 1947-2007,* Routledge, New Delhi, 2011, p. 470.
85. Kirti Nidhi Bista, no. 72.
86. For details, see Surya P. Subedi, "India's New Bilateral Investment Promotion and Protection Treaty with Nepal: A New Trend in State Practice,"*ICSID Review: Foreign Investment Law Journal*, 28 (2), 2013, pp. 384-404.
87. *My República*, August 15, 2013.
88. *My República*, September 22, 2013.

89. Ibid.
90. "Dahal and Delhi," Editorial, *The Kathmandu Post*, April 26, 2013.
91. Lok Raj Baral, *Nepal-Nation-State in the Wilderness: Managing State, Democracy and Geopolitics*, Sage Publications Inc., New Delhi, 2012, p. 184.
92. See "Salman Khurshid arrives in Nepal on day-long visit," *The Economic Times*, July 09, 2013, at http://articles.economictimes.indiatimes.com/2013-07-09/news/40469215_1_nepal-constituent-assembly-khil-raj-regmi. The Indian External Affairs Minister Salman Khurshid had also expressed the commitment of India to "working with the people of Nepal for a democratic, stable, peaceful and prosperous Nepal."
93. Prashant Jha, "In Nepal Visit, Khurshid to Press for Timely Elections," *The Hindu*, July 09, 2013, at http://www.thehindu.com/news/international/in-nepal-visit-khurshid-to-press-for-timely-elections/article4897577.ece.
94. Foreign Secretary of India Ranjan Mathai was reported to be talking to a group of Nepali journalists at his office in South Block. See *My Republica*, April 23, 2013.
95. "Politics in Nepal: Adhoc Country," *The Economist*, June 22, 2013, at http://www.economist.com/news/asia/21579882-election-called-political-stability-remains-distant-dream-ad-hoc-country.
96. Lok Raj Baral, no. 14, p. 79.
97. *The Economist*, no. 95. *The Kathmandu Post* on May 18, 2012 reported an Indian diplomat at the Consulate General of India in Birjung, Nepal, urging the political leadership of the Central Terai to take to the streets for the sake of Madhes and bring about "a storm in the Madhes before May 27," the last day of the term of the Constituent Assembly. Nepali media reports also pointed out that the UK Department of International Development (DFID), International Institute for Democratic, Electoral Assistance (IIDEA) and others are funding the Nepal Federation of Indigenous Nationalities (NEFIN) to form ethnic parties in Nepal. The formation of the Federal Socialist Party led by Ashok Rai, a former UML leader, is often cited in this regard. DFID in a Press Statement on May 12, 2012 claimed that funding under the Janajati Empowerment Programme (JEP) for greater economic, social and political inclusion ended in May 2011, when it became apparent that NEFIN was supporting *bandhs*.
98. *The Economist,* January 03, 1998. It describes geopolitics as "the maneuverings (*sic*) and counter-maneuverings (*sic*) of the world's big powers, and the question of who does what to whom around the globe, and why. It is a subject, you might think, that you ignore at your peril."
99. *The Economist*, no. 1. Chinese Premier Wen Jiabao reportedly remarked to the Nepali Prime Minister Baburam Bhattarai, "We (China) and India have been developing very cordial relations in the recent times and it would be better and fruitful for Nepal to maintain good relations with India."
100. K.V. Rajan, "Nepal," in J.N. Dixit (ed.), *External Affairs: Cross-Border Relations*, Lotus Collection: Roli Books, New Delhi, 2003, p. 97.
101. M.A. Thomas, no. 37, p. 201.
102. Lok Raj Baral, "India-Nepal Relations: Continuity and Change," *Asian Survey*, XXXII (9), September 1992, pp. 815-829.

7

Rising India and Bangladesh-India Relations: Mutual Perceptions and Expectations

M. Ashique Rahman

Introduction

The importance of Bangladesh-India relations in the ambit of Bangladesh's foreign relations is indisputable. Relations with India constitute the most important cornerstone of Bangladesh's external relations architecture. Geographical imperatives, socio-cultural affinities, historical ties and the shared South Asian civilisational heritages have created a natural bond of inter-dependence between the two close-door neighbours. They, however, could not augment this natural bond; and their bilateral relations did not follow a linear trend in the past, either. In spite of India's extraordinary assistance during the War of Liberation of Bangladesh both in terms of extending military assistance as well as providing refuge to the millions of Bangladeshis displaced during the War, Bangladesh-India relations for the last four decades have been beset with many strains and tribulations. As one scholar remarks, "The relationship has often been marked by occasional setbacks, thereby, making the bilateral ties rather lukewarm and uneven."[1] Many factors, ranging from unresolved bilateral issues to domestic factors of both the countries as well as regional/international geopolitical settings, are playing their respective part in forming and sustaining constraints in Bangladesh-India relations. While this is very natural that the two neighbouring countries sharing common borders will have their fare share of problems and uncertainties, in case of Bangladesh-India relations especially after a magnificent start following the Independence of Bangladesh in 1971, rocky relations in the last more than four decades have left analysts wondering and deliberating on the predicaments of Bangladesh-India relations.

Perceptions or for that matter misperceptions are often also highlighted as a significant variable responsible for creating and sustaining lukewarm relations between Bangladesh and India.[2] Whether relations in the past had been 'friendly' or 'un-friendly', the existence of unresolved bilateral issues[3] for long have created an environment of mistrust and suspicion rather than mutual trust and respect for each other. This mistrust and suspicion has got further amplified with how each country is perceived by the other. How the people of one country perceive 'the other' has an important bearing on how an act of foreign and security policy by one country is viewed and perceived thereof.

It is often said that the changing nature of Bangladesh-India relations profoundly impacts people's perceptions of India in Bangladesh. When there is bonhomie in bilateral relations, people's perceptions usually remain positive about India. It is normally expected that in a state of mutual understanding and friendly transactions, Bangladesh will receive more friendly treatment, and might also receive unilateral concessions regarding outstanding bilateral concerns. In an adverse state of relations, the expectations of a friendly treatment fall short of accomplishments leading to widespread disappointments which further germinate people's adverse perceptions about India. However, an exception was discernible during the last term of the present government. Despite 'very friendly' relations since early 2009, people's perceptions often did not follow the positive pitch made during 2009-2013 by the governments of both the countries. The reason in this case lies more in the gap that exists between the expectations and the achievements rather than the mood and disposition of their bilateral relations.

This expectations-achievements gap increases further in the context of India's rise both economically and politically. In contemporary times, few would argue against India's emergence as a major global power, and, this particular setting of emerging India has imparted a new dimension to the expectations and desires of its small neighbours. While some of India's neighbours, especially Pakistan and China, are critical of India's emergence at the regional and global levels, smaller neighbours of India including Bangladesh usually hold a position more propitious against such scenario. Bangladesh, not perceiving any threat from India in the traditional understanding of security, believes that India's rise will benefit the region and countries like Bangladesh. The people of Bangladesh, therefore, perceive that India with its rising status will emerge more magnanimous and compassionate as far as its smaller neighbours are concerned. The prevailing common expectations are that India will follow a friendlier neighbourhood policy while making utmost efforts to resolve all outstanding bilateral issues with its neighbours especially the smaller ones. The experience of last few years since 2009, however, does not fulfil those expectations. In spite of improving bilateral relations, India could not deliver on some of the issues or could not provide concessions in some areas that affect people's perceptions about India, often contributing to the persistence of negative perceptions in the minds of the people. Negative perceptions in turn create and sustain anti-India sentiments, constraining advancements in Bangladesh-India bilateral relations.

It is, therefore, imperative to analyse the roles of perception and/or misperception in Bangladesh-India relations especially in the context of India's contemporary political and economic rise. It is to be noted that we are discussing people's perception here, not Bangladesh's "threat perception" vis-à-vis India[4] although such a threat perception has crucial impact on the processes of public perception formation in Bangladesh. A good number of studies show that perceptions do matter in foreign relations.[5] Perceptions influence the decision-making process, and sometimes "decision-makers and negotiators find that their range of alternatives is constrained by (popular) moods and viewpoints."[6] In case of Bangladesh, it is difficult to ascertain direct linkages between people's perception and its impact in the foreign policy decision-making process especially given the underdeveloped and dysfunctional state of democracy in Bangladesh. How far leaders pay heed to popular attitude to a particular policy initiative is difficult to substantiate. Nevertheless, it can easily be assumed that a favourable mass would provide more political space for government's manoeuvring than a mass wielding adverse perceptions towards its policies. This is truer in case of Bangladesh-India relations. Given the importance of India in the domestic politics of Bangladesh as many political parties' use people's perceptions of India to garner popular support and score electoral advancement, decisions taken by the incumbent government needs to be driven and supported by the favourable attitude of the general masses. Therefore, the policy-makers and the decision-makers need to be well aware of the processes of perception formation concerning Bangladesh-India relations. A good grasp of how perceptions are shaped, and more importantly, how they are sustained in the long run will enable them to undertake informed policy initiatives.

Some very crucial questions, therefore, need to be raised and answered: To what extent perceptions do really matter in Bangladesh-India relations? How perceptions are formed and shaped in Bangladesh as far as India, particularly its global rise, is concerned? What are the key drivers, institutions, actors and stakeholders that are contributing in forming and shaping these perceptions and with what ends? And, finally, what is the way forward? Do addressing and fulfilling mutual expectations regarding many outstanding bilateral issues and immediate resolution of some very long-standing gridlocks, shred misperceptions between these two friendly (but strained) neighbouring countries? This paper follows a holistic approach towards understanding the key drivers, institutions, actors and stakeholders of perception formation in Bangladesh vis-à-vis India, thereby making an effort in providing an overall analysis of the process.

Four Decades of Bangladesh-India Relations: Changing Perceptions of India in Bangladesh

Relations between Bangladesh and India are complex, sensitive and multidimensional in nature.[7] Over the last more than 40 years of relationship, Bangladesh-India relations have experienced, contrary to expectations, many ups and downs, but as one analyst noted, "'India factor', as a positive force or a negative one, has remained constant and continued to affect Bangladesh's foreign policy behaviour."[8] Soon after the Independence of Bangladesh, bilateral relations commenced with a very close cooperative partnership which is generally dubbed as the "honeymoon period"[9] of Bangladesh-India relationship. The 1972 Bangladesh-India 'Treaty of Friendship, Cooperation and Peace,' popularly known as the Indira-Mujib Friendship Treaty, set the tone and texture of Bangladesh-India relations. The treaty was crucial for Bangladesh especially at a time when not many countries had recognised the newly born member of the community of nation-states and also against the international geopolitical order of bipolarity. The two countries had also been able to amicably resolve many of the outstanding issues, viz. the return of the Indian troops who entered Bangladesh territory during the War of Liberation, and the demarcation of land boundary through the 1974 Land Boundary Agreement (LBA). They also succeeded in inking agreements regarding cooperation on communications and trade and atomic energy development, thereby widening and deepening their areas of cooperation.[10]

In the period following 1975 military coup and the tragic assassination of the Father of the Nation Sheikh Mujibur Rahman, and with the Bangladesh-India "honeymoon period" ruined, the bilateral relationship plummeted into an irreversible discord and disparity. From the Bangladesh side, the two major contributing factors were: first, a significant shift in the foreign policy orientation of the post-1975 governments in terms of increasing their ties with the middle eastern countries as well as with China and the US bypassing India and, to some extent, using them as countervailing weight against India; second, the emphasis on the religious identity as a major component of Bangladeshi nationalism that had been construed by many as having an inherently anti-India connotation. Therefore, mistrust and mutual hostility were the dominant norms in Bangladesh-India relations during General Ziaur Rahman's regime.[11] However, some scholars maintain that notwithstanding the warm beginning, the two countries developed 'seeds of discord' on some issues in the later years of the Awami League (AL) tenure.[12] The creation of a para-military force by the AL Government called *Jatiyo Rakkhi Bahini* (national defence forces) were perceived by the Bangladesh Army as India's blueprint to keep the armed forces divided and weak in order to perpetuate its influence on Bangladesh. As also pointed out by Smruti S. Pattanaik, "India's training of *Jatioyo Rakhi Bahini*, the 10-mile-long free trade zone, the non-requirement of visas just after the liberation of Bangladesh and the signing of the 1972 friendship Treaty, all added to the suspicion regarding India's intentions."[13] However, it was the Farakka Barrage incident in the last year of the AL Government that contributed the most in forging 'suspicion' and 'mistrust' against India in the psyche of the general masses. The Barrage was constructed to divert water from the Ganges River to the Hooghly River for flushing out the Kolkata harbour. Bangladesh protested at the construction of the Barrage as it was assessed to have tremendous environmental and livelihood impact on Bangladesh. Paying due attention to Bangladesh's concern, India started operation of the Barrage on 'test basis' so that if it was found seriously harmful, India might consider termination of the operations. But in the later years, in spite of Bangladesh's severe concerns, India continued with the operation of the Barrage, and this severely added to the perception of India as 'not a trustworthy' country.

During General H.M. Ershad regime, Dhaka more or less followed a similar approach towards India as that of its predecessor, General Ziaur Rahman. In the aftermath of Ershad regime, Bangladesh witnessed the advent of democratic governance in the country after 16 years of autocratic rule. An elected government through widely acclaimed free and fair election led by the Bangladesh Nationalist Party (BNP) came to power in 1991. During the BNP tenure (1991-1996), Bangladesh-India relations still remained basically frozen. BNP was created by General Ziaur Rahman and it followed similar foreign policy orientation, emphasising religious identity and strengthening relations with the Muslim countries and China. It was widely believed that New Delhi also demonstrated little interest in improving relations with Bangladesh under the BNP Government; hence, the icy relationship continued.[14]

The relationship reverted to normalcy when the AL returned to power in 1996. Although falling far short of the historical ideal of the early 1970s, Bangladesh-India relations improved considerably under the first Sheikh Hasina regime (1996-2001). After decades of mistrust and discrepancy, the relationship started to thaw as both Dhaka and New Delhi began to pursue positive approaches towards each other. The conclusion of the Ganges water sharing agreement, which New Delhi had refused to sign with the previous governments, demonstrated the inclination for gradually improving relationship. Yet, there were limitations hindering further improvement in the bilateral relations. First, the AL had a thin majority in parliament, which resulted in diminished space for the government to manoeuvre against strong opposition from several political parties, mainly the BNP and the Jamat-e-Islami Bangladesh (JIB). Second, following the capture of power in India by the Bharatiya Janata Party (BJP) in 1998, the steady improvement in Bangladesh-India relations was stymied as the BJP Government strongly raised the controversial issue of 'illegal Muslim immigrants' from Bangladesh to northeast India.[15]

The Bangladesh-India relationship deteriorated again when BNP returned to power after winning the 2001 general elections. The policies of the two countries once again divulged discrepancies as they developed differences on security perceptions, owing in particular to India's suspicion of Bangladesh's hand in the insurgencies of northeast India, and in reverse, Dhaka's perception that New Delhi wanted to punish Bangladesh. Although there was some security cooperation during the period of indirect military rule from 2007-08, negative attitude and mistrust against each other continued in Bangladesh-India relationship. All that changed during the second tenure of Prime Minister Sheikh Hasina (2009-2013). Prime Minister Hasina initiated a radical departure in Dhaka's approach towards New Delhi, adopting a very India-positive foreign policy orientation in order to build a long-term irreversible bilateral relationship. New Delhi has also responded in similar fashion; consequently, the bilateral relationship has been on an upward trajectory since 2009, a trend that has been hardly evident since 1975.[16] Some maintain that it is natural for an AL Government, given the ideological similarity between itself and the Indian National Congress, to pursue a decidedly pro-India policy and get closer to India. However, as Bhumitra Chakma noted, the underlying causes of the second Hasina Government's India-positive foreign policy orientation run deeper being a consequence of multiple interactive variables emanating from three sources: personal, national and regional/international.[17]

Whatever are the causes, people's perception as far as AL and Bangladesh-India relations are concerned remains that during the AL Government bilateral relationship improves. Consequently, a widespread perception prevails that India favours AL over other political parties of Bangladesh. This has contributed to the negative perception that India pays little attention to the well-being of the people of Bangladesh by rather favouring a particular political party especially given the multi-party system of Bangladesh. Therefore, barring the period of the AL Government during 1996-2001, mistrust and suspicion has primarily characterised people's perceptions about India since the mid-1970s to the end of 2008. Even from 2009, in spite of tremendous improvement in the bilateral relationship at the government level, people's perception about India at the mass level, as already mentioned, has undergone little or no transformation owing to the lack of success by both the governments and especially by India to resolve many outstanding bilateral issues. During the second tenure of Sheikh Hasina which also coincided with the Congress regime in India, there were elevated expectations amongst the people that this is the most opportune moment for Bangladesh and India to take their bilateral relationship to a new height. Lack of success in that direction hardened people's perceptions about India.

Rising India: Bangladesh's Perceptions and Expectations

As pointed out by Rajesh Basrur, in contemporary times, "India's external relationships must be viewed from the larger perspective of its expanding strategic horizons and its emergence as an Asian and potentially global power."[18] Looking at India's regional relations through the prism of rising India assumes greater prominence as this has been a major contributing factor in enhanced expectations among the people of Bangladesh. India's rise has produced renewed expectations in Bangladesh that with its rising status and massive economic advancement, India will turn out to be more generous to its neighbours, especially the smaller ones, by providing more concessions or by being forthcoming in resolving various outstanding bilateral issues.

Rising India

Despite many vicissitudes, India's rise—economic and political at the global as well as regional levels—is now a reality. Overcoming many weaknesses, as predicted by Stephen Cohen in his celebrated book, *India: Emerging Power*,[19] a decade ago, or, to be more accurate, enduring those weaknesses, India is moving forward. Some of these weaknesses having contemporary relevance are: India's difficulty in translating its economic success into political and strategic influence; the economy is slowing down, and like many other countries, suffers from the general global economic stagnation; the dangers of ideological fanaticism are still there; and failure to resolve Kashmir dispute and establish a normal relationship with Pakistan, let alone not very inspiring advancement in bilateral dispositions with its smaller neighbours including Bangladesh.[20]

On economic front, India's advancement is more evident (see Table 1). In the last one decade, India has achieved significant improvement in the quality of life of its people. The GDP of the country has increased three times (in current US$) from US$ 618 billion in 2003 to US$ 1.85 trillion in 2012. The GDP per capita has also increased in similar fashion from US$ 565 in 2003 to US$ 1533 in 2012. This has been possible due to the average growth rate of 7.66 per cent in the last one decade with the highest growth of 10.26 per cent in 2010. The trade performance of the country is also very impressive. Trade as percentage of GDP stood at 55 per cent in 2012, nearly doubled from 30 per cent in 2003. Total exports of goods and services in 2012 was $443 billion (in current US$),

Table 1: Macro-Economic Performances of India during 2003-2012

	2003	*2004*	*2005*	*2006*	*2007*	*2008*	*2009*	*2010*	*2011*	*2012*
Population (in millions)	1,093	1,110	1,127	1,143	1,159	1,174	1,190	1,205	1,221	1,236
Gross Domestic Product (GDP) (current US$ billions)	618.3	721,5	834,2	949,1	1,238	1,224	1,365	1,708	1,880	1,858
GDP per capita (current US$)	565	650	740	830	1,069	1,042	1,147	1,417	1,540	1,533
GDP growth (annual %)	7.86	7.92	9.28	9.26	9.80	3.89	8.48	10.26	6.64	4.74
Trade (% of GDP)	30.07	36.86	41.31	45.30	44.88	52.27	45.48	48.31	54.08	54.73
Exports of goods and services (BoP, current US$ billions)	90	..	154	193	240	305	260	348	446	443
Imports of goods and services (BoP, current US$ billions)	95	..	181	225	278	379	328	439	553	579
ICT service exports (BoP, current US$ billions)	..	..	35	47	58	73	61	75	85	95
ICT service exports (% of service exports, BoP)	..	..	67.22	68.29	68.15	69.29	66.34	64.10	61.84	65.89
Total reserves (includes gold, in current US$ billions)	103	131	137	178	276	257	284	300	298	300
Military expenditure (in billion Rs.)	761	917	1,017	1,085	1,168	1,436	1,874	2,108	2,316	2,523
Military expenditure (% of GDP)	2.68	2.83	2.75	2.53	2.34	2.55	2.89	2.71	2.57	2.41

Source: World Development Indicators (Online Data Bank), *World Bank*, 2013.

nearly five times higher than the US$ 90 billion exports in 2003. Imports have shown similar growth from US$ 95 billion in 2003 to US$ 579 billion in 2012. An important aspect of India's exports is its export of ICT services which amounted to US$ 95 billion in the year 2012, and made up 66 per cent of the total services exports in the same year. The country's foreign reserves (including gold) now stand at US$ 300 billion. On a different plane, during the period 2008-2012, the country has also emerged as the largest arms importer[21] in the world although military expenditure as percentage of GDP hovered between 2.68 per cent to 2.41 percent during the decade of 2003-2012. In 2012, India's total military spending was US$ 46.1 billion (Rs. 2.5 trillion), giving it the status of seventh largest military spender in the world.[22]

Politically, India's global power status is yet to be certain, but as Peter R. Lavoy puts it, "Experts recently stopped asking if India will become a great power and began to wonder what kind of great power it will become."[23] Moreover, India's rise at the world stage is best captured by Amrita Narlikar, who argues that India would be the most potential negotiating partner of the West, i.e., the established world powers, although sided with the more cautionary segment of the debate.[24] Again, falling back to the analysis in one of the chapters in Cohen's book, "The India that Can't Say Yes," Narlikar upholds the view that India is learning very fast to say yes, thereby sketching out its position as a rising power at global stage.[25]

India's rise is positively viewed by Bangladesh. Bangladesh's "threat perception" vis-à-vis India has transformed in recent years. Bangladesh, in this age of mutual inter-dependence, no longer perceives traditional security threats from India. However, security concerns between the two countries remain. In fact, cross-border criminal activities, water resource security, smuggling and trafficking networks, environmental degradation, etc., have emerged as the new security concerns, and addressing them require India's active participation and cooperation. Bangladesh also believes that it will be benefited from India's economic advancement. An economically advanced India will pose for a market for Bangladeshi commodities at least in the north-eastern regions of India. From political point of view, Bangladesh's acceptance of India's global rise could also be observed in its unequivocal support for India's UN Security Council candidature as mentioned in the January 2010 Joint Communiqué. This can be construed as an indication that Bangladesh no longer perceives India as a regional hegemon against which it has to pursue a 'policy of bandwagoning' to secure its own national interest.

However, concomitant to the positive perception in Bangladesh vis-à-vis rising India is the expectation that India will also get rid of its old stereotypes, and perform like a growing power by undertaking initiatives to stabilise and settle its neighbourhood. A significant way of doing that is to be more forthcoming in resolving outstanding bilateral issues with its neighbours especially the smaller ones. Failure to do so could adversely impact the positive perceptions.

Processes of Perception Formation: Key Drivers, Actors, Institutions, Stakeholders

State of bilateral relations and dominant bilateral issues are the key drivers in shaping perceptions about India in Bangladesh. Moreover, outstanding issues, unresolved disputes and bilateral differences are all contributing to the formation and shaping up of perceptions, especially negative perceptions, in people's psyche in Bangladesh.

The Changing Nature of Dominant Issues and their Role as Key Drivers in Shaping Perceptions

Because of the dynamism in Bangladesh-India relations, dominant issues between the two countries also change. After Independence, demarcation of border, the Farakka Barrage, Ganges water sharing, etc., were some of the major issues of discord between Bangladesh and India. After successful completion of the Ganges Water Sharing Treaty in 1996, water sharing as a major focus of Bangladesh-India relations subsided. Border killings and informal migration from Bangladesh appeared as major outstanding concerns impacting and shaping each other's perceptions. In the early 1990s, due to Indian allegations of illegal immigration from Bangladesh, the "bilateral relations deteriorated to the extent that all negotiations on bilateral issues...came to a halt."[26] In 2000s, bilateral trade issues and trade deficit dominated Bangladesh-India discourse. In the mid-2000s, the Bangladesh-India formal trade which stood at about US$ 3.5 billion (see Table 2) and was nearly matched by the informal trade totalling US$ 7 billion, wherein the deficit was almost US$ 6 billion, had stirred people's perceptions of India as not a friendly country. Later, China emerged as the largest trading partner of Bangladesh and here again Bangladesh incurred huge trade deficit with China. This factor together with the emergence of other pressing issues subsequently made trade deficit issue less significant. For the last few years, sharing of Teesta River water, implementation of the border demarcation agreement and border killings have been dominating the discourse of Bangladesh-India relations. These issues that are dominant drivers, shaping perceptions about India in Bangladesh in contemporary times, are discussed below:

The Water Issue

Sharing of trans-boundary water resources remain at the core of Bangladesh-India relations. The process of water sharing and the successes and failures of the respective governments in resolving trans-boundary water-related discord, have been the major drivers of perception formation in Bangladesh. In the immediate post-Independence era, water issues, i.e., the Farakka Barrage and the sharing of Ganges River water, dominated Bangladesh-India relations. The issue was resolved with the conclusion of the Ganges Water Sharing Treaty in 1996. However, by then, years of disagreements over sharing of Ganges water and the debilitating socio-economic and environmental impacts[27] of the Farakka Barrage had contributed to the deep-seated mistrust and aversion against India among the people of Bangladesh. Even after the Ganges Treaty, on many occasions, there have been claims by Bangladesh that the water flow in the River Padma drops below the benchmark agreed in the treaty. Therefore, the perception of "lack of trustworthiness" created by the Farakka Barrage in the mid 1970s still continues in the minds of the people. However, for the last few years, especially since September 2011, the Teesta River water sharing issue has emerged as the dominant discourse leading to bitterness between Bangladesh and India.

Bangladesh and India share 54 trans-boundary rivers, and currently there is only one treaty, i.e., the Ganges Water Sharing Treaty. Both the countries are negotiating for the second one, the Teesta River water treaty. Bangladesh and India need to reach agreements for water sharing on at least seven of the rivers—Teesta, Dharla, Dudhkumar, Manu, Muhuri, Khowai and Gumti—immediately, with Teesta being the top priority. The two countries came very close to inking a deal on Teesta in September 2011. The progress for the agreement was very promising as the two countries agreed to sign a 15-year interim accord on sharing the waters of common rivers, such as Feni and Teesta, at a secretary-level meeting in January 2011.[28] The countries have also exchanged drafts of the interim agreement on the "Principles of the Sharing of Teesta waters During the Dry Season" at the 37th meeting of Bangladesh-India Joint Rivers Commission in New Delhi in March 2011.[29] Both sides reportedly agreed to a 50-50 sharing of the water,[30] and the agreement was expected to be signed during the visit of the then Prime Minister Manmohan Singh to Bangladesh in September 2011. But the agreement could not be signed as Mamata Banerjee, Chief Minister of West Bengal, refused to accept the water sharing formula agreed by the central government pointing out that it would severely harm her state's interests. Failure to conclude the Teesta Agreement generated enormous resentment and frustration among the people of Bangladesh. And since then Teesta water sharing issue has emerged as one of the key drivers of perception formation in Bangladesh vis-à-vis India. It contributed enormously to the negative perceptions of 'suspicion and mistrust' towards India and also a perception that there was 'lack of seriousness' on the part of India. Some arguments are put forward on India's failure in inking the Teesta Agreement as Indian states in recent times assume greater influence and power in the foreign policy decision-making of the country, and as state governments assert the legitimate right to defend state's interests.[31] While both arguments are valid, India cannot escape the fact that it had failed to do its own homework before advancing with the agreement. Moreover, nearly three years after the debacle, failure to make any progress towards achieving the Teesta Agreement sustains the adverse perceptions about India among the people of Bangladesh. Indian policy-makers have to take into cognisance the fact that extended delay in reaching the agreement will only harden negative perceptions about India in Bangladesh.

Apart from lack of success in sharing trans-boundary water resources, some of India's mega water resource development projects are also generating adverse perceptions in Bangladesh. Two of such projects have been the River Linking Project (RLP) and the Tipaimukh Dam. RLP is a mega project which envisages linking the Brahmaputra River with the Ganges to carry waters to Odisha and eventually to South India, thereby linking India's eastern peninsular rivers with the western peninsular ones. It will connect 38 rivers through 30 links, 9000 km long canals, 74 reservoir and several embankments. The project is estimated to cost between US$ 112 billion to US$ 200 billion.[32] If implemented, the project will cause severe impact in Bangladesh in terms of diminishing water flow in the downstream of Brahmaputra-Ganges river basins. Experts have estimated that Brahmaputra's flow will be reduced to 40,000 cusecs from its normal flow of 140,000 cusecs, while the combined flow of Padma and Brahmaputra at Maowa point in Bangladesh will also be reduced to 30,000-40,000 cusecs from the normal flow of 200,000 cusecs. As there will be very little or no water flow in many of the rivers of Bangladesh even during the regular monsoon season, the impact of the project for Bangladesh will be devastating.[33]

Tipaimukh Dam is another project envisaged by India on the Barak River in the state of Manipur to produce hydro-electricity, despite dire warning by experts regarding the dangers of such projects for the area and for lower riparian Bangladesh. The Dam was originally conceived for containing only flood waters, but later the focus shifted to hydroelectric power generation. The project would be built parallel to the border of Karimganj in Assam above the river Barak, which is also the main stream for the branch river Surma and Kushiyara that flow through Bangladesh and conjointly create the river Meghna. Therefore, implementation of the project would cause diminished water flow in three major rivers of Bangladesh—Meghna, Surma and Kushiyara—causing severe impact on Bangladesh. Increased rate of sedimentation due to diminished flow of water, dilapidated water carrying capacity of the river and aggravated rate of sudden and frequent floods in the region are some of the key devastating impacts that would be caused by the implementation of the project as per experts' estimation.[34] These effects will be seen in the Northeastern region and especially in the *Haor* areas of the country, which would totally transform the existing landscape of the area. The fertile land of the *Haor* would turn into desert, agriculture would be destroyed and some of the local rice varieties will be lost, impacting regional biodiversity.

India's unilateral planning and implementation of these projects without discussing and taking Bangladesh into confidence, the lower riparian country, has contributed to the perception that India is not a 'very friendly' country as it remains negligent about Bangladesh's concerns and the devastating impact of these projects on the country. These perceptions easily convert into anti-India sentiments. Being a big and 'not an enemy' country, India is expected to appropriately consult with Bangladesh and demonstrate its seriousness in paying due attention to the persistent hue and cry in Bangladesh against these projects.

The Border Issues

Bangladesh and India share 4,096 km of a porous land boundary—the longest of India's land border among its South Asian neighbours. Outstanding Bangladesh-India border issues consist of demarcation of the 6.5 km of borders, exchange of enclaves, resolution of the adversely possessed lands, border fencing, informal immigration, illegal movements, smuggling and trafficking along the border and the border killings.

Soon after independence, issues of undemarcated borders, exchange of enclaves and the adversely possessed lands were resolved through the 1974 LBA between Bangladesh and India. According to the constitution of both the countries, the agreement has to be ratified by their respective parliaments. Bangladesh Government was quick to ratify the agreement in 1975, and handed over the BeruBari enclaves to India. India, on the other hand, is yet to ratify the agreement in its parliament, thereby failing to implement provisions related to enclaves and adversely possessed lands. The two sides though signed a protocol to the agreement in 2011 to expedite implementation of the 1974 LBA, but it is yet to achieve success. India's failure to ratify the agreement in the parliament and implement it, again, germinates 'mistrust and suspicion' and the perception of 'not a trustworthy' country. There was huge possibility and expectation that the constitutional amendment bill would be passed in the Indian Parliament during the budget session of the Congress Government in 2013.[35] But with great dismay, it was found that the amendment bill could not be placed in the Indian Lok Sabha. In spite of the assurances by President Pranab Mukherjee, the then Prime Minister Manmohan Singh and the External Affairs Minister Salman Khurshid, the bill could not even be placed in the parliament due to the opposition of Trinamool Congress (TMC), Asom Gana Parishad (AGP) and the opposition BJP MPs.[36] While the opposition had reasons, as expressed by the BJP leaders, the fact that the ruling party went on to ink a deal with Bangladesh without consultation with the Opposition, and failure to place the Bill in the parliament despite assurances by the president and the prime minister, significantly contributed to the adverse perception about India in Bangladesh.

Other issues pertaining Bangladesh-India border include: a) India's claims that cross border movement of illegal immigrants from Bangladesh are transforming demographics in its north-eastern states and in many other parts of India, causing various socio-economic and political problems, and b) claims and counterclaims by both India and Bangladesh about hosting terrorist groups to conduct terrorist activities against the other. However, a significant border issue that acts as a key driver of perception formation about India in Bangladesh is the border fencing endeavour of the Indian authority. The 1974 LBA envisaged that no defensive structure would be erected within 150 yards of the Bangladesh-India border. After 1982, barbed wire fencing was erected by India, which has been viewed by Bangladesh as defensive structure. India argued that only walls or bunkers can be claimed as 'defensive structure' as those can impede movement of military vehicles. Since a tank can easily pass through a barbed wire fence, it does not contradict the 1974 LBA, rather the fencing is needed to restrict movement of 'illegal immigrants', 'smugglers', 'suspected militants', etc. While this may be true, India's unilateral construction of border fences, however, created suspicion and adverse perception among the people of Bangladesh.

Nevertheless, the most important driver of perception formation, especially the negative one, and sustaining it for long, has been the killing of Bangladeshis by the Indian Border Security Force (BSF) at the Bangladesh-India border. Although cross-border movements and related criminal activities, viz. smuggling and trafficking are highlighted as mainly responsible for such casualties, this is a "negation of the most elementary norms of inter-state behaviour unheard of in modern inter-state relations between two supposedly friendly countries having normal political, commercial and cultural relations."[37] According to a human rights body in Bangladesh, *Odhikar*, on an average one unarmed Bangladeshi is killed every four days on the Bangladesh-India border by the BSF.[38] These deaths at the Bangladesh-India border are germinating deep-seated resentments contributing to the persistence of adverse perceptions among the people of Bangladesh. Stressing the importance of border killings for Bangladesh-India relations, Shaheen Afroze noted, "(Border) killings (are) highly sensitive matter for Bangladesh. For every mile of progress made in respect of bilateral relations in other sectors, we regress two miles with the death of every Bangladeshi at the hand of the BSF."[39] A severe outcry was raised in early 2011 when a 15-year-old Bangladeshi girl named Felani Khatun was murdered at the Kurigram border, and her dead body was left hanging on the barbed wire fence for some days. This had created extreme resentment and anger in Bangladesh, tremendously hampering Bangladesh-India relations. The Indian Government launched a lawsuit against the perpetrators to bring them to justice. This led to some expectations in Bangladesh that perhaps for the first time a death at Bangladesh-India border will be awarded justice. The acquittal of the defendant in 2013 ditched that expectation, and the verdict of 'not guilty' engendered extreme frustration in Bangladesh. There were protests in Bangladesh, and some were of the opinion that the Indian court failed as it did not award even a single day jail time for the defendant. Therefore, the perceptions such as 'India not being serious' and 'does not care' prevailed in Bangladesh.

Trade Deficit

Bangladesh-India trade issues, particularly the trade deficit, remain a major driver of perception formation in Bangladesh. As can be seen from Table 2, Bangladesh's trade deficit with India has been a recurrent phenomenon. Bangladesh-India formal trade in 2012-13 was more than US$ 5 billion and the deficit was US$ 4.2 billion. If we add the informal trade, Bangladesh's trade deficit will be doubled. This deficit between Bangladesh and Indian trade continues as a major issue of discord and discussion. Tariff and Non-Tariff Barriers (NTBs) imposed by India are highlighted as the contributing factors generating and sustaining trade deficits in the bilateral trade. This has also contributed to the general perception that India wants to restrict its market for Bangladeshi products, thereby severely hampering national interests of Bangladesh.

Table 2: Bangladesh-India Bilateral Trade

Years	*Exports to India (In US$ millions)*	*% Change*	*Imports from India (In US$ millions)*	*% Change*	*Total Trade (In US$ millions)*	*Trade Deficit (In US$ millions)*	*% Change*
2003-04	101		1,602		1,703	1,501	
2004-05	187	85.15	2,030	26.72	2,217	1,843	22.78
2005-06	279	49.20	1,868	-7.98	2,147	1,589	-13.78
2006-07	289	3.58	2,268	21.41	2,557	1,979	24.54
2007-08	358	23.88	3,393	49.60	3,751	3,035	53.36
2008-09	277	-22.63	2,864	-15.59	3,141	2,587	-14.76
2009-10	305	10.11	3,214	12.22	3,519	2,909	12.45
2010-11	513	68.20	4,569	42.16	5,082	4,056	39.43
2011-12	498	-2.92	4,755	4.07	5,253	4,257	4.96
2012-13	521	4.62	4,741	-0.29	5,262	4,220	-0.87

Sources: Bangladesh Economic Reviews 2011, 2012 and 2013. Data for the year 2012-13 has been collected from the Bangladesh Bank.

For tariff barriers, India imposes a higher average tariff on Bangladeshi products compared to the tariff imposed on Indian products in the Bangladesh market.[40] For NTBs, the excessive requirements of documentation, varying methods of assessing duties, expensive mandatory certificates for meeting technical and health standards that need to be collected from distant locations such as Kolkata and Delhi, non-recognition of Bangladeshi certification and testing laboratories and India's ad hoc policy changes regarding tariff quotas, limited designated ports of entry, etc.,[41] are significantly constraining Bangladesh's competitiveness in the Indian market. These trade policies of India, intended to restrict its market for

Bangladeshi products, are generating adverse perceptions about India as 'not a very friendly country' in Bangladesh.

However, some positive initiatives were undertaken during and following the visit of Prime Minister Manmohan Singh. In 2011, India provided duty free access to 61 products from Bangladesh of which 47 were textiles. India also withdrew the NTBs on two jute products and acknowledged Bangladesh Standard and Testing Institution (BSTI) for 15 imported products. More progress has been made in the later years, as now almost all products, including Readymade Garments (RMGs), from Bangladesh except tobacco and liquor get duty free access in the Indian market. However, in September 2013, the Indian Government imposed a 12.36 per cent Countervailing Duties (CVD) for imports of branded readymade garments from Bangladesh.[42] While the Indian authority argues that the tax measure was necessary to provide level playing context for both Bangladeshi RMG exporters and the local manufacturers, as revealed in a study,[43] Indian manufacturers retain an advantageous position as they pay excise duty at the rate of 6 per cent. Question can be raised then, does the 12.36 per cent CVD is providing level playing field for Bangladeshi exporters? These ambiguities in India's trade policy vis-à-vis Bangladesh generate adverse perceptions in Bangladesh.

Shaping of Perceptions: Institutions, Actors and Stakeholders

Different actors, institutions, and stakeholders are involved in shaping and forming perceptions in Bangladesh vis-à-vis India. As for negative perceptions, various actors and institutions act according to their vested interests or to fulfil some narrowly defined agenda. The existence of unresolved bilateral issues as well as lack of success on both sides of the border in resolving them are providing greater scope for the actors and the stakeholders to mould and influence public perception in Bangladesh. It is to be noted that the terms—actors, institutions and the stakeholders—can be used interchangeably. For example, political parties are important institutions of a democratic system, but they are also key actors and inexorable stakeholders in the processes of perception formation in Bangladesh vis-à-vis India. In addition to political parties, the media and the civil society are the two other major actors, institutions and stakeholders of perception formation in Bangladesh.

The Media

Media in Bangladesh has been a key actor and institution in shaping people's perception in Bangladesh. Scholars and their theoretical works have extensively highlighted media's role in perception formation amongst the masses of a country. In fact, there is a general consensus among scholars that people's perception about any incident are shaped and sometimes destroyed by the media.[44] According to the communication theory, two very essential roles of media are issue-framing and agenda-setting in a particular community. Agenda-setting theory of media-effect suggests that the main effect of media is to influence people on what to think about and what not to think about.[45] Building on this agenda-setting theory, Noam Chomsky observes that media have a vibrant effect on manufacturing consent on any social issue.[46]

With regards to issue-framing role, scholars have agreed that media is a central agent in the construction of social frames about politics.[47] Isabelle Blondel, therefore, argues that how the media chooses to frame an incident can result in the media acting as either a catalyst in the escalation or de-escalation.[48] It can either magnify the importance of an actor's behaviour, giving positive or negative connotations, or *vice versa*. Media framing can also influence the level of credibility of political actors by defining their incompatibility and interpreting their behaviour.[49] Noelle-Neumann notes that media has the capacity to change one's perception of 'what is important'.[50] Similarly, Gerbner suggests that media 'cultivates' within users a particular view of the event.[51]

All this theoretical construction of the media's role in forming and shaping people's perception is particularly relevant and instrumental in case of people's perceptions in Bangladesh about India and Bangladesh-India relations. There are 566 national, 2,475 local newspapers and 26 television channels currently operational in Bangladesh.[52] However, only around three per cent of the total population constitute the circulation of Bangladeshi newspapers. Media plays both the issue-framing and the agenda-setting role in case of Bangladesh-India relations. For issue-framing role, media in Bangladesh mostly highlights the unresolved bilateral issues and more particularly the disputed nature of the issues. Often they focus more on failures or setbacks rather than the successes or improvements. For example, border killings are always greatly focused in the news media than the positive developments of Bangladesh-India relations.

For agenda-setting, media often sets the agenda according to the vested interests. Bangladesh-India relations inhabit enormous significance in the domestic politics of Bangladesh. Therefore, various groups with vested interests often use the print media to mould and influence people's perception and steer them in a particular direction to fulfil their narrowly-defined objectives. The agenda-setting role assumes greater significance when there is over sensitisation of some of the issues as well as desensitisation of some by the media, adversely impacting Bangladesh-India relations. The commercial interests of the news media also operate in this regard. A very senior Bangladeshi journalist, therefore, once remarked that the media in Bangladesh has to endure many hurdles such as government censorship, owners dictating the policy to safeguard their interests and threats of pressure groups.[53] Whatever the scenario, one way or the other, the media exerts tremendous sway over the perceptions of the people and, therefore, it is the most significant actor in shaping people's perception in Bangladesh.

Indian Media

An interesting aspect is that India's media also exerts tremendous influence on people's perception in Bangladesh. In terms of size, coverage and circulation, the Indian media is much larger than Bangladesh. Even the circulation of the Bangla daily *Anand Bazar Patrika* from West Bengal is higher than the total circulation of Bangladesh's all newspapers. Very often news reports in the Indian media either in newspapers or television channels make a tremendous impact on the minds of the people in Bangladesh, thereby contributing to the persistence of adverse perceptions against India.

Political Elites and Political Parties

Political elites and political parties are major actors, stakeholders and also institutions involved in forming and shaping people's perception in Bangladesh. Political elites and political parties to fulfil their political objectives often take advantage of the dwindling Bangladesh-India relations. Due to the significance of Bangladesh-India relations in the domestic politics, political parties also take advantage of it for electoral advancement. In both cases, vested political interests guide political parties' motive. And due to the emotive value of India in Bangladesh, political parties are significant actors shaping people's perception in Bangladesh.

If we look back, the very process of exploiting bilateral issues in shaping people's perception started as early as 1972 following the Indira-Mujib Friendship Treaty. The Treaty was criticised by the opposition political parties in Bangladesh as an instrument of Indian hegemony.[54] Similarly, in later years, the debacle of the Farakka Barrage, failure to implement the 1974 LBA, years of negotiation for sharing the Ganges water, border killings by the BSF, recurrent trade deficit and border fencing—all have been narrated by the opposition political parties in a way to portray India as an 'enemy country' of Bangladesh. Such narratives have also contributed to the approach of some of the political parties to view the entire gamut of Bangladesh's relations with India as "a zero-sum game."[55] The circumstances got further complicated with the existence of ideological divide in the domestic politics of both Bangladesh and India. The religion-based political parties of Bangladesh especially the JIB upholds a position disfavouring India. The reason lies in the processes of the genesis of the party as well as their particular ideological orientation which is antithetical to India. In all circumstances, political parties are major stakeholders and also significant actors in shaping people's perception in Bangladesh. However, a positive shift is evident in Bangladesh as the general masses in contemporary times are less inclined to follow the direction fabricated by the political parties. Rather, they would like to view outstanding bilateral issues from a national interest perspective and would like to see their immediate resolution.

Civil Society

Civil society in a country has similar agenda-setting and issue-framing role as far as shaping people's perception is concerned. In Bangladesh, civil society plays a significant role in shaping people's perception, thereby emerging as an essential actor in the processes of perception formation in the country. A significant way of participating in the process is through discussion sessions, seminars and conferences. Media comes to the aid of the civil society in this regard. In recent times, there has been an upsurge of the so called 'Talk Shows' in the media of Bangladesh where intelligentsia and members of the civil society participate in the discussion and analysis of a particular issue of concern. In view of certain outstanding issues dominating the Bangladesh-India relations, this sort of public discussion significantly impacts people's perception. The intelligentsia are respected as the knowledgeable section of the society; therefore, their opinion assumes greater significance in the psyche of the people.

Way Forward: Addressing the (Mis)perceptions and Meeting Expectations

Geographical imperatives and commonalities of interests necessitate mutual cooperation and shared responsibilities rather than hostility and indifference in Bangladesh-India relations. Mutual perceptions and how one country is perceived by the other impacts the success of the measures undertaken to advance Bangladesh-India relationship. Failure to resolve outstanding bilateral issues for long, functions as major drivers of adverse perception in Bangladesh against India. Therefore, it is absolutely essential that both the countries take initiatives to address the adverse perceptions of each other.

Resolution of all outstanding bilateral issues is the foremost way of addressing the adverse perceptions persistent in both the countries. The two countries need to pay due attention to the national interests and objectives of each other. India has to understand the importance of every bilateral issue, since lack of progress on any of the issues incites adverse perceptions and anti-India sentiments in Bangladesh. For instance, success of the Teesta Agreement would have gone a long way in improving Bangladesh-India bilateral relations and shredding adverse public perceptions in Bangladesh. Similarly, ending border killings and taking effective measures against the perpetrators of such hideous acts will tremendously impact negative perceptions and anti-India sentiments in Bangladesh.

Immediate implementation of some of the agreements and projects will also contribute in shredding misperceptions. India needs to make all-out efforts to see that it fulfils all its commitment on the various agreements signed during the high-level visits of 2011.[56] Immediate implementation of the 2011 Land Protocol in this regard can be a key driver in engendering positive perceptions about India in Bangladesh. The implementation process has made some great progress in recent times as the constitutional amendment bill is already approved by the Union Cabinet and highly acclaimed in Bangladesh. Passing the bill in the parliament will contribute enormously in addressing adverse perceptions in Bangladesh.

India also needs to grasp proper understanding of the expectations of its neighbours in the context of its rising status as a global power. It has to be more forthcoming in resolving bilateral issues and, if needed, should provide unilateral concessions to immediately resolve outstanding issues with its neighbours. India seems to lack a proper awareness of the politics and processes of perception formation in Bangladesh,[57] and how the action and policies of India often inadvertently generate anti-India sentiments in the country. Also, India often appears convinced that economics would remove the negative perceptions and take the Bangladesh-India relations forward on a sustainable basis, wherein Bangladesh, by becoming the subregional connectivity hub, would reap the benefits of cooperation with India. Such a perception fails to factor in the political divisiveness in Bangladesh where it does not have the luxury to wait for economics to launch bilateral relations, and delays mean playing into the hands of the Opposition, further constraining the Bangladesh-India relations.

A significant way forward, therefore, involves policy-makers or incumbent governments of both the countries undertaking measures to incorporate the Opposition into the policy-making process, at least as far as policies and initiatives regarding bilateral issues are concerned. Both Bangladesh and India assume special significance in the domestic politics of the respective countries. Opposition as a major actor and institution in the processes of perception formation has to be recognised and due consideration must be showed to them by the incumbent government to advance Bangladesh-India relations.

Media also has a significant role in moving forward Bangladesh-India relations. Media needs to be sensitised to the fact that they have a larger role to play. It has to realise that it needs to serve the greater purpose of contributing towards improvement and advancement of Bangladesh-India relations, and thereby serving the national interest, rather than pursuing parochial commercial and sectional interests.

It is inspiring to note that there has been some significant advancement in Bangladesh-India relations in recent times. Both the countries have been able to conclude an Extradition Treaty that will help them to address the long-standing allegations against each other of harbouring criminals. Bangladesh's initiatives to bring to justice some of the extremists who are involved in separatist movements in India's Northeast as well as measures taken to prevent them from using its territory to launch and instigate insurgencies in the north-eastern states of India, have contributed tremendously in improving India's confidence over Bangladesh. Since 2009, Bangladesh and India have signed 10 Memoranda of Understanding (MoU) and four other bilateral instruments (see Appendix). India's relaxation of the visa regime and easing the consular services in Bangladesh is an excellent initiative affecting people's perceptions in Bangladesh. Both the countries have also agreed to a Joint Border Management Plan which will have enormous impact in terms of reducing border casualties and unintended border incidents. However, in case of Bangladesh-India relations, there is no scope for complacency as due to the hyper sensitiveness of the relations, a trivial incident has the potential to undermine the achievements made so far. Both the countries, therefore, have to make continuous efforts to build on their successes while being cautious of not moving backwards in any circumstances.

Conclusion

Many factors in the last four decades have contributed in effecting divergences in Bangladesh-India relations. Regime changes, changes in the system of governance, change in foreign policy orientations and even changes in the constitutional principle of Bangladesh have contributed in creating and sustaining divergences between the two countries. On the other side of the border, India's own internal domestic factors have also played their respective roles in creating discrepancies between the two countries. However, from the foregoing discussion, some very crucial points have emerged as far as people's perception of India and Bangladesh-India relations are concerned. Perceptions of India in Bangladesh manifest through the image of India, i.e., how India is viewed or perceived in Bangladesh. India is 'not a friendly' country, 'lacks seriousness' when it comes to its relations with Bangladesh, 'not a trustworthy country' as it 'intends to impose its natural asymmetry in bilateral transactions with Bangladesh', etc., are some of the expressions illustrating people's perception of India in Bangladesh. Mutual mistrust and suspicion developed over the years have added to these adverse perceptions, in turn generating and sustaining anti-India sentiments in Bangladesh.

Outstanding bilateral issues are the key drivers in forming and sustaining people's perception; at the same time, media, political parties and the civil society are some of the crucial actors, institutions and stakeholders involved in perception formation about India. Gap in expectations and achievements in managing bilateral issues have further contributed to the anti-India sentiments. The historical baggage and the construction of the 'enemy image' both by the political vested interest groups and the media have their fair share in compounding the people's perceptions. The ideological differences are a key factor in Bangladesh-India relations as highlighted by some of the analysts,[58] but in an age of mutual interdependence, in the 21st century, bilateral issues and interests are to be managed and dealt with.

During the second tenure of the Sheikh Hasina Government (2009-2013), Bangladesh and India have been able to make tremendous advancements in their bilateral relations. They are now more confident about both the countries wanting to pursue cooperative partnership with each other. Moreover, both would certainly refrain from taking any initiative or policy measure that might hamper the national interests of the other while making every effort possible to address the grievances of the other. However, failure in resolving some of the issues, viz. the Teesta Agreement, implementation of LBA, continuing deaths at the border despite assurances from India at the highest level as well as sluggish progress in opening up of Indian markets for Bangladeshi commodities, continue to constrain Bangladesh-India relations. Policymakers and decision-makers of both countries, therefore, need to undertake immediate measures to resolve these outstanding issues which will enormously contribute in shredding Bangladeshi people's adverse perceptions of India, thereby sustaining the momentum achieved in the past to steer the trajectory of bilateral relationship towards a new height.

ENDNOTES

1. Shaheen Afroze, "Security Dynamics and Bangladesh-India Relations: Bangladesh Perspectives," in Smruti S Pattanaik (ed.), *Four Decades of India Bangladesh Relations: Historical Imperatives and Future Direction,* Institute for Defence Studies and Analyses, New Delhi, 2012, p. 217.
2. Ibid., p. 217. For instance, Shaheen Afroze noted, "It will not be an exaggeration to say that they (Bangladesh-India relations) plummeted to a low (level) of mutual mistrust and suspicion from the heights of very close friendship that lasted a brief period in the aftermath of Bangladesh's independence... Neither the warmth or nor the trust in the relationship could be sustained for very long. This uneven relationship appears to be caused by the misperceptions regarding each other in both countries." Similar observation was made by A.K.M. Abdus Sabur in early 1990s: "Relations between Bangladesh and India in real terms however reveal serious perceptional gaps." See A.K.M. Abdus Sabur, "Some Reflections on the Dynamics of Bangladesh-India Relations" in Iftekharuzzaman and Imtiaz Ahmed (eds.), *Bangladesh and SAARC: Issues, Perspectives and Outlook,* Academic Publishers, Dhaka, p. 131. Also, see Serajul Islam, "Indo-Bangladesh Relations: The Importance of Perceptions," *The Daily Star*, October 09, 2010, at http://archive.thedailystar.net/newDesign/news-details.php?nid=157691 (accessed October 20, 2013).
3. Bangladesh-India unresolved bilateral issues range from implementation of land boundary demarcation agreement, sharing of trans-boundary water resources, exchange of enclaves including the Tin Bigha corridor, problems of adversely possessed lands to the problems of trade concessions and the persistence of non-tariff and para-tariff barriers hindering bilateral trade.
4. For a comprehensive analysis of Bangladesh's 'threat perception' vis-à-vis India, see V.K.

Vinayaraj, "India as a Threat: Bangladeshi Perceptions," *South Asian Survey,* 16 (1), 2009, pp. 101-118.

5. Robert Jervis, *Perception and Misperception in International Politics,* Princeton University Press, New Jersey, 1976; Arthur A. Stein, "When Perception Matters," *World Politics,* 35 (4), 1982, pp. 505-526; Glen Fisher, *The Role of Culture and Perception in International Relations,* 2nd ed., Intercultural Press Inc., Yarmouth, 1997; Jack S. Levy, "Political Psychology and Foreign Policy" in David O. Sears, Leonie Huddy and Robert Jervis (eds.), *Oxford Handbook of Political Psychology,* Oxford University Press, New York, 2003, pp. 253-284; and Janice Gross Stein, "Threat Perception in International Relations" in Leonie Huddy, David O. Sear and Jack S. Levy (eds.), *The Oxford Handbook of Political Psychology,* 2nd ed., Oxford University Press, Oxford, 2013, pp. 364-394.
6. Glen Fisher, no. 5, p. 12, as quoted in Smruti S. Pattanaik, "India's Neighbourhood Policy: Perceptions from Bangladesh," *Strategic Analysis,* 35 (1), January 2011, p. 74.
7. V.K. Vinayaraj, no. 4, p. 103.
8. Bhumitra Chakma, "Bangladesh-India Relations: Sheikh Hasina's India-Positive Policy Approach," *RSIS Working Paper No. 252,* S. Rajaratnam School of International Studies, Singapore, 2012, p. 7.
9. Harun ur Rashid, *Bangladesh Foreign Policy: Realities, Priorities and Challenges,* revised ed., Academic Press and Publishers Library, Dhaka, 2010, p. 89.
10. The Agreements regarding telecommunication and trade were signed on March 27 and 28, 1972, respectively. The agreement on cooperation in the field of peaceful uses of atomic energy was concluded on August 27, 1973. Other instruments inked during this period included: November 01, 1972 Protocol on inland water transit and trade, November 24, 1972 statute of the joint river commission and January 04, 1973 Memorandum of Understanding (MoU) regarding joint power coordination board.
11. Bhumitra Chakma, no. 8. p. 8.
12. Akmal Hussain, "The Bangladesh-India Relations 1972-75: Seeds of Future Discord," in Muzaffar Ahmed and Abul Kalam (eds.), *Bangladesh Foreign Relations: Changes and Directions,* University Press Limited, Dhaka, 1989, pp. 9-19; Ishtiaq Hossain, "Bangladesh-India Relations: Issues and Problems" in Emajuddin Ahmed (ed.), *Foreign Policy of Bangladesh: A Small States Imperatives,* University Press Limited, Dhaka, 1984, pp. 34-51. Vinayaraj, no. 4, also maintains that Bangladesh-India relations began to show signs of stress and strain as early as 1972. He highlighted some very important factors: India's failure to realise the sensitivities and psychology of a people who had just emerged from a long history of colonial exploitation; the presence of the Indian army; the posture of the Indian bureaucrats who reminded Bangladeshis of the high-handed attitude of West Pakistani bureaucrats; visits by a large number of intellectuals from West Bengal who had migrated from East Bengal in 1947; the self-glorification of those Bengalis who had crossed the border during the liberation war; large-scale smuggling; the subservient attitude of Awami League leaders of Bangladesh and the alleged removal of abandoned Pakistani arms and ammunitions from across the border by the Indian army all aroused Bangladeshi suspicion.
13. Smruti S. Pattanaik, no. 6, p. 75.
14. Bhumitra Chakma, no. 8, p. 10.
15. Ibid., p. 10
16. Ibid., p. 1.
17. Ibid., p. 2. Chakma mentions that Sheikh Hasina's personal relations with the leadership of the Indian National Congress and the domestic political dynamics of Bangladesh have directed her India positive policy as far as personal and national level sources are concerned. For regional/international sources, India's regional and global emergence as economic power, improving India-China relations despite their outstanding border issues and India-US close

cooperation have greatly informed Sheikh Hasina's policy towards India.

18. Rajesh M. Basrur, "Global Quest and Regional Reversal: Rising India and South Asia," *International Studies*, 47 (2-4), 2010, p. 267.
19. Stephen P. Cohen, *India: Emerging Power*, Brookings Institution Press, Washington D.C., 2002, pp. xiii-xiv.
20. Ibid.
21. India's share in the world's total arms imports is 12 per cent; the second largest is China with 6 per cent share, i.e., half of India's imports. See Paul Holtom et al., "Trends in International Arms Transfers, 2012," *SIPRI Fact Sheet*, Stockholm International Peace Research Institute, Stockholm, March 2013, p. 4.
22. Sam Perlo-Freeman et al., "Trends in World Military Expenditure, 2012", *SIPRI Fact Sheet*, Stockholm International Peace Research Institute, Stockholm, April 2013, p. 2.
23. Peter R. Lavoy, "India in 2006: A New Emphasis on Engagement," *Asian Survey*, 57 (1), January-February 2007, p. 114.
24. Amrita Narlikar, "India Rising: Responsible to Whom?," *International Affairs*, 89 (3), May 2013, p. 595.
25. Ibid.
26. Vinayaraj, no. 4, p. 107.
27. Experts have found that water diversion at Farakka has severely affected the natural flow of water in the downstream of the Ganges, i.e., decreasing flow of water in the River Padma on Bangladesh side. Agriculture, navigation, irrigation, fisheries, forestry, industrial and economic activities have all been severely affected by the changes in the hydrological system of the Ganges basin in Bangladesh. Furthermore, salinity intrusion in the coastal rivers, ground water depletion, riverbed silting, coastal erosion and sedimentation are also directly or indirectly caused by the diminishing flow of water in Bangladesh.
28. Segufta Hossain, "Cooperation on the Water Issue: Bangladesh Perspectives" in Smruti S. Pattanaik (ed.), *Four Decades of India Bangladesh Relations: Historical Imperatives and Future Direction*, Institute for Defence Studies and Analyses, New Delhi, 2012, p. 155.
29. Ibid.
30. "Teesta Failure Unfortunate," *The Daily Star*, September 08, 2011.
31. For detailed analysis on this, see Anand Kumar, "Impact of West Bengal Politics on India-Bangladesh Relations," *Strategic Analysis*, 37 (3), 2013, pp. 338-352.
32. Segufta Hossain, no. 28, p. 151.
33. For elaborate discussion on RLP's probable impact on Bangladesh, see Mohammad Humayun Kabir and Sufia Khanom, "India's River Linking Project: Possible Implications for Bangladesh," *BIISS Journal*, 29 (2), April 2008, pp. 177-209.
34. Segufta Hossain, no. 28, p. 152.
35. In February 2013, the Union Cabinet gave their positive nod to the Constitutional Amendment Bill. See "Indo-Bangla boundary bill okayed by the Indian Cabinet," *The Daily Sun*, Dhaka, February 14, 2013.
36. Mahmood Hasan, "Delhi lets Dhaka down," *The Daily Star*, Dhaka, September 16, 2013.
37. M. Afsarul Qader, "Management of Bangladesh-India Border," Paper presented at the Roundtable on Bangladesh-India Relations: Exploring New Horizons, organised by Bangladesh Institute of International and Strategic Studies, Dhaka, January 09, 2010.
38. Shaheen Afroze, no. 1, p. 221.
39. Ibid.
40. Mahfuz Kabir, "Bangladesh-India Trade and Investment: Bangladesh Perspectives," in Smruti S. Pattanaik (ed.), *Four Decades of India Bangladesh Relations: Historical Imperatives and Future Direction*, Institute for Defence Studies and Analyses, New Delhi, 2012, p. 136.
41. Ibid., pp. 137-138.

42. Mahfuz Kabir, "Regional Trade Liberalisation and Non-tariff Barriers: The Case of Bangladesh's Trade with South Asia," *BIISS Journal*, 35 (2), 2014.
43. Ibid.
44. Richard West and Lynn Turner, *Introducing Communication Theory: Analysis and Application*, 2nd ed., McGraw-Hill, New York, 2004, pp. 376-380.
45. See John Zaller, *A Theory of Media Politics*, University of Chicago Press, USA, 1999.
46. E.S. Herman and N. Chomsky, *Manufacturing Consent: The Political Economy of the Mass Media*, Vintage, London, 1994.
47. Gadi Worfsfeld, *Media and Political Conflict: News from the Middle East*, Cambridge University Press, Cambridge, 1997.
48. Y. Isabelle Blondel, *Violent Conflict and Roles of the Media*, Uppsala University, Uppsala, 2003.
49. Jaap Ginneken, *Understanding Global News*, Sage Publications, London, 1998.
50. E. Noelle-Neumann, "The Theory of Public Opinion: The Concept of the Spiral of Silence" in J. A. Anderson (ed.), *Communication Yearbook 14*, Sage Publications, Newbury Park, 1991, pp. 256-287.
51. G. Gerbner and L. Gross, "Living with Television: The Violence Profile," *Journal of Communication*, 1976, pp. 172-199.
52. S. Rozana Rashid and Azharul Islam, "The Role of Media in Influencing Public Opinion on Violence against Minorities: The Case of Ramu in Bangladesh," *Journal of International Affairs*, 17 (1-2), June/December 2013, p. 2.
53. Reazuddin Ahmed, "Role of the Media in a National Crisis," Paper presented at the AMIC-SIDA Seminar on The Role of the Media in a National Crisis, Colombo, May 15-17, 1991, quoted in Ibid., p. 5.
54. Vinayaraj, no. 4, p. 106. The Treaty had the validity of 25 years with renewal option. However, in 1996, when it had to be renewed, both Bangladesh and India decided otherwise as they deemed it has lost its relevance due to the changed regional and international settings.
55. Smruti S. Pattanaik, no. 6, p. 74.
56. Ibid., p. 82.
57. Serajul Islam, no. 2.
58. Smruti S. Pattanaik, no. 6, p. 83.

APPENDIX

Treaties, Agreements and MoUs since 2009 (Total 21 Instruments)

Treaty

July 28, 2013: The Extradition Treaty

Agreements

January 12, 2010:

(1) Agreement on Mutual Legal Assistance on Criminal Matters
(2) Agreement on the Transfer of Sentenced Persons
(3) Agreement on Combating International Terrorism, Organized Crime and Illicit Drug Trafficking

September 07, 2011:

(1) Protocol to the Agreement Concerning the Demarcation of the Land
(2) Framework Agreement on Cooperation for Development
(3) Boundary Agreement between India and Bangladesh and Related Matters

[Total = Six Agreements]

MoUs

January 12, 2010: Memorandum of Understanding on Cooperation in Power Sector

September 07, 2011:

(1) Addendum to the MoU between India and Bangladesh to Facilitate Overland Transit Traffic between Bangladesh and Nepal
(2) Memorandum of Understanding on Renewable Energy Cooperation
(3) Memorandum of Understanding on Conservation of the Sundarban
(4) Memorandum of Understanding on Cooperation in the field of Fisheries
(5) Memorandum of Understanding on Mutual Broadcast of Television Programmes
(6) Memorandum of Understanding between Jawaharlal Nehru University and Dhaka University
(7) Memorandum of Understanding on Academic Cooperation between National Institute of Fashion Technology (NIFT), India and BGMEA Institute of Fashion and Technology (BIFT), Bangladesh.

February 16, 2013:

(1) Memorandum of Understanding for Establishment of Bangladesh-India Foundation.
(2) Memorandum of Understanding on establishment of Akhaura-Agartala Rail link.

[Total = 10 MoUs]

Others

January 12, 2010: Cultural Exchange Programme

2011

(1) July 30: Coordinated Border Management Plan
(2) September 07: Protocol on Conservation of the Royal Bengal Tiger of the Sunderban

July 28, 2013: 28 July: Revised Travel Arrangement

[Others = Four]

Sources: Collected and collated from websites of Ministry of Foreign Affairs, Government of Bangladesh and the Indian High Commission in Dhaka.

8

Indo-Afghan Relationship: Afghan Expectations and Indian Reluctance

Davood Moradian

Introduction

From the Buddhist heritage in the western Afghan city of Herat to the mausoleum of great Persian poet Mirza Abdul-Qader Bedil in the heart of Delhi, Afghan-India relations are almost unique in enjoying all elements of a truly historical and strategic partnership. India is an inspiring nation for Afghanistan's young democracy, its multicultural society and status as a developing nation. Delhi and Kabul share a number of identical interests and concerns, primarily in security and economic sphere. For the intertwined state-sponsored and transnational terrorism, Afghanistan and India are strategic targets. India's vast market presents golden business and economic opportunities for Afghanistan's emerging economy. Afghanistan's natural resources and its geo-strategic location as Asia's roundabout have made it a vital economic partner for India. However, Delhi and Kabul have failed to fully utilise their almost inseparable history and convergence of common values and shared political, security and economic interests and concerns. Delhi's cautious geo-strategic mindset and its entrenched bureaucracy is primarily responsible for a significant gap between the reality and the potential of Afghanistan-India's partnership; followed by West's Pakistan-centric and myopic understanding of the region and Kabul's transitioning political and institutional landscape.

India's popularity in Afghanistan is immense. People are fond of its Bollywood films and Indian actors are very popular among Afghans. There have been several opinion polls in which India stood out as the most favored and most popular nation among the Afghans. Since the American intervention in 2001, India has played an active role in the reconstruction and rehabilitation of Afghanistan. Its early engagement was seen as a strategy to undermine Pakistan by many in the West and in Pakistan, whereas preventing the return of Islamist government in Afghanistan is one of the core interests of India. The Islamist government, in India's view, may give strategic depth to Pakistan which will further encourage the Kashmiri and other militant groups to destabilise India. Therefore, India would like to closely engage with the democratically-elected Afghan Government and try to make sure that it does not fall after the drawdown of the NATO-led international force in 2014.

India actively engages the civil society of Afghanistan as well. India and the United States (US) cooperate mainly in the field of agricultural development and women empowerment in the NGO sector in Afghanistan. The Self-Employed Women's Association (SEWA) is an Indian NGO that has been actively working in Afghanistan since 2008. SEWA earlier achieved remarkable success in the Indian state of Gujarat. An estimated US$ 1 million is provided to SEWA by the United States Agency for International Development (USAID) for the vocational training of Afghan women. It is estimated that SEWA has trained over 3,000 Afghan women so far, and despite two fatal terrorist attacks on its staff it continues its mission in Afghanistan. The US provides around US$ 3 million in the field of agricultural development including various scholarship and exchange programmes while linking Afghan students studying in Afghan agricultural colleges with the Indian universities. Moreover, a trilateral dialogue between the US, Afghanistan and India took place in September 2012, which could result in further cooperation between India and the US towards the social and economic development of Afghanistan.

In 2011, the Steel Authority of India Limited (SAIL)-led consortium, during a bid, won the mining rights of three iron ore blocks in Hajigak in Afghanistan. It is believed that some of the members of SAIL were wary of the deal due to the uncertain security situation in Afghanistan. However, the Indian Government encouraged the bid as part of its economic diplomacy. SAIL was planning to invest about US$ 10.8 billion initially but later reduced it to US$ 1.5 billion, apparently due to the last-minute refusal of the Indian Government to finance the deal for security reasons.

There is a possibility that Afghanistan could become a means for building confidence and cooperation between the arch rivals India and Pakistan. Pakistan can benefit financially if it agrees to allow the transit of iron ore from Afghanistan to India. This could lead to improved relations among the three countries. However, Pakistan military's hard stance against India leaves it with no other option but to look for alternative ways. The development of Chabahar Port of Iran and the Zaranj-Dehlaram Road built by India is one such alternative to lessen dependence on transit via Pakistan. The Iranian port permits the transportation of iron ore and would act as a hub of transportation of various goods between India and Afghanistan.

The Strategic Partnership Agreement (SPA)

The two countries signed a Strategic Partnership Agreement (SPA) during President Hamid Karzai's visit to India in 2011. It is the first ever agreement where Afghanistan has formally entered into a strategic partnership with any country. With the international security forces scheduled to withdraw at the end of 2014, the timing of the SPA could not have been better, which increases its significance many times.

In the region surrounding India and Afghanistan, there is a conflicting interplay of interests. It is obvious that the responses to the Indo-Afghan partnership by various nations in the region differ substantially. The problem is further aggravated when the different nations follow different objectives and agendas. However, the people of Afghanistan and its government both view SPA as an outcome of strong historical ties between the two nations. In a more practical view, there is a growing consensus in Afghanistan that the country needs assistance in the reconstruction of its economy. India, being a growing economy, is perceived to be in a much better position to help Afghanistan in reviving its economy shattered by decades of conflict. On its path towards developmental assistance to Afghanistan, India has already committed nearly US$ 2 billion in aid so far. Apart from the developmental assistance, the government of Afghanistan sees India as a means to alleviate the insecurity, which could possibly deteriorate after the withdrawal of international forces. India has cultivated goodwill among the Afghan people by involving itself more in the developmental activities, such as development of roads, telecommunication and power generation, in addition to investing in the field of education, health care and future leadership programmes. Afghanistan believes that Pakistan is nowhere close to competing with India's contribution regardless of whether it is in the field of developmental activities or foreign policy, where India is seen as a more mature and trustworthy partner.

Moreover, in September 1964, the government of India launched the Indian Technical and Economic Cooperation (ITEC) programme—a bilateral programme of assistance that covers a large number of countries, which are in need of assistance around the world. Afghanistan has been a beneficiary of this programme for many years. The agreement on the strategic partnership might seem to reaffirm the past ties between the two countries; however, it mainly aims at propelling the relationship between India and Afghanistan beyond the aid relationship. An important and integral part of the agreement is training of the Afghan National Security Forces (ANSF). The stability in Afghanistan and sustenance of its democratic set up is a critical element of India's security interest. Therefore, to contribute towards building up the capacity of the Afghan Government to tackle the security issues on its own is the first step from the Indian side to pursue its objective of security interest in Afghanistan.

In India, two completely opposite views prevail when it comes to engagement in regional affairs, especially in regards to Afghanistan. One view suggests that if India wants to emerge as a regional superpower, it would have to step up its engagement in regional affairs to show its preeminence in various fields. This view further suggests that India should grab the opportunity provided by Afghanistan to project itself in the region. In contrast to this, there are others who believe India should refrain from any direct involvement in regional affairs and especially in Afghanistan where Britain, USSR and the US have failed miserably in the past. As per the second view, it is believed that India should first solve its internal conflicts and secure its borders with hostile neighbors. Only when it is secure internally, it can engage itself more proactively in regional and global affairs.

To the US and the Western powers, SPA came as a surprise and questions were raised as to why Afghanistan chose to sign a strategic partnership with India in the first place. This paper identifies three factors to explain why Afghanistan chose India as a strategic partner.

The first factor is convergence of certain values. It is a well known fact that India is the largest democracy and a great example for pluralistic and multi-cultural societies. Afghanistan needs democracy and development to bring lasting peace and stability in the region. Since Afghanistan is a young democracy, there is a lot to be inspired from the model of Indian democracy. India is currently a developing nation but until few decades back it too was poor and underdeveloped. India had to bear the trauma of partition and faced severe crisis from within. The society was largely rural and mostly based on agricultural economy. Afghanistan today faces several of such challenges and there is lot that it can learn from India's model of democracy, governance and development.

The second reason Afghanistan sees India as a strategic partner is the convergence of national interests of both the countries. For Afghanistan, terrorism presents the biggest threat on a daily basis. The country is confronted with and threatened by terrorists who have the power to disseminate their radical ideologies across the region. India too is troubled by terrorist activities in its northern, north-eastern and central regions. A regional cooperative approach is needed to tackle this menace of terrorism. This suggests that there is something beyond the historical and cultural relations between the two countries that bind them together.

The third primary reason is that the economies of the two countries are compatible as they complement each other. India with its huge human resource is a large market for Afghan products and at the same time Afghanistan has a wealth of natural resources that can offer plenty to India's rising economy. Afghanistan acts as a land bridge between South Asia and Central Asia. For India, Afghanistan is a gateway to Central Asia and a part of Middle East; in a similar manner, India can be the gateway for Afghan products. Thus, it is the above-mentioned three reasons—shared values, common national security interests and complementary economy—that bind India and Afghanistan as strategic partners.

Afghanistan's Expectations and Concerns

Except for the short span of five years from 1996 to 2001, when Taliban controlled Kabul, the two countries have long shared cordial relations. Currently, Afghanistan is concerned about India's weaknesses and not about its rise. Earlier, three presidents of Afghanistan had an excellent relationship with India: Sardar Mohammad Daoud Khan, Mohammad Najibullah and Burhanuddin Rabbani were great friends of India. However, India could neither prevent the fall of their governments nor could it protect them against the threats that they were confronted with. All three Afghan presidents had virtually pleaded for India's support; but, despite its good intentions, the Indian power was not sufficient enough to protect their governments. There is a considerable amount of fear in Afghanistan that the same forces that toppled the previous three governments are again giving a tough time to Kabul. It would be interesting to see whether India will repeat the same or will it approach the Afghan crisis in a different manner this time.

Afghanistan does not need or expect any muscular support from India. Kabul has a functioning army that is capable enough to defend the nation. Peace and stability in Afghanistan is of vital national interest to India too and, therefore, India should provide necessary equipment required by the Afghan national army to tackle terrorism on its soil. Also, India can help Afghan army in training and consultation on security and defence matters. Moreover, India can help Afghanistan in the field of modern education and health care. India is a fast developing nation and has made several advancements in the field of science and technology while Afghanistan, being rich in mineral wealth, needs expertise not exploitation for developing its mineral wealth. The infrastructure required for establishing a modern industrial base in any country is the need of the hour and Afghanistan is not an exception to it. India has a great potential in this sector and can help Afghanistan in this respect as well. Furthermore, in order to revive the economy of Afghanistan, it has to be integrated with regional economies. In the ancient and even medieval times, Afghan economy has done better than the regional economies when there were centers of trade around Afghanistan. The role of India,

China, Russia and Pakistan is very crucial in this regard. There is an urgent need for a strong regional consensus on building connectivity and infrastructure in and around Afghanistan.

The problem here is that the government of India has taken a very cautious approach in Afghanistan. Even the strategic partnership to some extent came as a surprise. India needs to cooperate whole-heartedly with Afghanistan without bothering about what Pakistan or other countries think. Also, India does not have a regional policy except towards Myanmar and Afghanistan. It seemed to be more interested in developing strategic partnership with the US and other global powers. Except for the time of Inder Kumar Gujral's government in the mid-90s—arguably the best phase in India's relationship with regional countries—India did not have an explicit regional policy approach. However, after 2004, the Congress-led government had shown a renewed commitment to engagement in regional affairs. India's foreign policy towards Afghanistan is frequently justified in these terms. India believes that a socially and economically developed Afghanistan is crucial for regional stability.

Initially, the US was concerned about India's growing influence in Afghanistan mainly reflecting Pakistani concerns. Recently there seems to be a shift in the US stance, as it wants more involvement from the Indian side but without their military presence in Afghanistan, which it acknowledges, would concern Pakistan. However, it is very unlikely that India will send its troops to Afghanistan on a peacekeeping mission, as it has no desire to take a unilateral security role in Afghanistan. It is because of the fact that India is yet to forget the long-standing memories of its failed peacekeeping mission in Sri Lanka from 1987-90, and also more importantly India does not want to alarm Pakistan by its troops' presence in Afghanistan.

India's Reluctance

Due to India's overall reluctance to engage in regional affairs, there are fears in Kabul that India might not be able to help the country for the fourth time in succession. The first manifestation of that reluctance is the language that has been used by the Indian establishment to describe Indo-Afghan relationship. After 2010, the language was one of a developmental partnership between the two countries, and a strategic partnership was considered a taboo in the establishment and the strategic community of India. Despite the fact that the strategic partnership has already been signed, India is still reluctant to fully implement it as one component of that partnership is security cooperation between Afghanistan and India. It was very disappointing for the Afghan administration when their request for stronger defence and security cooperation was not received warmly by Delhi. India needs to recognise the difference between Afghanistan and African or Latin American nations. Afghanistan is an important strategic country, not only for India but also for the region as a whole, and it is hard to imagine that India is reluctant to fully engage with Afghanistan on security and defence matters.

Another point of concern is that, with respect to Afghanistan, India does not have an independent foreign policy. Moreover, India's engagement with Pakistan and the US shapes the Indo-Afghan relationship to a large extent. Therefore, Kabul does not see an independent Indian foreign policy, one that is irrespective of Pakistani concerns, Western wishes and perceptions of its other partners.

The other problem between the two countries is the existence of the socialisation gap. It is a well-known fact that Afghan politicians, academics, journalists and travelers visit India on a regular basis unlike the Indians who hardly show up in Afghanistan. Therefore, this socialisation gap needs to be addressed if the two countries want to promote cooperation in various fields. The other concern in Kabul is India's obsession and appeasement of Pakistan which prevents it from whole-heartedly involving itself in Afghan affairs. It is time both India and Afghanistan realised that appeasing Pakistan has not helped so far and nor will it help any side in the near future. Pakistan needs to be confronted for its policies and actions.

To further understand the Indian reluctance to engage fully in Afghanistan, this paper identifies five probable reasons. The first reason is the Gandhian legacy of non-violence which is an integral part of India's national psyche and character. However, the Gandhian legacy emphasised various principles and Mahatma Gandhi himself was not afraid of confronting difficult issues. The Gandhian legacy has resulted in a kind of strategic autonomy, i.e., the ability to work independently, in India's foreign policy approach.

The second probable reason is that India is an evolving and a rising power and is in the process of transition to becoming a full-fledged global power. It is unfortunate for Afghanistan to be caught in the middle of this transition period because rising powers are often not very predictable. Also, they are often reluctant and sometimes they overdo or underdo things as it is the nature of transition which does not provide predictability.

The third probable reason is a sort of trust deficiency between the two countries. India is not sure about its own capacities and is not confident enough to fully assert or involve itself on the international stage. There is a kind of internal doubt about India's capabilities and part of that is reflected in its trust deficiency in the future Afghan leadership and the future of Afghanistan as a whole. The Afghan Government too is partly responsible because some of the statements made by top government officials and foreign policy makers do not enforce trust in the Indo-Afghan relationship.

The fourth probable reason is the resource constraint. There are high expectations and demands from other developing nations in India's neighborhood. India does not have the resources to simply meet all of their demands.

The fifth probable reason is the institutional inefficiency of the Indian bureaucracy, which further adds to the problem. India's Ministry of External Affairs (MEA) is not structured in a way that is compatible with the dynamic world of the 21st century. It is somehow a static bureaucracy. India's foreign policy has to be more dynamic and adaptable if India is keen enough to involve itself as a major power in regional or international affairs.

The Way Forward

The way forward for both countries is all about building trust in each other. To build trust means that the two countries should be more confident and have self-belief that they can get things done without worrying about how their actions are perceived by other nations in the region. India has been a great civilisation for centuries now and continues to be one. Therefore, any doubt or uncertainty about how to deal with the region is not justified here. Moreover, India needs to actively take part in regional initiatives. Turkey took the opportunity to co-initiate the Istanbul Process, also known as the Heart of Asia Process. India could have taken on the role of the co-steward following the third conference of Heart of Asia Process in Almaty, but instead stayed back while China showed more commitment, allowing it to become the co-steward of the most comprehensive regional initiative ever initiated by Kabul.

India needs to understand that it has the capacity to lead the regional initiatives. Its proximity to Afghanistan gives it prominence over Turkey; hence, it must step up its involvement in regional security and stability initiatives. India is a well respected country and with the exception of Pakistan, every other nation respects India's role in coordinating regional efforts. Furthermore, there is the need for India to engage itself more with the US. The US is currently facing a difficult situation; it has an identity crisis when it comes to its regional and/or global objectives. India can help Washington to have a better relationship and a more effective policy in South Asia; and particularly in the context of Afghanistan, could help in working towards creating a trilateral process consisting of India, Afghanistan and the US.

Last but not the least, Afghans are Muslims by faith. India enjoys the status of being a country with second largest majority population as Muslims. The Afghans have been at war for decades now. Indian Muslim scholars can help their Afghan brothers in reengineering their mindset in accordance with the teachings of Islam—the religion of peace. India is unique among all the Muslim countries and enjoys supremacy in this regard. It can work wonders in transforming Afghanistan into a peaceful, developed country and a model for other Muslim countries. It is noteworthy that the great Muslim scholar of the erstwhile India, Muhammad Iqbal, had once referred to Afghanistan as the 'Heart of Asia'. A peaceful and developed Afghanistan could revitalise Asia including India. Afghanistan has the potential and it only needs unfolding. It would be interesting to see if India is willing and ready to play its historical role.

9

Shift in Maldivian Perception Towards India During the 2012 Political Crisis

Mohamed Naahee Naseem

As proposed by Tim Junio, "*State's perception of one another in the international system stems from how individuals in the states view one another.*"[1] This paper aims to shed light on the perceptions of the Maldives towards its regional neighbour India, with an emphasis on how this perception had been impacted by the Maldivian political crisis following the unprecedented transfer of power in February 2012.[2]

The Maldives and India have shared a strong cultural, economic and social bond that dates back far beyond the establishment of formal diplomatic ties in 1965.[3] In the past few decades, India has undoubtedly become a strong regional partner in the course of development in the Maldives. This continued friendship has arguably benefited the Maldives more than India. As of today, on the one hand, a number of Maldivian families reside in different regions of India for purposes that primarily include higher education and better health care, wherein the Maldives still lags behind, and on the other, a sizable portion of the Maldives' expatriate workforce comprise Indians who work in almost all major sectors in the country including the construction industry, education and health sector as well as the lucrative tourism industry which makes a significant contribution to the Maldivian economy.

Similarly, following the ascension of the country's first democratically-elected President Mohamed Nasheed in 2008, a number of privatisation projects were initiated. These primarily included large Indian investments in the Maldives through Indian corporations such as TATA Projects, Tatva Global and most notably GMR Group, which brought in the single largest foreign investment through the privatisation of the Ibrahim Nasir International Airport (INIA). Hence, the stakes and interests remained high for both countries in almost all aspects.

However, as mentioned before, the Maldives went into a political crisis in February 2012 following the unprecedented fall of the government that was elected in 2008. President Nasheed stepped down following days of continued anti-government protests that were later backed by both the police and the military. Nasheed subsequently claimed that he had been ousted in a bloodless *coup d'état*, but that was eventually dismissed as a baseless claim in a report released by the Commission of National Inquiry (CoNI)—a commission formulated by the incoming government to investigate the circumstances surrounding the controversial transfer of power.[4]

Nasheed was succeeded by his Vice President Dr. Mohamed Waheed Hassan Manik with the backing of the then opposition led by former President Maumoon Abdul Gayoom's Progressive Party of Maldives (PPM) and other smaller parties including the Jumhoree Party (JP) led by business tycoon Gasim Ibrahim and religiously conservative Adhaalath Party. The incoming President Waheed Hassan—whose legitimacy to remain in power was consistently challenged[5] by Nasheed's Maldivian Democratic Party (MDP)—led an unstable government up until the 2013 presidential elections.

One of the most predominant justifications given by Nasheed's opponents in removing him from power was that he had, through his privatisation plans, attempted to sell off country's major national assets to foreign states and corporations. They were particularly critical about the privatisation of INIA in November 2010.[6]

Nasheed's government, through a competitive international bidding process managed by the International Financial Corporation (IFC)—an arm of the World Bank, had awarded India and Malaysia Airports Berhad (MAHB), a consortium of the GMR Group, the concession of INIA, whereby GMR-MAHB was to manage and develop the airport within a period of 25 years, extendable for an additional 10 years.[7] The tri-party agreement—entered between the Government of Maldives, the Maldives Airports Company Limited (MACL) and the GMR-MAHB—was strongly opposed by then opposition political parties, which had announced country-wide protests against the decision.[8] After the agreement had been signed, series of protests took place in the next two years largely led by a national front called *GaumeeHarakaai* (translated as National Movement).

When Waheed assumed power with the backing of *GaumeeHarakaai* and political parties opposed to Nasheed, he was pressurised to decide on the fate of the concession agreement of INIA and GMR-MAHB. The *GaumeeHarakaai*, meanwhile, continued with its protest. During some of these protests, senior government officials and leaders of the *GaumeeHarakaai*—who also held key political positions in Waheed's government—made slanderous remarks towards the Indian High Commission including the High Commissioner D.M. Mulay. These contemptuous remarks alleged that the Indian High Commissioner was involved in bribery and was heavily influenced by the GMR-MAHB consortium.[9] Allegations were also levied against GMR-MAHB, claiming that it had tried to induce opposition politicians including parliament members to defect to the government by promising financial benefits.[10]

Despite concerns raised by the Indian High Commission, the government failed to take any measures, let alone condemn the remarks made by its own officials. Instead, the Waheed Government issued a statement disassociating from the remarks made by its very own officials—including the president's office spokesperson and the minister of state for home affairs.[11]

In November 2012, Waheed Government publicly announced the repudiation of the agreement in a press conference broadcast live on state television. The government argued that it had to terminate the agreement primarily on two grounds: Firstly, the government claimed that the contract was not lawfully entered as per the existing laws of the Maldives and, therefore, it was *void ab initio*, that is, invalid from the outset. Secondly, the government claimed that the contract had become 'frustrated' due to decisions made by the Maldivian courts of law.[12]

The previously mentioned two incidents—the ridiculing of the Indian diplomatic presence in the Maldives and the repudiation of the GMR-MAHB contract by the government—hit hard both the Indo-Maldives ties as well as the general Maldivian public perception towards India.

India's decision to change the interpretation of the agreement signed between India and Maldives regarding the granting of visas for Maldivians travelling to India, which increased the visa processing time (resulting in long queues at the Indian High Commission), further added to the negative view towards India, which had already been initiated by the *Gaumee Harakaai*.[13] In addition, local media reports on restrictions placed by the Indian Government on Maldivian imports, particularly construction materials including construction sand and aggregate, further contributed to the shift in the perception.[14]

Moreover, deposed President Nasheed's decision to seek refuge in the Indian High Commission in Male when the Hulhumale' Magistrate Court ordered the police to summon him to the court, on charges of arresting the Chief Judge of Criminal Court Abdulla Mohamed[15] during his final days in power, led to a public perception that India was meddling in the domestic affairs of Maldives by siding with Nasheed and his party MDP. This was particularly to the dismay of parties supporting the Waheed Government.[16]

Despite efforts by the Indian High Commission to dismiss these allegations and disassociate itself from the allegations made, the local media continued to link these events to the government's decision to evict GMR-MAHB from INIA. This did not fare well for the diplomatic ties between the two countries as well as the perception of Maldivians towards India—particularly among those who opposed Nasheed and his government—leading to noisy anti-Indian rhetoric.

However, as the Maldives entered into the 2013 presidential election campaigning, the focus quickly shifted towards partisan politics and flaws within the judiciary. The 2013 presidential election was continuously interrupted by interventions of the Supreme Court.[17] Following the elections, which voted former President Gayoom's half-brother, Abdulla Yameen Abdul Gayoom, into power,[18] the Maldivian Government made positive efforts to mend the strained ties with India.

The 2012 political crisis may be over, but the incidents during 2012-13 period show how critical India remains for the Maldives as a neighbour. Critical in the sense, a sizable number of Maldivians rely on India in terms of trade and commerce, healthcare and education. Similarly, India too has its interests in the Maldives. In order to further avoid such instances, both the Maldives and India need to realise and understand their obligations, responsibilities and duties towards one another in protecting each other's interests. The Maldives has benefited from the famous Gujral Doctrine, but that does not exempt it from its obligation towards protecting Indian investments and Indian people working and residing in the country. The Maldivian media should also realise the critical role that it could play in shaping up perceptions. A stronger coordination by the Indian High Commission with the Maldivian media would prove extremely helpful, not only in avoiding misreporting on bilateral issues, but also in strengthening the media for informed, independent and impartial reporting.

ENDNOTES

1. Timothy J. Junio, "The Role of Social Autonomy in Perceptions of 'Other' in the International System," *APSA 2009 Toronto Meeting Paper*, at http://ssrn.com/abstract=1450311
2. J. J. Robinson, "Maldives Government Changes in Dramatic Scenes after Police Elements Join Opposition Protest," *Minivan News*, February 07, 2012, at http://minivannews.com/politics/live-police-join-opposition-protests-attack-military-headquarters-31592
3. N. Sathiya Moorthy, "India and Maldives: Towards Consolidation," *IPCS Issue Brief*, 145, March 2010, at http://www.ipcs.org/pdf_file/issue/IB145-Maldives-Sathiyamoorthi.pdf
4. J. J. Robinson, "No Coup, No Duress, No Mutiny: CNI Report," *Minivan News*, August 30, 2012, at http://minivannews.com/politics/no-coup-no-duress-no-mutiny-cni-report-43074

5. Mohamed Naahee, "Sacked Human Rights Minister Files Case in Court to Declare Waheed Government Illegitimate," *Minivan News*, March 21, 2013, at http://minivannews.com/politics/sacked-human-rights-minister-files-case-in-court-to-declare-waheed-government-illegitimate-54943
6. Ahmed Nazeer, "DRP Plan 'For Sale' Protest," *Minivan News*, September 16, 2010, at http://minivannews.com/politics/drp-plan-for-sale-protest-11237
7. J. J. Robinson, "Government Signs Male International Airport to GMR-Malaysia Airports Consortium," *Minivan News*, June 29, 2010, at http://minivannews.com/politics/government-signs-male-international-airport-to-gmr-malaysia-airports-consortium-8720
8. Ahmed Nazeer, "Airport Opposition Seeks Injunction over GMR Deal," *Minivan News*, June 30, 2010, at http://minivannews.com/politics/government-signs-male-international-airport-to-gmr-malaysia-airports-consortium-8720
9. J. J. Robinson, Mohamed Naahee and Mariyath Mohamed, "Televised Allegations by President Spokesperson against Indian High Commissioner Spark Diplomatic Incident," *Minivan News*, November 11, 2011, at http://minivannews.com/politics/televised-allegations-by-president-spokeperson-against-indian-high-commissioner-spark-diplomatic-incident-47174
10. Neil Merrett, "Gasim Calls for Public Vigilance over Political Parties Trying to Buy MPs," *Minivan News*, June 30, 2013, at http://minivannews.com/politics/gasim-calls-for-public-vigilance-over-political-parties-trying-to-buy-mps-60489
11. Luke Powell, "President's Office Spokesperson 'Stands by' Comments against GMR, Indian High Commissioner," *Minivan News*, November 18, 2012, at http://minivannews.com/politics/presidents-office-spokesperson-stands-by-comments-against-gmr-indian-high-commissioner-47534
12. J. J. Robinson, "Cabinet Voids US$511 Million GMR Contract, Gives Airport Developer Seven Day Ultimatum to Leave," *Minivan News*, November 27, 2012, at http://minivannews.com/politics/cabinet-voids-us511-million-gmr-contract-gives-investor-seven-day-ultimatum-to-leave-48023
13. Luke Powell. "'No choice' But to Wait, Maldivians Facing Overnight Queue for India Medical Visas," *Minivan News*, December 24, 2012, at http://minivannews.com/politics/no-choice-but-to-wait-maldivians-facing-overnight-queue-for-india-medical-visas-49538
14. "Construction Companies Experiencing Aggregate and River Sand Shortage," *Minivan News*, March 21, 2013, at http://minivannews.com/news-in-brief/construction-companies-experiencing-aggregate-and-river-sand-shortage-54923
15. Eleanor Johnstone, "Chief Judge Held 'in Good Condition' at MNDF Training Center Girifushi," *Minivan News*, January 19, 2012, at http://minivannews.com/politics/chief-judge-held-in-good-condition-at-mndf-training-center-girifushi-30952
16. N. Sathiya Moorthy, "What after Nasheed's 'Refuge' in Indian Mission?," *Minivan News*, February 14, 2012, at http://minivannews.com/politics/comment-what-after-nasheeds-refuge-in-indian-mission-52955
17. J. J. Robinson, "Supreme Court Annuls First Round of Presidential Elections," *Minivan News*, October 08, 2013, at http://minivannews.com/politics/supreme-court-annuls-first-round-of-presidential-elections-67952
18. J. J. Robinson, "Abdulla Yameen Wins Maldives 2013 Presidential Election with 51.39 Percent of the Vote," *Minivan News*, November 17, 2013, at http://minivannews.com/politics/abdulla-yameen-wins-maldives-2013-presidential-election-with-51-39-percent-of-the-vote-71981

10

Myanmar's Perception of India

Denzil Abel

Myanmar is located at the strategic crossroads of South and Southeast Asia. It is nestled between two giants, India and China—with populations of roughly 1.2 billion each and areas of over 3 million sq. km and 9 million sq. km, respectively. The GDP of India is almost US$ 2 trillion and that of China over US$ 8 trillion. In comparison, Myanmar's GDP is just over US$ 55.416 billion. It is 676,578 sq. km in area and has an estimated population of only 50 million. Hence, the perception in Myanmar of being sandwiched between two giants and treating the two with considerable respect. After all, one can choose one's friends but not one's neighbours.

Myanmar is India's only land bridge with Southeast Asia and is largest of all the mainland states of Association of South East Asian Nations (ASEAN) in terms of land area. Myanmar and its people are oriented towards Southeast Asia in terms of perceptions. Myanmar does not see itself as a South Asian country, rather sees itself as an observer looking in from outside.

However, Myanmar's links to India go back to antiquity. They are deeply embedded in history, culture, religion, literature, law, tradition and in the psyche of the people. The very word 'Burma' is derived from 'Brahma,' the god of creation and one of the Hindu trinity. Hence, 'Brahmadesa' was the name given to this land. The art of writing came from India. The Hmannan Yazawin royal history compiled during the last Myanmar Dynasty—the Konbaung—gives the account of the first Myanmar city of Tagaung as being founded by Indian princes of the Sakya race. Myanmar kings were called 'rajas' and queens 'devis'. Kings and cities carried Sanskrit or Pali names. The links between the two countries in antiquity are undeniable.

The people of Myanmar view India as the birthplace and cradle of Buddhism. The vast majority of the people of Myanmar are followers of Theravada Buddhism, which reached Myanmar from India via Sri Lanka. Famous Buddhist pilgrimage sites including Bodh Gaya continue to draw thousands of Myanmar pilgrims from all strata. Moreover, Myanmar's leaders usually visit the pilgrimage sites at Bodh Gaya before conducting their official business in New Delhi.

In antiquity, the Indians came to Myanmar in two streams, one by overland route through Assam to Upper Myanmar, and the other by sea from South India to lower Myanmar. Hence the word *Ka-la* or *Ka-laar*, derived from the root word *kur-la*, meaning "to cross over". An alternative explanation is that the word means 'people who adhere to a caste system'.

The pre-colonial environment and setting underwent a major transformation during the colonial period. Burma became a province of India ruled from Calcutta (now Kolkata) as part of British India between 1886 and 1937, following three Anglo-Burmese Wars. In the British colonial era, Indians freely crossed over the Bay of Bengal to find their fortunes in what was known as the 'Golden Land'. Interestingly, it is during the British colonial time that the word *ka-la* took on a pejorative meaning.

The British brought Indians to assist them in conquering Myanmar and in governing the new and rich provinces. The Indians were substantively engaged in administration, police, education, trade and agriculture. They were extensively used by the colonialists in enforcing law and order and maintaining security, thus putting them in the unenviable role of oppressors of the occupiers. As the Indian community grew after the First World War, the lucrative business and industry fell increasingly into its hands, creating further resentment and dissatisfaction. Particularly, the Chettiars from South India, who were prominent moneylenders, caused immense unrest and ill will as a result of their foreclosure on lands held by the Myanmar farmers in the vast Irrawaddy Delta in the wake of crash in the rice prices during the great economic depression of the 1930s. It led to nationwide anti-Hindu and anti-Muslim riots.

At the start of the Second World War, more than 16 per cent of the country's population was estimated to be ethnically Indian. Half-a-million Indians fled the country overland into Assam as a result of the Japanese Invasion in 1942. After independence, in 1948, Myanmar's law saw the Indian community as 'resident aliens'. The 1982 Myanmar citizenship law restricted the citizenship to groups which had immigrated before 1823, largely excluding Indians from acquiring Myanmar citizenship.

Thus, it was from the colonial period onwards that the pejorative perception of Indians, irrespective of their religion, Christian, Hindu or Muslim, took a firm hold in the minds of the people of Myanmar. Unfortunately, it still exists among the majority of the Myanmar people. At the same time, two important events continually remind the Myanmar and the Indian people of their common suffering as a consequence of British colonialism. First is the exile until death of India's last Mughal Emperor Bahadur Shah Zafar in Yangon, and that of Thibaw, the last King of Burma, in Ratnagiri in India. Second is the story and accompanying image of General Aung San in a long coat that Jawaharlal Nehru insisted on getting his personal tailor stitch for him on his way to London for Independence talks, is still recalled with much pride by the people of Myanmar.

Myanmar's and India's struggle for Independence from the same colonial master helped promote solidarity among the leaders of the two countries. Myanmar drew as much inspiration from Mahatma Gandhi, the apostle of non-violence, as from Subhash Chandra Bose who set up the Indian National Army (INA) to liberate India from the colonial rule.

Post-Colonial Era

Relations with India following Independence can be classified generally into four periods: the U Nu era (1948-62), the Ne Win era (1962-88), the transition (1988-90) and the military-dominated era (1990-2010), and the current period.

The U Nu Era

The era immediately following the independence of the two new nation states from colonial bondage is considered by many as the 'Golden Age' of the Indo-Myanmar relations. The then premiers of Myanmar and India, U Nu and Jawaharlal Nehru, had a high degree of intellectual affinity and commonality of interests in charting and managing their respective nation states' orientation amidst the superpower rivalry at the time. Together with Chou En-Lai of China, they pioneered the five principles of peaceful co-existence as the fundamentals of international relations and were the founding fathers of the Non-Aligned Movement of the newly independent Asian and African states. The two countries and people had positive perceptions of each other in spite of critical post-independence adjustment issues. The Indian Government even airlifted a planeload of armaments for the beleaguered new government in its battle against the communist and the Karen insurgency that had swept over the newly born state of Myanmar.

The Ne Win Era

In the Ne Win era that followed, however, relations cooled perceptibly. General Ne Win who seized power in a military coup in 1962 immediately began isolating Myanmar from the outside world in a bid to preserve Myanmar's hard won independence from what was then seen as right and left-wing plots to drag the country into one of the two opposing blocs. People of both Chinese and Indian ethnicity were greatly affected by the isolationist socialist policies of the Ne Win regime. The wholesale nationalisation of private businesses in 1964 led to the emigration of over 300,000 ethnic Indians to India. Although personal relations between Indira Gandhi and Ne Win remained good, the overall relationship was one of mutual neglect and estrangement. Indians in particular became the target of discrimination and oppression by the military junta. Later, the visit of the then Indian Prime Minister Rajiv Gandhi to Myanmar in 1987 raised the expectations for better ties. However, the events of 1988 in Myanmar put paid to such aspirations.

The Transition and the Military-Dominated Era: 1988-2010

In 1988, Myanmar experienced a nationwide uprising and protests of epic proportions against the one-party state's inept policies that had reduced Myanmar to a Least Developed Country (LDC) status. In mid-September, the military seized power and brutally put down the nationwide protests.

India condemned the suppression of the demonstrations and extended strong support to the pro-democracy movement. In 1992, India even sponsored a UN resolution calling on the military junta to respect the 1990 election results and restore democracy. The military regime perceived India as having strayed from the five principles of peaceful co-existence. It viewed India as a major regional player whose support for the democracy movement could be a game changer. Myanmar-India bilateral relations had reached their lowest point ever with open mutual recrimination.

Only China maintained close ties with the regime at that point of time. As a consequence, China's influence in Myanmar surged dramatically in the absence of a counterbalancing element. However, beginning from 1992, successive Indian governments changed the policy course and began to establish warmer relations with Myanmar as part of a wider effort to deepen India's engagement and influence in Southeast Asia in the light of the surging influence of China. This came to be known as the 'Look East Policy'.

This policy re-orientation on the part of India was perceived by the pro-democracy movement in Myanmar with much disappointment. The military regime of course welcomed the Indian move as an opportunity to rebuild bilateral ties while simultaneously redressing the imbalance that had crept in its relations with China.

In Myanmar's perception, following are the reasons for change in India's policy stance:

1. India has finally come to recognise the importance of Myanmar for the successful realisation of its ambitious Look East Policy.
2. India's four Northeastern states of Arunachal Pradesh, Nagaland, Manipur and Mizoram border on Myanmar's Kachin State, Sagaing Region and Chin State.

And, the Indian Government places importance on Myanmar-India bilateral relations because of the following reasons:

1. India wishes to fulfil its energy needs from Myanmar which has vast oil and gas reserves.
2. India desires to gain the cooperation of Myanmar in the suppression of armed rebellions seeking secession or autonomy in its Northeastern states bordering Myanmar—Arunachal Pradesh, Nagaland, Manipur and Mizoram.
3. The Government of India has analysed that the traditionally friendly relations between Myanmar and India were overtaken in the past few decades by closer ties of Myanmar with China, and therefore, wishes to rectify the situation in its favour.
4. India realises Myanmar's strategic position as the bridge connecting it with the ASEAN states in order to implement its Look East Policy by furthering its cooperation with Southeast Asian nations for economic, commercial and energy security.
5. India recognises that Myanmar is the gateway for the development of its Northeastern states, which it recently incorporated in the Look East Policy framework.
6. India believes that it has to cooperate more closely with an increasingly influential ASEAN in its bid for a leading role in the international community. This is the reason why India is paying greater attention to Myanmar as a member state of ASEAN and its role as ASEAN Chair in 2014.
7. The Government of India supports the democratic transition process and the political, economic and social reforms undertaken by President U. Thein Sein's Government.
8. India does not want to lose the opportunity presented by the open door economic policy of Myanmar.

Current Period

Myanmar has been undergoing major transformation since 2011 when the military handed over power to a newly constituted parliament following the 2010 elections held under the new constitution of 2008. As a result of this ongoing process, the government under President U. Thein Sein has embarked upon reforms in the political, economic, and social and media sector, and is currently deeply engaged in administrative reforms. These reforms are needed because of the state the country is in as a result of decades of isolation, mismanagement, Western sanctions and enforced deprivation.

As a consequence of these reforms, the locus of power is gradually moving away from the military to power centres based upon the constitutional structure of the country. Significant developments include the participation in parliament of the National League for Democracy (NLD) and its Chairperson Daw Aung San Suu Kyi as a result of the 2012 by-elections in which the NLD swept 42 of the 43 seats contested. The next general elections are scheduled for 2015.

As the transition to democracy gained recognition from India, the Myanmar-India cooperation too has been re-ignited. The visit of President U. Thein Sein to India in October 2011 and that of the then Indian Prime Minister Manmohan Singh in May 2012, have substantively laid the basis for a much closer and realistic relationship between the two countries. A quarter of a century had passed since an Indian prime minister had visited Myanmar. Prime Minister Singh also held talks for the first time with democracy icon Daw Aung San Suu Kyi.

Analysts see the developing ties between India and Myanmar as having particular significance, even with some wider strategic importance for Southeast Asia and the international community as a whole. However, as it comes out of isolation, some others see Myanmar as bypassing India and turning to the West, especially the US, to balance China's growing influence. India is seen as only a defensive power, incapable of contesting Chinese influence in Myanmar. ASEAN and Japan seem to have done more for Myanmar in this period. Myanmar analysts to this day point out that India was not around when it was needed most to counter China's surging influence.

Trade

In contrast with the rich base for economic growth provided by rapidly developing neighbouring Chinese province of Yunnan, the states on both sides of the Myanmar-India border are among the poorest in each country. Border trade alone cannot be expected to lead to a large growth in bilateral trade and investment. Besides, the trade routes to the more dynamic domestic markets in both countries are longer and much less developed along the Myanmar-India border, thereby making other markets more attractive.

In the fiscal year 2012-13, the bilateral trade was valued at US$ 1.324 billion, with Myanmar exports accounting for US$ 1.019 billion and Indian exports at only US$ 304 million. It is far short of the nearly US$ 5 billion estimated trade value with China. A Myanmar-India two-way target of US$ 3 billion by 2015 may not seem ambitious, but even that may not be achieved. Also, India is a less attractive market for Myanmar's business community. China, Southeast Asia, Japan and Korea are seen as preferred opportunities.

Defence and Security

The visit of Vice Senior General Min Aung Hlaing, Commander-in-Chief of Myanmar Armed Forces, to New Delhi in August 2012 and his meeting with the then Indian Defence Minister A.K. Anthony, and the latter's visit to Myanmar in January 2013, marked the growing bilateral defence cooperation. Following the commencement of democratic reforms in Myanmar in 2011, military leaders from both sides have exchanged visits to enhance military-to-military cooperation and enter into a dialogue on border security threats and challenges.

In the past few years, three Indian service chiefs have visited Myanmar to foster a closer defence relationship. Land and maritime security concerns were, in all likelihood, among the topics discussed. The cooperation included provision for training facilities, visits by naval ships, and supply of equipment. However, at this point, it cannot measure up to the existing level of cooperation between Myanmar and China. Someone once said that Myanmar goes to China for arms and India for salvation. Another aspect is that with the opening up of the country and ongoing democratic reforms, the Myanmar Tatmadaw is eager to tap into Western training facilities and even purchase arms from them. Some analysts think defence ties with India will continue to be under-developed because they are constrained by India's past anti-Myanmar military policies.

In terms of soft power, India is more than on equal terms than China, given the legacy bequeathed by antiquity and the positive aspects of the colonial association. As the cradle of Buddhism, India does have a special place in the hearts of the Myanmar people. Yet this advantage is being eroded. While India has been idle, China has stepped up its cultural diplomacy by regularly sending the Sacred Tooth Relic of the Buddha from Beijing to Myanmar for veneration. It should also be noted and analysed that the sacred Buddhist monuments in Bodh Gaya are being meticulously replicated by the government in Naypyitaw for veneration.

Future

The democratic transition underway in Myanmar offers a welcome opportunity for a new beginning in India-Myanmar relations. Bilateral high-level visits have started a new dialogue and shared perceptions and plans have been recorded in joint statements for implementation. The two countries share similar perceptions on regional or subregional cooperation. India has a unique opportunity and role to play in supporting the success of Myanmar's Chairmanship of ASEAN in 2014.

In all of these worthy endeavours, a cautionary note needs to be sounded. The colonial experience has scarred Myanmar's perception of Indians. Two perceptions exist in parallel. One is that the Indians who were themselves enslaved by British colonialism acted in turn as the instruments of British colonial rule, suppression and oppression. The other perception is that that the vast majority of Indians were of the menial class—coolies, sweepers, rickshaw pullers, pony cart drivers, *malis* and *durwans* and usurious moneylenders (Chettiar). As a consequence of this *Kala* syndrome, even today Indians are consciously or unconsciously looked down upon and continue to bear the brunt of discrimination. The result is that Myanmar consistently attaches lower priority to its ties with India.

11

Bhutan and Its International Collaborations-2013

Pema Tenzin and Chhimi Dorji

Bhutan came out of its self-imposed isolation only in the late 1960s when the outside world had already undergone centuries of modern development and interactions. Bhutan has been through rapid socio-economic development in the last four decades. The Gross National Happiness (GNH) philosophy, conceptualised sometime in the 1970s, is a very earnest system that the government is committed to and working on. From an absolute monarchy since 1907, year 2013 saw the second democratically-elected government take charge after the fourth King started the process in 2006.

India was and is still the largest economic partner and supporter to the country. Bhutan has also started opening up to the outside world wherein tourism is a high contributor to the national income, but well behind the hydropower electricity sale to India which is about 45 per cent of the national revenue. The last decade also saw Bhutan taking even further interest in foreign direct investment (FDI) and international collaborations. Bhutan currently has diplomatic relations with some 50 countries, a noticeable increase from mere 20 until a few years ago. Even with just less than 700,000 people in the country and with some 50,000 foreign workers, the government is also considering joining the World Trade Organisation (WTO), opening a big education city, and further expanding the scope of FDI to diversify and amplify the economy. Bhutan has also been very keen on South Asia cooperation and further strengthening the regional collaborations.

Background of Bhutan

Bhutan is a small landlocked country with 38,394 sq. km area on the eastern Himalayas between China and India. It is divided into 20 administrative districts with some 700,000 people.[1] The district administrations are housed in forts called *Dzongs*, which are both centres of local administration and religion. There are 205 gewogs/panchayats/counties across the country.

It is located on a very fragile Himalayan topography. The terrain ranges from tropical foothills in the south at 200-300m to extremely rugged high mountains in the north, which are more than 7,000m. Winters are generally cold and dry with occasional snow in some parts, while the summers are warm and wet. The country basically consists of three physical zones with the sub-tropical foothills in the south, the inner Himalayas in the middle, which has temperate state, and the higher Himalayas that are of sub-alpine and alpine conditions.

More than 70 per cent of the country is under forest coverage, and there are strict environmental regulations such as requiring 60 per cent of forest coverage to be maintained for all times to come. There are also nine protected areas in Bhutan that cover more than 50 per cent of the country's total area. Bhutan is home to 7,000 species of vascular plants, 700 bird species and 167 mammal species including some globally endangered species such as tiger, snow leopard, golden langur, white-bellied heron and black-necked crane.[2]

Dzongkha is the national language of Bhutan, while English is the medium of instruction in schools and the language of communication in offices. Buddhism is the most common religion, and a strong Buddhist culture is showcased in most parts of the country. Preservation and promotion of tradition and culture is considered as a very important national identity. The Bhutanese men and women wear their national dress, *Gho* and *Kira*, respectively, on a daily basis. The national tree is Cypress, national animal is Takin, national flower is the Blue Poppy, national bird is Raven, and national sport is archery which is very popular among men.

Agriculture is the predominant occupation with about 69 per cent of the population depending on subsistence farming. Most farming methods are still very manual and labour intensive. Hydropower sale is the country's biggest national revenue earner followed by tourism. Currently, the country has about 1500MW power capacity from which about 85 per cent is exported to India. There are major investment plans to harness 10,000 MW by 2020.[3]

History of Bhutan

History of Bhutan can be basically divided and explained in three simple, yet major periods. The first period, or the earliest history of Bhutan, dates back to 746 A.D. when Guru Rimpoche, the Buddhist master, considered as the second

Buddha, came to Bumthang, Bhutan, from India. He sowed the seeds of Tibetan Buddhism in Bhutan. It is also believed that he hid numerous treasures around the valley that were later revealed by treasure discoverers called *Tertons*. Future *Tertons* discovered the treasures and further transmitted Buddhism in Bhutan for many years through their lineages. The most notable is Terton Pema Lingpa in Bumthang (1450-1521), who is renowned for knowing all the 13 traditional Bhutanese artesian skills.[4]

The second period of the history of Bhutan dates to the 17th century. Bhutan was unified under one rule by Zhabdrung Ngawang Namgyel, a Buddhist Lama who fled from Tibet in 1616. Zhabdrung established the dual system of governance, whereby authority was shared between a secular and a religious leader. He is also the one who set up all the centres of administration and religion through the construction of fortresses called *Dzongs* in all major valleys in the country. The dual system of governance (1651-1907) was carried forward by 54 secular administrative heads called *Druk Desi*, also known as "Deb Raja", and religious chief abbots called *Je Khenpos*.

The third major period was 1907 onward when Bhutan became a monarchy with Sir Ugyen Wangchuck as the first hereditary King of Bhutan (1907-1926). The country thereafter was ruled by King Jigme Wangchuk (1927-1952) and King Jigme Dorji Wangchuk (1952-1972). The Third King of Bhutan is known as the "Father of Modern Bhutan" for leading the country to the outside world, ending centuries of isolation.

King Jigme Singye Wangchuk (born 1955), who became the world's youngest leader at the age of 19 in 1974, abdicated the throne at the age of 51 years for his young prince Jigme Khesar Namgyal Wangchuk in 2006 when he was only 26 years of age. King Jigme Singye Wangchuk initiated the process of decentralisation by starting the District Development Committee in 1981, having an elected cabinet of ministers from the national assembly in 1998 and the drafting of the constitution. The current king is His Majesty King Jigme Khesar Namgyel Wangchuk (born 1980).

Exactly after 100 years of the Wangchuk Dynasty's reign, Bhutan transitioned into a democratic constitutional monarchy in a peaceful process in 2008. The first parliamentary elections were held in 2008 and the National Council of Bhutan and the National Assembly were formed the same year. Bhutan adopted a written Constitution on July 18, 2009. The Druk Phuensum Tshogpa ruled the country from 2008-2013 under the leadership of Prime Minister Jigme Y. Thinley. The second parliamentary elections were held in 2013, and currently the People's Democratic Party (PDP) is the ruling government that is headed by Prime Minister Tshering Tobgay who was the former Opposition Leader.

Current Economy

Bhutan, even as a poor developing country, provides free health care and education to all its citizens. The government even bears the cost of medical treatment including travel and living expenses for patients, along with escorts, who are referred outside the country for specialised tertiary level care. The employees of the civil service are also given paid 'medical leave' for one month to enable them to escort their relatives who are referred outside the country for medical treatment. The medical personnel make periodic visits to religious institutions, schools and prisons to conduct medical check-ups and impart health education on various topics of interest to beneficiaries. As of 2005, life expectancy is 68.9 years with a literacy rate of 63 per cent. The maternal mortality ratio is 255/100000.[5]

The government provides free education to all children right from the pre-primary level. Besides tuition, even stationary, textbooks, sports items, boarding facilities and meals are provided free based on needs. There are plans for universal education by 2020.

Bhutanese economy was traditionally confined to subsistence farming and animal husbandry. Today, around 70 per cent of the country's population has access to electricity with 1500 MW of hydropower capacity, which contributes to almost 45 per cent of the national revenue. There are plans to build 10,000 MW of hydropower projects by 2020 through collaboration with the Government of India from the total potential of 30,000 MW.

Other industries are minimal and labour intensive, such as the production of handicrafts, ferro-silicon, cement and export of minerals. Tourism, the largest hard currency generator within the services sector, earns on an average US$ 35 million annually with 27,000-41,000 visitors per annum. The tourism policy of Bhutan is 'High Value, Low Volume' with a minimum tourist all-inclusive royalty of US$ 200/person/day.

The Gross Domestic per capita income has increased from US$ 51 in 1961 (the lowest in the world at that time) to US$ 870 in 2005 and US$ 1055 in 2011. Poverty has also decreased from 23 per cent in 2008 to 12 per cent in 2012. Unemployment in Bhutan in 2012 was 2.7 per cent. Currently, Bhutan has a money reserve of US$ 906 million as of 2011[6] as shown in Table 1.

Trade

Bhutan has a fixed exchange rate with the Indian rupee, and both countries share a free trade agreement. India is Bhutan's largest trading partner, absorbing over 90 per cent of Bhutan's exports consisting of fruits, crops, electricity, timber, spices and gemstones. Imports, of which nearly 75 per cent originate in India, consist primarily of petroleum products, machinery and vehicles.

Table 1: Bhutan's Key Socio-Economic Indicators

Sl	*Title*	*Figure*	*Category*	*Source*	*Year*	*Posted*
1	Life Expectancy at Birth	68.9 years	Key Indicators	Population Projecions-2005-2030	2005	May 14, 2013
2	Literacy Rate	63%	Key Indicators	Bhutan Living Standards Survey 2012	2012	May 13, 2013
3	Poverty Rate	12 %	Key Indicators	Bhutan Living Standards Survey 2012	2012	May 13, 2013
4	Maternal Mortality Ratio	255/100000	Key Indicators	National Health Survey	2000	March 15, 2013
5	Gross Domestic Product (US$Million)	1055.48	Key Indicators	National Accounts Statistics, National Statistics Bureau (NSB)	2011	March 15, 2013
6	Money Reserves	906.0	Balance of Payment	NSB	2011	January 08, 2013

Bhutan has been an exporter of hydroelectricity to India since 1986, and since the construction of additional facilities the exports have only increased. The ability to harness hydropower with close collaboration with India marked the beginning of bilateral cooperation in strengthening Bhutan's energy security and water resource management. The export has increased by 45 per cent from 2004 to 2012. About 77.66 per cent of the total electricity generated (from 2004 to 2012) was exported to India, out of 49903.17GWh of energy harnessed. It has been contributing to significant growth in countries' Gross Domestic Product (GDP) with the Average Annual Growth Rate (AAGR) of 14.5 per cent since 2003 (as per World Economic Outlook, International Monetary Fund). In 2011, the largest share to country's GDP was from hydropower with 17.05 per cent of the total revenue. The sectoral revenue from electricity was 24 per cent with revenue from sectors constituting 73.01 per cent of total revenue.[7]

Bhutan's share in world trade in goods and services has so far been negligible, given the small size of its economy. Its merchandise exports were $133 million in 2003, which was an increase of 23 per cent over the previous year 2002. However, the annual percentage increase of exports growth has been 3 per cent between 1995 and 2003. Imports, on the other hand, were to the tune of $249 million, an increase of 51 per cent over 2002. The annual percentage increase of imports during the period 1995-2003 was 11 per cent.

Besides hydropower, the other main exports from Bhutan are agricultural products, followed by manufactures and mining products. The main destinations of these exports are India, Bangladesh, the US, Nepal and the European Union

(EU). On the import side, manufactures account for the maximum share of its total exports. The main importing countries are India (about 75 per cent), Singapore, Japan, Thailand and EU.

Bhutan's Foreign Relations

The Department of Foreign Affairs of Bhutan was established in 1970, which was upgraded to a full-fledged Ministry in 1972. Currently, there are formal diplomatic relations with 52 countries and the EU. The oldest relationship is with India dating back to 1968; whereas bilateral ties with 31 countries have been established in the last five years.[8] Bhutan is also a signatory to many UN, international and multinational organisations.

There are three foreign embassies in Bhutan, which are India, Bangladesh and Kuwait. Countries such as Thailand, the Netherlands, Denmark and Japan have consulate offices. Bhutan has embassies in India, Bangladesh, Thailand, Kuwait and Belgium (an EU member state). Most diplomatic relations with other countries are through the Royal Bhutanese Embassy in New Delhi and Thailand.

The UN has an office in Bhutan and Bhutan has permanent missions in Geneva and New York to the UN. As a principle of state policy, the Royal Government of Bhutan strives for cooperation with all nations, respects international law and treaty obligations, and promotes settlement of international disputes by peaceful means in order to promote international peace and security.

According to the Ministry of Foreign Affairs of Bhutan, the objectives of Bhutan's foreign policy are as follows[9] :

Political

- Enhance and maintain national security.
- Promote world peace and security by engaging in meaningful dialogue with the international community.
- Promote and contribute towards international understanding and cooperation as well as international peace and security on the basis of peaceful co-existence.

Economy and Trade

- Develop and expand mutually beneficial bilateral, regional and multilateral economic and trade co-operation.
- Contribute towards the development of a dynamic and a sustainable economy through mobilisation of external resources.

With the support of India, Bhutan joined as a member of the UN on September 21, 1971. As a small country located in a geo-politically sensitive region, Bhutan's admission as a member of the UN reaffirmed its status as a sovereign independent country and laid the foundations for cooperation with the UN and its specialised agencies.

Over the years, Bhutan's status as an active and responsible member of the UN has gained prominence through its involvement in the numerous bodies of the UN. Bhutan has served on many important posts such as the Vice President of the UN General Assembly (New York), President of the Trade and Development Board, UN Conference on Trade and Development (UNCTAD, Geneva), two terms as member of the UN Commission on Human Rights (Geneva), two terms as member of the Economic and Social Council (ECOSOC, 1993-1995), Executive Board of United Nations Children's Fund (UNICEF), World Health Organisation (WHO) and Chairman of the Third Committee during the 50th Anniversary Celebrations of the UN (New York, 1995).[10] Bhutan had also bid for a non-permanent member seat in the Security Council of the UN in 2012, which was unfortunately unsuccessful.[11]

Current Donors and Relations

Foreign aid plays a very important role in the socio-economic development of Bhutan. Between 2005 and 2010, external grants amounted to about 15.5 per cent of the GDP, and on an average Bhutan received about US$ 175 million a year as shown in Table 2.[12] In the financial years 2008-2010, Official Development Assistance (ODA) funded 39 per cent of the total expenditure and 74 per cent of capital expenditure in Bhutan.[13] India contributes to about 70 per cent of the external fund every year. Other major donors include bilateral development partners such as Austria, Denmark, Japan, Netherlands and Switzerland and multilateral partners like the UN Agencies, EU, the World Bank, Asian Development Bank (ADB), International Fund for Agricultural Development (IFAD), etc.

Table 2: Grants, FDI and GDP in Bhutan

Indicator	*2001-2005*	*2006*	*2007*	*2008*	*2009*	*2010*
Grant Inflows in Million Nu.	4,169 (average)	6011	5,935	6,575	10,423	13,314
Grant Inflows as % of GDP	16.4% (average)	13.8%	16%	12%	17%	18%
FDI in Million Nu.	262.8 (average)	3,238	1,198	710.8	534.6	580
Remittances in Million Nu from NRBs	-	70	77.8	147	191.9	-

Source: MoF, BPFSS.

There is a strong consensus among development partners that aid has been highly effective in Bhutan and has been catalytic in the country's extraordinary socio-economic transformation from among the poorest nations to one that today is among the fastest growing economies in Asia and stands as a medium human development country.[14]

Policy and Plans in View of GNH

GNH is the development philosophy of Bhutan that puts a wholesome and holistic achievement of materialistic, spiritual and social needs at the centre of decisions and plans. Instead of comparing the country's development to traditional GDP values, Bhutan is advocating and implementing a valuation of the happiness index of people to gauge its success or failure.

Foreign Direct Investment, though marginal in Bhutan, is mainly associated with the tourism sector, particularly for starting new hotels and resorts. The FDI policy and its revision in 2010 also highly encouraged environmentally conscious investments, and FDI in other sectors with certain limitations and conditions[15] are permissible. Currently, there are FDIs in the tourism, banking, agriculture and security services in Bhutan. The Government of Bhutan is also investing in a mega education city project in Thimphu to attract foreign investors and students in a 1000 acre FDI project. The city is expected to host some 15,000 students at the campus from Bhutan and abroad.[16]

Bhutan has also made preliminary assessments to join the WTO. The newly formed government, the People's Democratic Party, has pledged to join the WTO within their term considering the benefits to the economic development of the country.[17] Bhutan is also considerably interested in furthering diplomatic and economic collaboration with its South Asian neighbours and is looking for further interaction to the existing ties such as the South Asian Free Trade Area (SAFTA), Bay of Bengal Initiative for Mutli-sectoral Technical and Economic Cooperation (BIMSTEC) and Preferential Trade Agreement with Nepal and Thailand.[18]

Conclusion

Bhutan has a very interesting physical location. The country is surrounded by the two most populous and culturally distinct nations in the world. This is further aggravated by the fact that the country is very mountainous where one community is isolated from another. This has shaped Bhutan in the sense that there are more than 27 different languages spoken in such a small area; further, its population is smaller than a district in India.

Furthermore, it is very fortunate that the donor community supports the development of the country. The recent policies and programmes are all geared towards making the country self-reliant in the next decade or two, which is indeed timely as donors are also pulling back with the improvements shown in Bhutan. Bhutan on itspart seems to be making cautious steps, but at the same time embracing globalisation and realising the need to have more and better international collaboration.

The SAARC Development Goals (SDG) report 2011[19] shows that Bhutan is on track on most of the SDG indicators. Under the livelihood theme, Bhutan has fared well in the areas of reducing poverty, reducing inequality, increasing rural infrastructure, increasing access to justice and in mainstreaming concerns of women and children. However, challenges do remain in addressing rising unemployment, especially among the youth, with 3.1 per cent unemployment in 2011. The report also reveals that child and maternal health have improved. In the area of education, gross enrolment ratio has exceeded 100 per cent with 117 per cent in 2010.

ENDNOTES

1. 2012 Annual Report, *National Statistics Bureau (NSB)*, Bhutan.
2. Climate Change in WCP, *WWF*, 2011.
3. DGPC 2013, at www.drukgreen.bt
4. History of Bhutan, Ministry of Education, Bhutan.
5. no. 1.
6. Bhutan and Its Socio-Economic Development, *EU Country Strategy Paper 2012.*
7. "National Revenue Report 2011-2012," *Department of Revenue and Customs, Ministry of Finance, Royal Government of Bhutan*, at http://www.mof.gov.bt/wp-content/uploads/2014/07/nr2011-2012.pdf
8. "Bilateral Relations," *Ministry of Foreign Affairs, Royal Government of Bhutan*, at http://www.mfa.gov.bt/foreign-policy/bilateral-relations
9. "Bhutan's Foreign Policy," *Ministry of Foreign Affairs, Royal Government of Bhutan,* at http://www.mfa.gov.bt/foreign-policy/bhutans-foreign-policy
10. "Multilateral Relations," *Ministry of Foreign Affairs, Royal Government of Bhutan,* at http://www.mfa.gov.bt/foreign-policy/multilateral-relations
11. "A non-permanent seat to the UN Security Council", *Kuensel Online*, at www.kuenselonline.com
12. "Turning Vision into Reality: The Development Challenges Confronting Bhutan," Eleventh Round Table Meeting, *Gross National Happiness Commission (GNHC), Royal Government of Bhutan,* at http://11rtm.gnhc.gov.bt/RTMdoc/RTM_Text_Final15July2011.pdf
13. "Budget Policy & Fiscal Framework: Bhutan's Macro-economy and Public Finances in the Medium-Term," Eleventh Round Table Meeting, *Ministry of Finance, Royal Government of Bhutan*, September 02, 2011, at http://11rtm.gnhc.gov.bt/presentations/daytwo/Final%20Version%202011.09.01.pdf
14. no. 6.
15. "Economic Development Policy of the Kingdom Of Bhutan, 2010," *Royal Government of Bhutan*, at http://rtm.gnhc.gov.bt/wp-content/uploads/2013/10/EDP.pdf
16. Bhutan Education City, *DHI Infra*, at http://www.dhiinfra.bt/

17. Manifesto, People's Democratic Party, at www.pdp.bt and "The Mineral Sector Is Our 'Low Hanging Fruit,'" *Kuensel Online*, September 30, 2013, at http://www.kuenselonline.com/the-mineral-sector-is-our-low-hanging-fruit/#.VLxIasnvn3E
18. Ibid., Manifesto.
19. "Mid-Term Review Report 2011," SAARC Development Goals (SDGs), *Gross National Happiness Commission (GNHC), Royal Government of Bhutan*, at http://www.gnhc.gov.bt/wp-content/uploads/2011/12/SAARC-DEVELOPMENT-GOALS-BHUTAN.pdf

PART III

Perceptions on Regional Cooperation

12

South Asian Economic Integration: Potential, Challenges and the Way Forward

*Nagesh Kumar**

The Context

Regionalism became a very important trend in the world economy in the 1990s with the rise of very important blocks like the European Union (EU), North American Free Trade Agreement (NAFTA) and other regions following their lead—Mercosur in South America, the South African Development Community (SADC) in Africa and Association of Southeast Asian Nations (ASEAN) in Southeast Asia. Although the South Asian Association for Regional Cooperation (SAARC), the Economic Cooperation Organisation (ECO) and the Bay of Bengal Initiative for Multi-Sectoral Technical and Economic Cooperation (BIMSTEC) were formed in Southern Asia, the region has been slow in exploiting the potential of regional economic integration and has largely been relying on rising demand for its products in the advanced economies to support its growth over the past two decades. However, the region now faces a new, dramatically altered, economic context in the aftermath of the global financial crisis of 2008/09.[1] The US and the Eurozone economies currently face a subdued and uncertain medium-term outlook with high-levels of sovereign debt build-up and ageing populations. It is clear, therefore, that the world economy is unlikely to go back to the "business as usual" scenario

---

*This paper represents the text of the presentation made at the 7th IDSA South Asia Conference held in New Delhi on October 30-31, 2013. Views expressed should not be attributed to the United Nations or its member states.

that existed before the onset of the crisis. The Asian and Pacific economies will have to look for alternative engines of growth to support their dynamism in the coming years. Regional economic integration can play the role of a new growth engine for sustaining the Asia-Pacific region's dynamism over the coming decades.[2]

Another factor that makes regional economic integration a viable development strategy is the emergence of large and dynamic markets in developing Asia, including in South Asia, which are contributing significantly to global growth. Significant complementarities exist across the region and subregions as the patterns of development over the years have diverged between countries. This creates space for development of vertically integrated regional production networks that can enable the region to harness economies of specialisation and economies of scale. The eight countries of South Asia share cultural, ethnic, linguistic and historical commonalities that can facilitate integrated production networks.

The relevance of regional economic integration for the South Asia region also arises from its potential to contribute to a balanced and equitable regional development benefiting smaller and poorer parts of the region more. It has been demonstrated that regional economic integration leads to a process of efficiency seeking industrial restructuring across borders, aimed at exploiting the economies of vertical specialisation and regional value chains. The industrial restructuring takes place in such a manner that relatively smaller and lesser developed parts get more of this and so it needs to balance regional development, and some literature which has come on the experiences of the regional groupings around the world has actually documented that it does lead to that kind of industrial restructuring which is of a more balanced type.[3]

The South Asian subregion turns out to be among the least integrated in the world, and much of the potential for regional economic integration remains unexploited. While a number of initiatives have been taken over the past decade, the time has come to expedite implementation schedules, consolidate progress and move on to new initiatives in view of the new international context. Regional economic integration can lead to more balanced outcomes and experiences are now available from different countries and regions that can benefit South and South-West Asia, as the subregion seeks to design its own plans of cooperation.

Finally, an integrated South Asia would be in a better position to play its due role in the broader Asia and the Pacific market alongside the formation of transcontinental mega-Free Trade Agreements (FTAs) like Trans-Pacific Partnership (TPP) and Transatlantic Trade and Investment Partnership (TTIP). Apart from deepening its own integration, ASEAN is driving the formation of a broader Asia-Pacific integrated market by consolidating ASEAN+1 FTAs with six dialogue partners—Australia, China, India, Japan, Republic of Korea and New Zealand—through the Regional Comprehensive Economic Partnership (R-CEP).

R-CEP is widely seen as the nucleus of an incipient, broader Asia-Pacific integrated market.[4]

Taking into consideration the new international context for regionalism, this paper summarises major initiatives for regional economic integration undertaken in South Asia, their limitations and challenges. It presents some proposals for the future on how to exploit the potential of regional economic integration in a mutually beneficial, inclusive, balanced and sustainable manner.

Initiatives for Regional Economic Integration in South Asia

The South Asian subregion has a number of multilateral frameworks for regional economic cooperation and integration. SAARC came into being in 1985, but did not adopt a programme of economic cooperation until 1991 when the Committee on Economic Cooperation (CEC) was formed. It created a SAARC Preferential Trading Arrangement (SAPTA) in 1995, and in 2004 eventually agreed to create a SAARC Free Trade Area (SAFTA) to be implemented over 10 years from 2006. The 16th Summit held in Bhutan in 2010 adopted a SAARC Agreement on Trade in Services (SATIS) and established the SAARC Development Fund (SDF).

Initiatives together with other subregions in Asia and the Pacific also include ECO initially formed with Turkey, Iran and Pakistan in 1985, but later expanded to cover Afghanistan and six Central Asian countries—Azerbaijan, Kazakhstan, Kyrgyzstan, Turkmenistan, Uzbekistan and Tajikistan. ECO established the ECO Trade Agreement (ECOTA) in 2003 which became effective from January 2009 and seeks a phased reduction of tariffs on 80 per cent of tariff lines over eight years to a maximum of 15 per cent. It is likely to evolve ultimately into a FTA. In 2006, ECO also set up an ECO Trade and Development Bank based in Istanbul with a capital base of Special Drawing Rights (SDR) 300 million contributed by Turkey, Iran and Pakistan, and plans to admit new members.

Another notable initiative is BIMSTEC involving five South and South-West Asian countries (Bangladesh, Bhutan, India, Nepal and Sri Lanka) and two South-East Asian nations (Myanmar and Thailand), bridging the two subregions. BIMSTEC adopted a Framework Agreement for an FTA to be implemented within 10 years at its first summit held in Bangkok in July 2004.

Besides the above subregional and inter-subregional arrangements, bilateral preferential trading arrangements also exist between India and Nepal (transit and trade), India and Bhutan (transit and trade), India and Sri Lanka, Pakistan and Afghanistan (transit and trade), as well as Pakistan and Sri Lanka, which contribute to economic integration in the South Asian subregion.

These are complemented by the Asia-Pacific Trade Agreement (APTA) (earlier called the Bangkok Agreement) which was signed under the auspices of the United

Nations Economic and Social Commission for Asia and the Pacific (UNESCAP) in 1970s with some of the South Asian countries like India, Bangladesh and Sri Lanka under which member countries exchange tariff preferences between them.

Together, SAARC, ECO, BIMSTEC and APTA present overlapping sets of multilateral frameworks for regional cooperation in South Asia (see Figure 1). However, among them, SAARC presents the most comprehensive framework combining the eight countries with a functioning FTA that has been under implementation since 2006. The effectiveness of the SAARC framework in achieving its objectives is worth examining.

Figure 1: Regional Cooperation Frameworks in Southern Asia

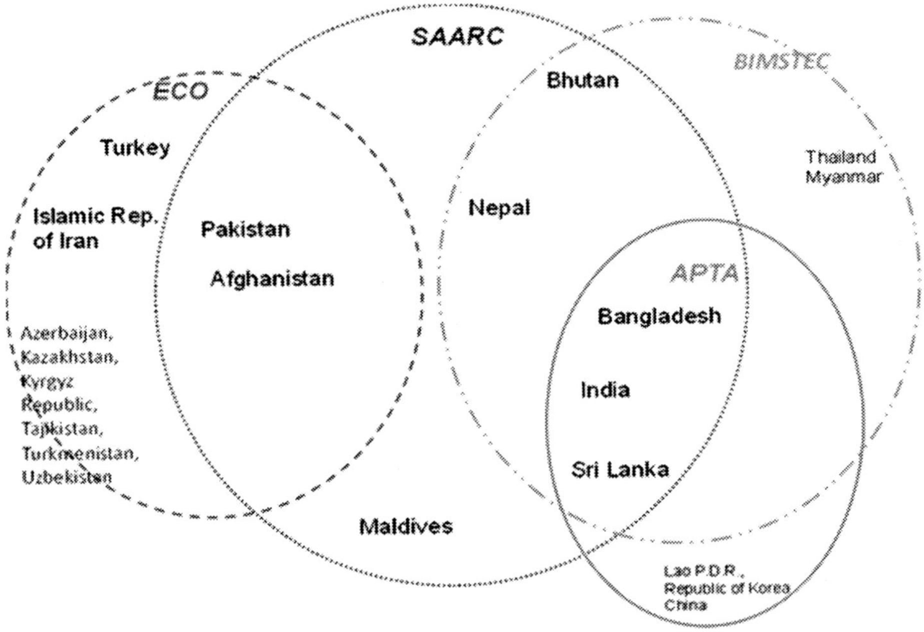

Source: ESCAP.
Note: Countries outside South and Southwest Asia are shown using a relatively smaller font.

SAFTA and Regional Economic Integration in South Asia

SAFTA is being implemented from 2006 in a phased manner over a 10-year schedule. However, the proportion of intraregional trade in SAARC countries' total trade has been one of the lowest among the regional groupings. This has been seen as an indicator of the poor potential of SAARC and of SAFTA's ineffectiveness. The share of intraregional exports in SAARC countries' global exports has fluctuated around 5 per cent between 2002 and 2011. However, if Indian exports are excluded, the intraregional share of other SAARC countries' exports to all SAARC countries (including India) is on a rising trend, and fluctuates between 8 to 10 per cent.

Country-wise detail presented in Table 1 suggests that smaller countries like Afghanistan, Bhutan, Maldives and Nepal have a greater proportion of their exports directed to the subregion. Furthermore, since the signing of SAFTA in 2004 and the beginning of its implementation in 2006, the share of intraregional trade among the individual South and South-West Asian countries has already increased for a number of countries in the subregion. Table 1 show how intraregional exports since 1995 have nearly tripled their share of Afghanistan's exports and almost increased fourfold as a share of Nepal's exports and of Pakistan's exports. Figure 2 additionally shows a rising trend in India's share in Nepal's and Bangladesh's exports. Thus, there are distinct signs that trade within the subregion is growing. Yet the overall proportion of intraregional trade in SAARC is low compared with other groupings like ASEAN where it stands at around 22 per cent.

Table 1: Intraregional Exports Trade as Share of Total Trade (in per cent)

	1995	*2000*	*2005*	*2010*
Afghanistan	17	44	44	46
Bangladesh	3	2	3	3
Bhutan	91	93	85	92
India	5	4	5	5
Maldives	23	14	16	12
Nepal	19	40	70	74
Pakistan	3	5	11	13
Sri Lanka	3	3	10	7

Source: ESCAP-SSWA (2012).

Figure 2: Indian Share of Exports from Two Trading Partners (in per cent)

A. Nepal **B. Bangladesh**

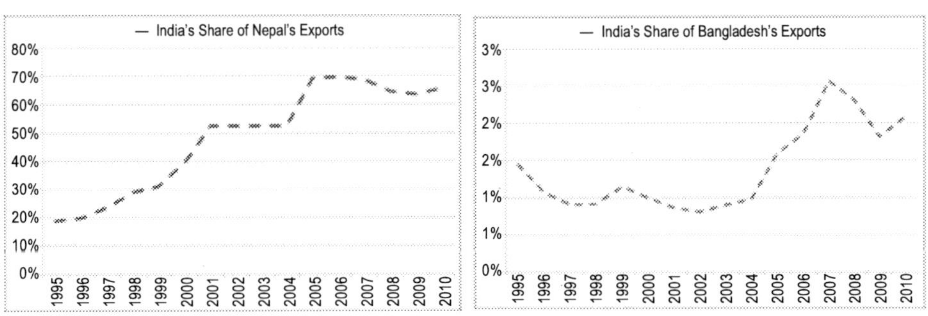

Source: ESCAP-SSWA (2012).

The present low level of intraregional trade, however, is neither an indication of low level of complementarities between the member countries nor is it a sign of SAFTA's ineffectiveness. The ESCAP analysis shows that South and South-West Asia has substantial complementarities within it. The value of the complementarity index for intraregional trade within the subregion is 37 compared with the maximum value of 64 for intraregional complementarities within Asia-Pacific's subregions.[5] It is also important to remember that complementarities are a dynamic concept and change over time with changing economic structures. In fact, SAFTA represents the case of a regional trade agreement with unexploited potential.

Potential of SAFTA and the distribution of welfare gains

The complementarities that exist within the subregion provide for a much higher level of intraregional trade than has been realised to date. ESCAP estimates that the US$ 16 billion in intraregional exports of SAARC countries in 2010 only partly achieved the full potential of US$ 37.5 billion in intraregional exports. Therefore, nearly 57 per cent of the potential of intra-SAARC trade remains to be exploited. The estimations of potential intraregional trade summarised in Table 2 use an augmented gravity model, which suggests that the bulk of the potential of intra-SAARC trade remains to be exploited. ESCAP estimations also show that by 2017, the intraregional export potential could double to US$ 72.4 billion.

Table 2: Underexploited Trade Potential in South and South-West Asia

		Export potential in South and Southwest Asia (in millions of US$)		
Country	*Actual export to SAARC country 2010*	*Potential export 2010*	*Potential export 2017*	*Unexploited (percentage)*
Afghanistan	271.0	718.0	1,635.7	62.3
Bangladesh	427.9	2,112.7	4,229.8	79.7
Bhutan	591.9	1,149.8	2,549.5	48.5
India	11,104.7	26,146.8	48,240.4	57.5
Maldives	48.2	285.6	585.3	83.1
Nepal	473.9	996.6	2,662.9	52.4
Pakistan	2664.3	4572.5	8,928.3	41.7
Sri Lanka	589.0	1564.2	3,630.2	62.3
SAARC	**16,170.8**	**37,546.2**	**72,462.1**	**56.9**

Source: ESCAP-SSWA (2012).

Among SAARC countries, in most cases, more than half the export potential remains to be utilised. The proportion is particularly high for Maldives (83 per cent to be exploited) and Bangladesh, with nearly 80 per cent untapped potential remaining.

Empirical studies have analysed the welfare gains from implementation of SAFTA for the participating countries and the rest of the world. In general, studies conducted using computable general equilibrium models and the Global Trade Analysis Project (GTAP) database have found SAFTA to be trade creating, leading to stronger growth and enhanced welfare for its participants.[6] Furthermore, estimated welfare effects from SAFTA are distributed equitably with relatively poorer countries receiving a greater proportion of welfare gains when normalised by the size of the economies. The largest gains accrue to Bangladesh, Nepal, Bhutan and Maldives. The studies showed many favourable effects of SAFTA on the participating economies in terms of opportunities for vertical specialisation, exploitation of economies of scale, expanded inflows of FDI by 30 per cent, formation of regional production networks and strengthened overall competitiveness.[7] Table 3 summarises findings of another recent study computing welfare gains from trade liberalisation and trade facilitation under SAFTA for member countries normalised by their GDP. This study corroborated the previous findings that poorer countries benefit proportionately more from SAFTA.[8]

Table 3: Welfare Effects from Trade Liberalisation and Facilitation in SAFTA as a Proportion of GDP of the Participating Countries

Countries	*Total welfare gain (in millions of US$ in 2007 price)*	*GDP (in millions of 2007 US$)*	*Welfare gains as a percentage of GDP*
Bangladesh	1,431.5	65,398	2.2
India	5,761.9	1,004,750	0.6
Nepal	1,769.0	8,858	20.0
Pakistan	2,887.4	122,550	2.4
Sri Lanka	2,160.4	28,064	7.7
Other South Asian countries (Afghanistan, Bhutan and Maldives)	1,324.8	10,842	12.2

Source: ESCAP-SSWA (2012) based on Raihan (2012) and ESCAP online database 2012.

Not just producers and industry, but consumers as well will gain from the integration of South Asia—studies of SAARC integration have additionally predicted some US$ 2 billion in static gains to South Asian consumers.[9] This could be an underestimate since it is purely in terms of price adjustments and wage improvements and does not count the potential knock-on effects that a better investment climate, stronger cross-border supply chain integration, and other positive externalities will bring.

Reasons for low level of intraregional trade in South Asia

The level of intraregional trade remains below its potential, owing to structural barriers such as high transport costs and other non-tariff and tariff barriers. The low level of intraregional trade can also be explained in terms of a number of factors described as follows:

High-level of under-reported or informal trade

While official trade statistics show South Asia to be one of the most underexploited areas for intraregional trade, it is important to realise that an enormous amount of informal trade goes unreported. South West Asian countries share long borders and given their shared history, language and culture, and despite political barriers to trade, a great deal of informal trade is thriving, particularly in border areas. Measuring informal flows poses a significant amount of methodological difficulties and often relies on small or limited sample sizes. However, most estimates agree that the scope of informal trade in South Asia is in many cases comparable to formal flows, in some cases even exceeds them.

As India is the largest and most centrally located country in South Asia, most informal trade in the subregion occurs between India and its neighbours. While India has a trade surplus based on the official figures with all of its neighbours, taking into account informal trade, it would still have a moderate trade surplus with Bangladesh, Bhutan and Pakistan, but a trade deficit with Nepal, and a balanced trade with Sri Lanka.[10] Estimates of informal trade between Pakistan and India ranged between $ 500 million and $3 billion in 2005, well above that of formal levels.[11] Similarly, informal trade between India and Nepal is estimated to be approximately eight to 10 times the official trade, while informal trade flows between Bangladesh and India are estimated to be twice as large as official flows.[12] However, informal flows between India and Sri Lanka are somewhat lower in magnitude, mostly owing to the fact that goods must travel via sea or air. The armed conflict that prevailed in the north of Sri Lanka for much of the last three decades may also have constrained informal trade.

Simple estimates of the current magnitude of informal trade between India and its largest neighbours can be made. UN-ESCAP-SSWA (2012) estimated that exports of Bangladesh, Nepal, Pakistan and Sri Lanka to India in 2011 may have been underestimated by nearly $8 billion and their imports from India by $3.8 billion.[13]

Further regional trade liberalisation will help formalise many of the trade flows currently taking place informally in South Asia. Nonetheless, the difference between the composition of informal flows and the composition of products traded formally indicates that even under a free trade regime, many of the goods traded may still take place off the books. This is because many of the goods traded are low value-added products and consumer goods like food items and textiles, rather than high value-added, complex manufactured and capital goods.

In addition to informal cross-border trade, South Asia also experiences a great deal of "third-country trade" to overcome the official trade barriers. This is the case for example of many trade flows between Pakistan and India. While the main channel of official trade flows between the two countries occur along the narrow Amritsar-Lahore corridor, a potentially larger amount of trade between the two countries takes place via the more indirect routes passing by Dubai and Iran or by Singapore, as a number of products that were not on the positive list governing Pakistan's imports from India were imported through these third countries. That however should change now with Pakistan moving towards granting India the Most Favoured Nation (MFN) status and scrapping the positive list in favour of a negative list.

Poor transport connectivity leading to high trade costs

SAARC countries are contiguous neighbours, however, the trade costs encountered by intra-SAARC trade at 113 per cent of import prices are higher than those encountered by SAARC countries trading with far distant markets like the EU, at 101 per cent, and the US, at 99 per cent (see Table 4). Furthermore, while trade costs for exports to different regions have declined between 2007 and 2009, there has not been such a movement for intra-SAARC trade. It is clear that the intra-SAARC trade has not been able to exploit the benefit of geographical proximity and is incurring costs greater than those applicable to distant locations. To further lower trade costs, physical connectivity and trade facilitation needs to be improved.

Table 4: Non-Tariff Intra- and Extra-Regional Trade Costs in Asia-Pacific, 2007-09 (as percentage of import prices)

Region	*ASEAN-4*	*East Asia-3*	*North and Central Asia-6*	*SAARC-4*	*Australia-New Zealand*	*EU-3*
ASEAN-4	79 (-10)					
East Asia-3	73 (-6)	47 (-21)				
North and Central Asia-6	291 (-14)	187 (-33)	149 (-21)			
SAARC-4	134 (-0)	119 (-3)	270 (-22)	113 0		
Australia-New Zealand	90 (-12)	78 (-16)	270 (-22)	130 (-3)	45 (-24)	

(*Contd.*)

Region	*ASEAN-4*	*East Asia-3*	*North and Central Asia-6*	*SAARC-4*	*Australia-New Zealand*	*EU-3*
EU-3	97 (-5)	70 (-19)	149 (-26)	101 (-3)	89 (-17)	32 (-33)
United States	77 (-0)	53 (-14)	165 (-17)	99 (-1)	82 (-11)	51 (-18)

Note: Trade costs may be interpreted as tariff equivalents. Percentage changes in trade costs between 2001-2003 and 2007-2009 are in parentheses. ASEAN-4: Indonesia, Malaysia, the Philippines and Thailand; EastAsia-3: China, Japan and Republic of Korea; North and Central Asia-6: Armenia, Azerbaijan, Georgia, Kazakhstan, Kyrgyzstan and the Russian Federation; SAARC-4: Bangladesh, India, Pakistan and Sri Lanka; EU-3: France, Germany and the United Kingdom.

Source: ESCAP Trade Cost Database (version 2).

Poor supply capabilities and potential of regional trade liberalisation in augmenting them

One of the reasons for persistent trade imbalances between India and the SAARC countries has been the poor supply capabilities or productive capacities in Least Developed Countries (LDCs) and other SAARC countries for the products of import interest to India. A recent study found that with duty free access to India, Bangladesh could be a potentially competitive supplier for nearly $6 billion worth of India's exports.[14] However, existing supply capabilities will permit additional exports of a few hundred million dollars. A similar situation holds for other countries. ESCAP analysis shows that productive capacities in South Asian LDCs have actually decreased in relative terms compared with other countries in terms of technical complexity and product variety.[15]

The India-Sri Lanka Free Trade Agreement (ISFTA) could be indicative of the potential of SAFTA in creating balanced regional development and addressing the poor supply capabilities through flows of FDI between the FTA partners. As ISFTA has been operational since 2000, it is possible to analyse the impacts on trade flows and their balance, flows of FDI and build-up of supply capabilities. ISFTA has led to massive expansion of bilateral trade while reducing imbalances.[16]

The FTA has enabled Sri Lanka to export value-added goods often produced by Indian companies in Sri Lanka through FDI, which has created more supply capabilities. For instance, an Indian tyre company set up a joint venture with a Sri Lankan company to produce automobile tyres in Sri Lanka for export to South Asia and the rest of the world, capitalising on the availability of natural rubber at a cheaper price in the country.

FDI is now flowing from Sri Lanka to India as well and is creating supply chains for the textiles and clothing industries. This includes a huge special economic zone in India being set up by the company Brandix to bring together the entire supply chain in textiles and clothing industry in a single location.[17] It is this kind of efficiency-seeking industrial restructuring that produces supply capabilities and jobs in relatively lesser developed locations, and also helps in strengthening the overall international competitiveness of products, exploiting economies of scale and specialisation.[18]

Recent Initiatives Towards Deepening Economic Integration

Over the past year, a number of favourable developments have unfolded that are likely to help remove some barriers to regional economic integration. These include movement by Pakistan towards granting MFN trading status to India sometime soon (Pakistan already enjoys MFN status in India since 1996). When granted, this would be an important step in normalising the trade relations between the two countries and towards the full implementation of SAFTA. It would also help avoid routing of trade through third countries rather than directly importing from the neighbouring country, thus saving on freight costs and raising consumer welfare. India has also allowed investments from Pakistan to be made in the country, a move that would assist in formation of joint ventures as a part of the efficiency-seeking industrial restructuring between the two countries.[19]

Another development has been a series of meetings and official visits since early 2010 between the Prime Ministers of Bangladesh and India as well as other high level representatives, which culminated in the announcement in September 2011 that India was removing all 46 textile lines which are of interest to Bangladesh from India's negative list for LDCs under the provisions of SAFTA. This reduced the applicable duty rate in India for the goods from Bangladesh to zero with immediate effect. Bangladesh, in response, conveyed its appreciation for this major step on improved market access aimed at reducing the existing trade imbalances.

Interestingly, at the same time, the trend growth of Bangladeshi exports to India increased dramatically. UNESCAP-SSWA (2012) showed how India recorded nearly three times the import volumes from Bangladesh in the period following the beginning of those discussions, than the previous eight years. India has subsequently removed all the products from the negative list for LDCs under SAFTA barring 25 items of a prohibited nature like alcoholic liquor and cigarettes.

Harnessing the Potential of Regional Economic Integration in South Asia

Expediting the Implementation of SAFTA

The regional trading arrangements in South Asia, viz. SAFTA has a rather long implementation schedule, long lists of sensitive or negative products and other restrictions that do not allow the process of liberalisation and industrial restructuring to take place. Having committed to regional economic integration, the participating States should compress the implementation schedules. The subregion can take cues from the ASEAN's experience which advanced the implementation of ASEAN FTA from the original deadline of 2008 to 2002 in the aftermath of the Asian financial crisis. SAFTA includes a provision for accelerated implementation.

Besides the lengthy implementation period, the scope for tariff liberalisation among SAFTA trading partners is reduced by large sensitive lists of products that remain outside the tariff cuts under SAFTA. One way forward to expand the scope of trade liberalisation is for member countries to cut down on the sensitive lists. In this context, India's recent initiative to virtually eliminate the sensitive list for the LDCs is encouraging. This may hopefully encourage other non-LDCs such as Pakistan and Sri Lanka to follow suit. The sensitive lists should also be reduced for non-LDCs. Removal of non-tariff barriers also merits urgent attention, as they could become instruments for protection despite the phasing out of tariff barriers.

Exploiting the Potential of Regional Trade in Services

South Asian countries have vibrant services industry and their trade in services is growing fast. Another observation is that services capabilities are more balanced and complementary than the goods trade, where India dominates the productive capabilities of the subregion.[20] For example, India specialises in computer and information services, while other economies in the subregion—particularly the least developed countries—specialise in traditional services such as travel and transport. This indicates outstanding potential for mutually beneficial trade in services within the subregion. Some of the trade is already vigorously happening. For instance, following the liberalisation of air services and the visa facility between India and Sri Lanka, India has emerged as the biggest services market for Sri Lanka.[21] Significant trade also takes place in health and education services, although barriers preventing its full potential from being exploited remain.[22]

A key reason for the limited level of intraregional trade in services is the failure to liberalise intraregional service trade including removal of "behind-the-border" barriers. A SAARC Agreement on Trade in Services or SATIS was signed at the 16th SAARC Summit held in Thimphu in 2010. However, the actual liberalisation of trade through national schedules within the framework of SATIS needs to be expedited.

Facilitating Intraregional Foreign Direct Investments

The real gains from a regional trading arrangement result from efficiency-seeking industrial restructuring, which also builds productive capacities in relatively lesser developed economies. Therefore, many new FTAs combine trade in goods and services with investment liberalisation.[23] In South Asia, some countries are now emerging as the sources of FDI. In this context, the South Asian Agreement on Promotion and Protection of Investments, a draft of which has been nearly finalised, needs to be signed at the earliest. A SAARC Limited Multilateral Agreement on Avoidance of Double Taxation and Mutual Administrative Assistance in Tax Matters has already been signed. SAARC could also adopt the SAARC Industrial Cooperation (SICO) Scheme. Under this scheme, the products of joint venture projects (set up with involvement of intraregional investments) could be accorded duty-free access in the home countries without waiting for the implementation of the SAFTA schedule of trade liberalisation to facilitate industrial restructuring.

Strengthening Banking and Financial Links

Banking and financial links play a very important role in facilitating trade and investments between the countries. The absence of reciprocal banking links makes it difficult for banks to accept letters of credit issued by exporters' banks. The subregion has very perfunctory cross border banking links. Liberalisation of banking services could be prioritised under SATIS. However, even without waiting for negotiations to take place, South Asian countries could expedite the liberalisation of banking and financial linkages by providing national treatment to designated banks originating in the subregion on a reciprocal basis.

Capital Raisings and Development Finance

One of the constraints on industrial development and supply capabilities, especially in LDCs, is their access to capital as local capital markets are shallow, if they exist at all. The access to international capital markets is constrained by poor sovereign credit ratings and currency risk problems. Raising capital at the stock exchanges of the advanced countries by enterprises registered in developing countries is made difficult by high initial expenses. These include getting them listed and making an initial public offering as well as bearing the high costs of compliance with accounting standards and other regulations. Only a handful of larger well-known enterprises from countries like India have been able to raise capital at the Western bourses like New York Stock Exchange, NASDAQ or Luxembourg. In that context, allowing enterprises from South Asian LDCs to list and raise capital in more developed capital markets in the subregion such as in India, Pakistan or Sri Lanka may be fruitful. The cross-listing of securities on the subregion's various stock exchanges should also be encouraged as that would provide more options for raising capital to enterprises.

The SAARC Development Fund is an innovative scheme for development financing in the subregion. It was set up in 2010 as a part of SAARC financial cooperation with an authorised capital of SDR one billion and paid up capital of

$300 million. The Fund will finance infrastructure projects in the subregion, including the preparation of feasibility studies. It has three windows for financing, namely, the social window for poverty alleviation and social development projects; the infrastructure window for projects in the energy, power, transportation, telecommunications, environment, tourism and other infrastructure areas, and the economic window devoted to non-infrastructural economic projects. The Secretariat of the SDF has been established in Thimphu, Bhutan.

In view of the huge infrastructure deficits faced by the SAARC countries, it may be appropriate to focus on infrastructure. However, considering rather small capital base of $300 million, SDF should focus on playing the role of catalysing rather than funding infrastructure projects. A useful model in this respect is that of ASEAN Infrastructure Fund (AIF). AIF has been created as a part of an ASEAN initiative to mobilise resources for infrastructure development in 2010 with an initial equity base of US$ 485 million, of which $335 million will come from ASEAN members and remaining $150 million being provided by the Asian Development Bank. Malaysia with $150 million and Indonesia with $120 million are major contributors of the equity capital of the AIF. Based in Malaysia, AIF will function as a limited liability company and hopes to have a total lending commitment of $4 billion by 2020 which will be co-financed by ADB to the tune of 70 per cent. Therefore, it expects to catalyse more than $13 billion in investments in realising the Master Plan on ASEAN connectivity adopted in 2010. AIF will be administered by ADB in terms of due diligence of the projects identified for funding.[24]

SAARC can also establish a SAARC Development Bank, as advocated by ESCAP-SSWA (2012), catalysing much bigger projects that are of critical importance for regional connectivity and subregional development needs through a co-financing arrangement with ADB among other financing institutions. As a regional institution, it should help prioritise the regional projects that may otherwise remain unfunded or underfunded. It could also be more effective if it undertook to catalyse regional infrastructure development projects that would have a larger impact across the subregion rather than in any one member state.

Strengthening the Asian Clearing Union Mechanism

Nine countries of the region (Bangladesh, Bhutan, India, Iran, Maldives, Myanmar, Nepal, Pakistan and Sri Lanka) are members of the Asian Clearing Union (ACU), headquartered in Tehran, a grouping which heavily overlaps those of SAARC and ECO. ACU provides a useful mechanism for promoting intraregional trade by reducing the need to transfer hard currencies for mutual trade. It provides for settlement of balances in hard currency in a settlement period. It operates as an association of the central banks of the nine members. It also provides a swap facility enabling the members with a deficit to draw upon the reserves of other members for taking care of the short-term liquidity problems. ACU is an important mechanism for regional cooperation and needs to be strengthened. It might consider opening its membership to Afghanistan to have all SAARC countries on board. It might be a useful vehicle for financial and monetary cooperation in South Asia. It should also coordinate with the SAARC Finance which is a body of SAARC Central Banks.

Strengthening Transport Connectivity and Trade and Transport Facilitation

Trade and transit facilitation measures need to complement the removal of tariff and non-tariff barriers to be effective. SAARC is addressing the issue of simplification and harmonisation of customs operations and standards with the establishment of the SAARC Standards Organisation (SARSO) in Dhaka. An innovative way of trade facilitation could be to consider creating a SAARC Single Window which would allow SAARC goods to pass through customs more rapidly. Transit and connectivity along with trade facilitation are important issues in the subregion. There are important opportunities for developing extended transport corridors to not only facilitate intra-regional trade but also to make the subregion a hub of East-West trade that it was in the days of Silk Route.[25] Among the specific opportunities available include extending the Istanbul-Tehran-Islamabad (ITI) container train corridor to Dhaka and beyond through Delhi and Kolkata (DKD) making it a vital trunk route for intraregional trade with feeder routes to Afghanistan, Bhutan, Nepal, Sri Lanka and Maldives. Besides facilitating intraregional trade, it could help the subregion harness its strategic location to emerge as a hub of the East-West trade in the Eurasian region.[26]

Longer-term Vision and Target-setting

For regional groupings, it is important to adopt a long-term vision and objectives and to take incremental steps to achieve those goals. In the case of SAARC, the Eminent Persons Group had proposed a long-term vision of a South Asian Economic Union to be achieved by 2020. SAARC may revisit those proposals and articulate a vision of the grouping to be achieved by a certain year. ASEAN has successfully moved towards the goal of ASEAN Economic Community that is now set to be achieved by 2015 and was advanced from the initial 2020 target. ECO could develop a similar vision for itself.

Furthermore, SAARC should take note of the broader trends in Asia-Pacific regionalism. For example, ASEAN is adopting a framework on RCEP of East Asia that will bring together six FTA partners of ASEAN in a single Regional Trade Agreement (RTA) with itself. SAARC will have a better chance to play an important role in the incipient broader regionalism through its own deeper integration.

Concluding Remarks

This paper has shown how despite large potential for intraregional cooperation in South Asia, intraregional trade in goods and services and intraregional investment remain low. In fact, South Asia has been one of the least integrated subregions in the world. From such a low level, however, trade flows and increased cooperation are growing in magnitude. Spurred on by common historical backgrounds, shared languages and existing informal trade links of impressive size, there are increasing reasons for South Asians to be optimistic about the prospects for regionalism.

The most important reason for South Asian countries to pursue further regional integration is to facilitate efficiency-seeking investment and industrial restructuring. Building an intraregional trading network that exploits complementarities across the subregion's various countries in both merchandise and service trade can pave the way not only for improved trade balances with the rest of the world but also improved productive capacity, particularly in the subregion's LDCs.

The obstacles facing increased subregional cooperation are not economic, but rather are political in nature. Overcoming these political barriers has increasing relevance and importance today, given the geopolitical situation prevailing in the subregion, and given faltering demand in the subregion's principal trading partners in the developed world.

For far too long, politics has held back the progress in the subregion. The time has come for letting economics to play a greater role and for regional cooperation to finally take the centre stage in South Asia. Despite long-standing political differences between some countries, the pressures of faltering demand in developed markets due to the crisis, and the prospect of higher costs in the world's workshop of East Asia, are opening a door of opportunity for South Asia to regain its former position as a crossroad between the East and the West.

ENDNOTES

1. "Growing Together: Economic Integration for an Inclusive and Sustainable Asia-Pacific Century," *UNESCAP*, United Nations, Bangkok, Thailand, 2012a.
2. Ibid. Also, see "Economic and Social Survey of Asia and the Pacific 2012," *UNESCAP*, United Nations, New York, 2012b.
3. UNESCAP, 2012a, no. 1.
4. Ibid.
5. "Economic and Social Survey of Asia and the Pacific 2011,"*UNESCAP*, United Nations, New York, 2011, pp.112-113.
6. "Quantification of Benefits from Regional Cooperation in South Asia," *UNCTAD-India and ADB*, 2008, as cited in "South Asia Development and Cooperation Report," *Research and Information System for Developing Countries (RIS)*, Oxford University Press, New Delhi, 2008.

7. Ibid.
8. Selim Raihan, "SAFTA and the South Asian Countries: Quantitative Assessments of Potential Implications," *MPRA Paper # 37884*, 2012, at http://mpra.ub.uni-munchen.de/37884/
9. Bipul Chatterjee and Joseph George, "Cost of Economic Non-Cooperation to Consumers in South Asia," *CUTS International and The Asia Foundation*, New Delhi, February 01, 2012.
10. Nisha Taneja, "Informal Trade in SAARC Region," *Economic & Political Weekly*, March 17, 2001, pp. 959-964.
11. Shaheen Rafi Khan, "Can Illegal Trade between Pakistan and India Be Eliminated?," *SDPI Research and News Bulletin*, 12 (3), May-June 2005, at http://www.sdpi.org/research_and_news_bulletin/Vol.%2012,%20No.%203%20%28May%20-%20June%202005%29/can_illegal_trade%20.htm
12. Nisha Taneja and Sanjib Pohit, "Characteristics of India's Informal Trade and Formal Trading with Nepal: A Comparative Analysis," *Indian Economic Review*, New Series, 37 (1), January-June 2002, pp. 69-89.
13. "Regional Cooperation for Inclusive and Sustainable Development: South and South-West Asia Development Report 2012-13," ST/ESCAP/2644, *UNESCAP-SSWA*, United Nations and Routledge, New Delhi and New York, October 2012.
14. See RIS, no. 6.
15. UNESCAP-SSWA, 2012, Chapter 9, no. 13.
16. See S. Kelegama, "Regional Economic Cooperation and Connectivity in South and South-West Asia," *Development Paper Series No. 1205*, UNESCAP-SSWA Office, New Delhi, 2012; and UNESCAP-SSWA, 2012, Chapter 4, no. 13.
17. UNESCAP-SSWA, 2012, no. 13.
18. Nagesh Kumar, "Investment Provisions in Regional Trading Arrangements in Asia: Relevance, Emerging Trends, and Policy Implications," *Working Paper Series*, 46, Asia-Pacific Research and Training Network on Trade, October 2007, at http://www.unescap.org/tid/artnet/pub/wp4607.pdf
19. Sujay Mehdudia, "Now, Pakistanis Can Invest in India," *The Hindu*, New Delhi, August 01, 2012, at http://www.thehindu.com/business/Economy/article3712510.ece
20. Nagesh Kumar, R.U. Das and Prabir De, "Potential for Trade in Services under SAFTA," *SAARC Regional Study*, SAARC Secretariat, Kathmandu, 2008.
21. S. Kelegama, no. 16.
22. Rupa Chanda, *Integrating Services in South Asia*, Oxford University Press, New Delhi, 2011; Safdar Sohail, Noorulain Hanif and Maliha Quddus, "Liberalization of Trade in Services under SAFTA: Prospects and Challenges for Pakistan," in Sultan Hafeez Rahman, Sridhar Khatri and Hans-Peter Brunner (eds.), *Regional Integration and Economic Development in South Asia*, Edward Elgar, Chaltenham, United Kingdom, 2012.
23. Nagesh Kumar, no. 18.
24. UNESCAP, no. 2.
25. See UNESCAP-SSWA, 2012; and "Towards Seamless Connectivity in South and South-West Asia," *UNESCAP-SSWA Office*, 2013, at http://sswa.unescap.org/pdf/Towards_Seamless_Connectivity_in_South_and_South_West_Asia.pdf
26. Ibid. For more details of the ITI-DKD container train corridor.

13

Stepped-Up Inter-State Dialogue as a Key to Improving SAARC Development Prospects

Gabriel Ian Lynn Ockersz

The Challenge for SAARC

'Another Chola invasion'—these are the disconcerting terms in which a Sri Lankan english language weekend newspaper had sometime back described the alleged incursion into Sri Lankan territorial waters of fishing boats from Tamil Nadu. The 'illegal fishing problem' is one of several issues which need to be sorted out in Indo-Lanka relations, but such a process would be stymied by the absence of a constructive dialogue between the political leadership of the countries, besides other relevant opinion-making sections. In addition, this quote is adequate proof that we are still some distance from launching and sustaining a dialogue process of this nature.

In the realm of inter-state ties in South Asia, perceptions could prove to be of vital importance and are perhaps more decisive in their impact than reality. It could be seen from just the above quote how decades long prejudices continue to mar perceptions that influential sections in Sri Lanka have been having about India in general and the state of Tamil Nadu in particular. In other words, India is being viewed through lenses which are centuries-old. We are left to conclude that nothing very positive has been done by both Sri Lanka and India to rectify these misperceptions over the years. However, the new Indian Prime Minister Narendra Modi has clearly stated that he is for improving the inter-state SAARC ties. This could bode well for the South Asia region if it is put into practice in earnest, and if he wins the ready support of the rest of the SAARC members on this score.

What is true of Indo-Lanka ties is also true of India's relations with many of its neighbours in the post-independence times. While security issues such as 'cross-border terrorism' figure strikingly among the contentious ones between India and many of its neighbours, territorial disputes, sharing of river waters and movement of displaced people across state boundaries, particularly, emerge as divisive issues in their bilateral relations.

Nothing particularly new would be said by taking-up the position that these divisive questions in the bilateral ties between India and its neighbours have, among other things, got in the way of the South Asian Association for Regional Cooperation (SAARC) graduating into a successful exercise in regional co-operation and solidarity.

The case of Sri Lanka indicates that prejudices regarding India among some sections in Sri Lanka could be even centuries-old and are very much part of the collective memory of the Lankans. This is very much a matter for the Lankan state and other sections, such as higher education authorities, which need to concern themselves with educating the consciousness of the public. If Sri Lanka needs better relations with India, misperceptions and prejudices about India among Lankans need to be dislodged through a process of public education. That is, a mindset change about India needs to be effected. This is a long-term undertaking which needs to be taken on by mainly educated and responsible sections in Sri Lanka, including the state, and it is hoped that forums, such as the current one, launched by the Institute for Defence Studies and Analyses (IDSA), New Delhi would contribute towards this positive change in attitudes.

However, in the short-term, both India and Sri Lanka would need to engage in confidence-building measures continually to improve bilateral relations, and thereby put their relations on a better footing so as to benefit mutually from qualitatively improved ties. The consequences of these long and short-term measures aimed at improving bilateral relations could be a closer bonding between India and Sri Lanka. This process could contribute towards fostering regional amity, which is so essential for the smooth functioning of the SAARC.

The initiation of confidence-building measures between the two states in this region needs to be premised on the launching of a bilateral dialogue process which would thereafter be sustained. The challenge before our states in South Asia is to engage in constructive dialogues among each other in a spirit of openness. Very often, the constructive element is missing in these bilateral and even multilateral exchanges, and the result is usually a further straining of inter-state ties, especially if these relations are already far from cordial. Accordingly, the South Asian states would need to have an eye on the quality of their dialogues and exchanges.

However, the above aims could be achieved even to a relative degree if the SAARC provides the forum for the broaching of issues which are seen as dividing the South Asian states at the bilateral and multilateral levels. Right now, this exercise is not provided for under the SAARC Charter. While it could be argued that this stipulation could help in keeping the SAARC process afloat in view of the disruptive impact an unconstructive airing of controversial issues could have on the process of regional cooperation, the non-resolution of controversial questions in a spirit of openness and constructive engagement would not be of much help either because unaired and unresolved grievances tend to get in the way of full-blown regional cooperation. Stifled, unarticulated grievances or those that are 'swept under the carpet' of diplomatic niceties and graces, only tend to simmer within the consciousness of state representatives, for instance, and mar the atmosphere attendant on inter-state engagements and diplomatic exchanges.

Accordingly, a case could be made for a degree of openness in the relations among the SAARC Eight. There was the encouraging news when in 2013 an Indian parliamentary delegation had visited Pakistan and engaged in fruitful and informal discussions with its Pakistani counterpart. It had helped in easing out some strain in the India-Pakistan ties, and it goes without saying that more of such exchanges among even other states of the SAARC region could help in bringing a degree of unprecedented cordiality to the inter-state relations in this part of the world.

It needs to be recognised that democratisation in South Asia has been taken several notches higher with a democratic administration in Pakistan completing its term of office for the first time in that country's post-independence history. This is a most positive development, and it is hoped that India would make the most of this opportunity to strengthen ties with Pakistan, bearing in mind that, usually, relations among democracies are of a cordial kind. SAARC needs to put to good use this relatively widespread spirit of democracy, although this region is also deeply troubled by divisive political forces such as the identity politics.

Therefore, Track Two diplomacy and other forms of informal interaction among the SAARC states and the people need to gather pace, while formal diplomatic exchanges and engagements continue among the countries as well. It is hoped that Track One would be nourished by Track Two and informal interactions.

Accordingly, this spirit of informality and openness needs to inform the SAARC deliberations too because as long as the task of resolving bilateral contentious issues is approached by the association in a constructive and cooperative spirit, there is a possibility of SAARC narrowing these seemingly intractable differences among its membership.

Momentous Opportunities

SAARC needs to 'grab this moment' because India and numerous countries of the 'South' are on an unprecedented economic growth trajectory. As is well known, while the economic fortunes of the 'developed world' are currently on the decline, the growth prospects of the 'developing world' are on an unprecedented upswing. Today, it is the 'South' or the developing countries which are evincing the highest growth rates and are proving to be the 'engine of growth' of the global economy.

A recent vital document of the international community that needs to be studied in depth is the UNDP's Human Development Report 2013. Subtitled, *The Rise of the South: Human Progress in a Diverse World*, a summary of the report states thus:

> Although most developing countries have done well, a large number of countries have done particularly well—what can be called the 'rise of the South'. Some of the largest countries have made rapid advances, notably Brazil, China, India, Indonesia, Mexico, South Africa and Turkey. But there has also been substantial progress in smaller economies, such as, Bangladesh, Chile, Ghana, Mauritius, Rwanda and Tunisia.[1]

Elaborating on the growth prospects of the 'South', the summary goes on to state:

> The middle class in the South is growing rapidly in size, income and expectations. The sheer number of people in the South—the billions of consumers and citizens—multiplies the global human development consequences of actions by governments, companies and international institutions in the South. The South is now emerging alongside the North as a breeding ground for technical innovation and creative entrepreneurship. In North-South trade, the newly industrializing economies have built capabilities to efficiently manufacture complex products for developed country markets. But South-South interactions have enabled companies in the South to adapt and innovate with products and processes that are better suited to local needs.[2]

Touching on the importance closer regional integration in its concluding observations, the summary further states:

> New institutions and partnerships can help countries share knowledge, experiences and technology. This can be accompanied by new and stronger institutions to promote trade and investment and accelerate experience sharing across the South. One step would be to establish a new South Commission to bring a fresh vision of how the diversity of the South can be a force for solidarity.[3]

SAARC needs to take its cue from these observations. Certainly, a new South Commission would be welcome and prove timely, but more vitally, we need what may be called a 'South Asia Commission' which would seek to address the issue of how the South Asian region could harness its economic growth and vibrancy on an equitable basis for the material advancement of the SAARC Eight.

But there is no need to re-invent the wheel. SAARC would be playing a role that is most appropriate to it by discharging the functions of this envisaged 'South

Asia Commission'. This is how SAARC needs to see itself in current times. It should take on anew the task of ensuring, to the extent possible, the advancement of regional growth and prosperity on an equitable basis, for this was seen as one of its primary tasks, although it did not live up to the expectations over the decades.

However, SAARC would be resurgently functional and effective only to the degree to which it is rendered so by its membership and to the extent to which it enjoys the latter's wholehearted backing. Accordingly, in order of priority, SAARC needs to be rejuvenated and rendered dynamic and effective before it takes on the momentous responsibilities outlined above, such as ensuring shared and exceptional material advancement for its member states.

Eschewing Short-term Gains

All South Asian eyes inevitably turn towards India and Pakistan at the very mention of the aforementioned challenges. It goes without saying that the advancement of the SAARC region would depend on the degree to which these regional heavyweights put their shoulders to the wheel of the SAARC development agenda. They would be enabled to do so only if they keep their sights on long-term development goals and eschew short-term political gain in particular.

Admittedly, this is no easy task, but it must be made to work if even a degree of shared economic gain is to accrue to the region and conflicts among states are to be better managed. However, these times are propitious because the Nawaz Sharif Government in Pakistan is on record that it is for improved ties with India. Political relations have also improved with parliamentarians from both sides establishing closer and cordial contact. Hopefully, Track Two diplomacy and people-to-people contact between India and Pakistan would improve too.

Both India and Pakistan too need to seize this moment. Apparently, the Indian and Pakistani polities need to be convinced of the need to keep in mind the larger picture of a South Asian region which is at relative peace with itself, conducting its relations in a spirit of amicability, bearing in mind the greater good that would accrue to it through expanded and intensified economic cooperation. Such 'conversations' are starkly lacking in almost all the polities of South Asia, including Sri Lanka. Consequently, it should not come as a surprise if misunderstandings, misperceptions and prejudices persist in the inter-state relations of this region.

The South Asian governments, in short, should relay the vital importance of good neighbourliness and cordial inter-state ties to the general public. This 'conversation' needs to be eloquent, vibrant, and consistent, and the material benefits which could be reaped from it clearly underscored for the purpose of winning public support for the attendant programmes of the SAARC economic cooperation.

This 'development conversation' needs to supersede all divisive concerns in the ties among the countries in South Asia. For, of the present international situation, it could be said with considerable justification that 'economics drives politics'. Moreover, if South Asia is lagging behind in the development race among regions, it should not come as a surprise because most states in this region have permitted divisive inter-state issues to cloud the larger aim of regional economic cooperation.

Therefore, an effort needs to be made on the part of governments to effect a change in their political cultures which are currently, in the main, of a populist bent. Such political tendencies and habits would enable political parties to win power, but would not help in efforts to mend fences with neighbours. This observation applies to Indo-Pakistan and Indo-Lanka relations in particular.

There are security issues figuring in India-Pakistan ties, for instance, which have been thus far leading to accusations and counter-accusations between the two countries. With Pakistan making an effort to stabilise democracy within its borders, amid a number of internal challenges, including those emanating from a politicised military, obligates India to relate to Pakistan with exceptional patience. Ideally, 'incidents' on the India-Pakistan border should not lead to an acrimonious exchange of allegations which strains ties very disconcertingly.

However, joint security arrangements need to be in place on the common border to minimise the occurrence of 'incidents' that tend to mar Indo-Pakistani ties. There should not be a tendency on the part of the two governments to resort to populist politics on these issues. Majoritarian chauvinism, a species of populist politics, needs to be strongly guarded against by governments, but this norm is usually observed more in the breach because of the obvious importance to ruling parties, in particular, of their vote banks.

SAARC has to take upon itself the task, as mentioned, of fostering democracy-friendly ideals and values in this region which would help in blunting the impact of populism and majoritarian chauvinism. But this must be effected very unobtrusively and delicately. Nevertheless, for now, we need to focus on the need for stepped-up economic interaction among the SAARC countries which would prove mutually-beneficial.

The International Situation

The importance of the latter process is underlined, among other things, by the strong economic and political links the West has been forging with India. Over the past few years, both the US and Britain have made it plain that they intend bolstering business, trade and investment ties with India. This is on account of India's strengths as a global economic power. But to the extent to which economics drives the West's efforts to build strong bridges to India, to that extent are *realpolitik* considerations being diluted in the West's ties with Pakistan and other countries of this region. This is on account of the primacy of India in the West's policy outlook for the region.

There was a time when security and strategic considerations propelled the West to foster close ties with Pakistan rather than India. Those were the heydays of the Central Treaty Organisation (CENTO) and the South East Asia Treaty Organisation (SEATO), and it could be argued that security issues continue to determine, to some extent, the West's ties to Pakistan down to the present times. For example, the West needs the assistance of Pakistan to manage its issues in Afghanistan. But it is India that is steadily acquiring primacy for the West in South Asia.

Some South Asian commentators have been quick to notice the changed international situation in the Asian region. Today, it is 'the Eagle, the Dragon and the Elephant' which are seen to be the principal players in the region. That is, the US, China and India are seen as playing a pivotal role in the Asian strategic landscape. Commenting on current global realities, analyst Jasjit Singh, for instance, had stated: "But within this larger complex landscape, and for a variety of reasons, three key players—the United States, China, and India—and their relations among themselves and the rest of the world—stand out as the *core strategic triangle* of the future that would exercise increasing influence on the world at large, and security issues in Asia, in particular."[4]

These crucial changes in the international situation, involving mainly economic, strategic and material considerations, need to be taken cognisance of by the SAARC countries. India and China are the most important economic, military and political actors on the Asian stage, and SAARC should set its priorities right in this changing situation. There are vast markets to be tapped in India, for instance, and India's neighbours would have only themselves to blame if they let these opportunities go.

But prior to doing so, they must relate with increasing cordiality to India, and for this purpose India and its neighbours need to recognise each other's sensitivities and core concerns and fashion their ties accordingly. So, continuing inter-state 'conversations' are of the first importance and the SAARC should, ideally, facilitate this process.

Quality Dialogue

It should be plain to see that it is quality in inter-state dialogue that would prove pivotal in improving the tone and timbre of regional relations. As suggested earlier, such dialogue or 'conversation' should be constructive in orientation, and it is the constructive element that imparts quality to the envisaged dialogue process. From this point of view, what needs to be eschewed in inter-state dialogue is destructive criticism of each other by states.

India's neighbours need to see that although it is easy and even 'fashionable' to destructively criticise India over the plethora of contentious issues that keep the SAARC region divided, what is needed, if the emerging economic strengths of this region are to be equitably tapped, is a constructive approach to India.

Sections in India habitually call for the dismantling of what they allege are jihadist militants' training facilities in primarily Pakistan and to a lesser extent in Nepal. It is made out by some that such jihadists of Pakistan origin are even in Sri Lanka, aiming to infiltrate India from Sri Lankan shores. These are recurring security questions, as mentioned, which keep some SAARC states divided. Besides some security-linked irritants, Sri Lanka has a plethora of issues with India, including those related to the West-initiated human rights-linked accountability questions being probed by the UN Human Rights Council.

Unless handled constructively and imaginatively by the states concerned, these bilateral issues could lead to irrevocable rifts among the SAARC Eight. The record, thus far, regarding the handling of these issues by the states concerned, leaves very much to be desired, and this is the reason why inter-state dialogue needs to be conducted within a value structure which would be adhered to region-wide.

SAARC as Humanising Influence

In effect, SAARC has its work cut out for itself. It needs to strongly consider making itself a vehicle of open and constructive dialogue among its membership, within reasonable limits, so that even divisive issues could be aired and discussed. SAARC should ensure that such 'conversations' are conducted in a constructive, civilised fashion and do not degenerate into finger-pointing acrimonious debates. It needs to set the rules and guidelines for these dialogues and ensure they are observed.

'Easier said than done', the cynics may argue, but this would not prove an uphill task if a SAARC consensus is formed for a united vision and action. Such unanimity could be forged if vibrant efforts are made by the leaders of the SAARC to underscore the collective gains which could be reaped by the region in the current international economic and political milieu. India and Pakistan would need to put principles above politics and take upon themselves the bulk of this undertaking, since they are the pivotal states in the SAARC.

SAARC also needs to take on itself a humanising and civilising mission. As indicated earlier, democratic ethos is currently pervading SAARC, although divisive politics remains. The most number of countries in the South Asian region are democracies and apparently, understand democracy's basic norms and values. Why cannot these values underpin our dealings with each other?

This is a long gestation project, but needs to be undertaken right now. Slowly but surely, divisive political ideologies and beliefs that keep people divided, domestically and internationally, must be eschewed. In order to achieve this, the costly consequences of division must be underscored. Such programmes could be undertaken by the SAARC, without necessarily referring to them as being aimed at 'democratisation', since the sovereign rights of states must be respected. Public education programmes could be imaginatively devised to achieve these aims, and SAARC needs to take on such challenges.

Accordingly, a degree of revamping of the SAARC is necessary to meet some of the challenges just outlined. For one, the constitution of SAARC must be amended to provide for the constructive discussion of issues that are being viewed as divisive by its members, but which have, in fact, stymied the growth of the association. This provision should be underpinned by a carefully thought out regime of unanimously accepted rules. However, before such issues are taken up formally by the SAARC, they need to be subjected to informal trouble-shooting discussions among the relevant parties to the dispute, under the arbitration of, perhaps, the SAARC Secretary General, or some such eminent official of the SAARC.

Furthermore, the interests of the SAARC region would be served, if the organisation could adopt a Regional Convention on the Humanisation of Domestic and International Politics. This could help in the process of 'civilising' the politics in this region because, as noted, there are far too many destructive political forces at work in this region. There is, of course, no guarantee of the ready acceptance and adoption of these ideas, but they must be tried out if this region is to accept the challenges of the current age. We certainly cannot forge ahead as a region if communalism and fascism, for instance, are winked at by states under the assumption that we live in 'free' societies. What needs to be provided, for the development of societies, are human values which are the defining essence of democracy, as generally understood.

We need to take a page from the European Union (EU), which is, today, a success story in regional cooperation. What has undergirded the success of the EU is democracy and its values and ideals. Despite some occasional differences, the EU has forged ahead as a regional body and its successes in regional economic cooperation speak for themselves. Besides, the EU has been single-minded in its pursuits. It has not, for instance, adopted conventions and done little about them. But SAARC has adopted quite a number of conventions over the years, and one wonders how successfully and effectively they have been implemented. There was a convention for the adoption of a regional food reserve some time back, for instance, but what is the current position with regard to this valuable initiative?

Therefore, SAARC needs to take stock of its achievements as it goes along and see itself as a change agent. Public education programmes and such tools must not only be devised to ingrain democratic values, such as the respect for life and the 'Other', in the consciousness of the rulers and the ruled, the urgency of collective economic well-being too must be clearly underscored. In other words, the cruciality of SAARC unity must be ingrained in the minds and hearts of the people of the region.

ENDNOTES

1. "The Rise of the South: Human Progress in a Diverse World," *Summary UNDP Human Development Report 2013.*
2. Ibid.
3. Ibid.
4. Alyssa Ayres and C. Raja Mohan (eds.), *Power Realignments in Asia: China, India and the United States,* SAGE Publications, 2009.

14

China and South Asian Cooperation Under SAARC

S.D. Muni

In order to understand China's role in the South Asian regional cooperation and how this role is being perceived within South Asia, we must begin by looking at the drives behind China's engagements with and interests in South Asia. China has been South Asia's neighbour, though a new one, since its military absorption of Tibet in 1951. Not that China did not have historical contacts with the South Asian countries before absorbing Tibet, but such contacts were sporadic, confined to political and trade matters generally, and made nominal impact on each other. There was hardly any engagement at the level of societies and people. Geographical distances and barriers, which have started melting away under technological innovations, played dividers too.

China now has a strong desire to engage with the South Asian countries for three specific reasons. First of all is its sense of vulnerability in relation to its western periphery, comprising Tibet and Xinjiang. Both these outlaying regions of China are restive and unstable. Despite its massive administrative control, financial investments, and military presence, Tibet erupted into a major revolt in 2008, marring China's otherwise masterly organisation of Olympic Games. The vehemence and anger with which the Chinese authorities react to His Holiness the Dalai Lama reflects their inherent sense of insecurity. Like Tibet, Xinjiang also has been simmering with discontent for a long time. Islamic upsurge has further complicated China's internal security concerns in Xinjiang so much so that President Xi Jinping has been initiating special measures to deal with the situation, even by spreading nets "from earth to sky" to catch the "terrorists"—"thugs influenced by religious extremist ideology."[1] Since both these peripheral regions of China share borders with South Asian countries, China has to cultivate these countries to ensure that the discontented and rebellious groups do not receive support and encouragement from across the borders.

Second, there is an economic drive pushing China's increasing engagement with South Asia. The rising Chinese economy is looking for opportunities of investments and natural resources all over Asia and the world, and its neighbouring South Asian region cannot be an exception. More so as South Asia is the world's most populous sub-region with 1.5 billion population and growing economies. China cannot neglect this region in the interest of its own continuing prosperity and growth. In this context, let us recall China's drive to develop Yunnan, which led to closer engagement with the countries surrounding the south-western province, i.e., Myanmar, Laos, Vietnam, and Cambodia.[2] Yunnan's further growth and development would also require connectivity and cooperative relations with some of the South Asian countries like Bangladesh and India. Similarly, if Tibet and Xinjiang have to grow economically, they will need South Asian outlets. The noticeable emphasis in China's efforts on connectivity with the neighbouring regions can also be explained by the hunger of the Chinese infrastructure companies that are facing some sort of saturation in opportunities internally. Chinese leadership has clearly shown its intent to boost the infrastructure sector and thus the Chinese economy.

The third drive is obviously strategic which may have multiple objectives ranging from keeping India boxed within South Asia to securing transit and access points in the Indian Ocean/Bay of Bengal region. This access will also cushion its so called Malacca dilemma to ensure uninterrupted flow of trade and commerce. China's investments in developing ports like Humbantota in Sri Lanka, Chittagong in Bangladesh, Gwadar in Pakistan, Kyaukpyu in Myanmar and building economic/transit corridors in Pakistan and Myanmar are indicative of this objective. China's proposals to develop new Maritime Silk Road and the Silk Road Economic Belt are also a part of it. Under these proposals, China wants to connect with whole of Asia and access its markets and natural resources, creating new opportunities for its infrastructure sector as well in the process. While ostensibly commercial and economic projects, these accesses and facilities will also establish a strategic Chinese presence in the Indian Ocean, and the Asian region, curtailing strategic space that naturally exists for other countries including the US and Russia.

Driven by these three objectives, China is approaching the South Asian countries both bilaterally and regionally as a group. China's phenomenal economic rise and growing military muscle has given it a new confidence, allowing it to engage with the South Asian region assertively. According to one assessment, South

Asia is third priority, after East and South East Asia, vis-à-vis China's strategic engagement with Asia.[3] South Asian Association for Regional Cooperation (SAARC) being the only viable regional organisation for development cooperation in South Asia, China has been interested in it from the beginning.

There are two different ways in which the South Asian countries look at China's interest in South Asia. One is led by India, and the other by almost all other countries of the region, mainly Pakistan, Nepal and Bangladesh. One may take Bhutan as an exception to this as it has so far generally followed Indian lead in critical strategic aspects of the SAARC development. It was during the 1970s that early moves were made to explore the possibility of regional economic cooperation for development in South Asia. These moves were sponsored by the European funding agencies, the United Nations Development Programme (UNDP) and the Asian Development Bank (ADB) for undertaking studies for regional cooperation. Pakistan and Nepal since then have been interested in getting China involved in regional initiatives. The imperative was more political than economic development, whereby China was expected to provide a political counterweight to India in regional affairs. While Pakistan wanted to contain India's rising stature in the region following the emergence of Bangladesh, Nepal had been feeling uncomfortable with India for its overall dominance in bilateral affairs and strong resistance to Nepal's country-specific proposals like "Nepal as a Zone of Peace." King Birendra's proposal initiated in 1975 was meant to erode the burden of the bilateral Treaty of 1950 with India which underlined a kind of 'special relationship' between the two countries. China was perhaps not that keen at the time to engage with the South Asian regional affairs, as its economic development had not yet begun in any serious manner. However, China was always forthcoming in assuring Pakistan and the other neighbours of India that it would stand by them against any pressure and interference from India.

When SAARC came into existence in 1985, and even when it was being formed, there was a very strong plea made by China's South Asian supporters that China should be involved. The argument extended was not only based on using China as a counterweight to India, but also on the basis of China's growing economic strength and advantages of making it South Asia's development partner. Reference was to China's emphasis on economic growth under Deng Xiaoping's reforms.

The efforts of some of India's neighbours to get China involved in SAARC did not succeed until 2005 largely because of India's resistance. SAARC functions on the basis of unanimity in decision-making, which in effect means a veto right to every member of the grouping to abort a given decision. However, in 2005, at the 13th SAARC summit, China was granted an Observer status along with many other countries including the US, Japan, the European Union, South Korea,

Australia, Myanmar, Mauritius and Iran. It is interesting to note that in 2005, India became a member of the East Asia Summit (EAS) and was also accepted as an Observer in the Shanghai Cooperation Organisation (SCO) comprising China, Russia and the Central Asian countries. Both in the EAS and the SCO, India's entry was being resisted by China.

One wonders if there was any informal swap between India and China regarding the organisations involved. If there was any, it is interesting to speculate its implication for the current developments as China has offered India to participate in the Asia Pacific Economic Cooperation (APEC) and also supports its full membership of the SCO.[4] India may still find it difficult to concede the SAARC membership to China as decision-making processes are widely different in the SAARC from the APEC and the SCO. China attended the 14th SAARC summit in 2007, first as an Observer. In his statement, the Chinese Foreign Minister Li Zhaoxing had described SAARC as "an important organisation for regional cooperation...as well as peace and stability in South Asia." He added that "China respects the aspirations of SAARC countries and the principles of equality, mutual trust and win-win cooperation and is ready to carry out exchanges and expand practical cooperation with SAARC..."[5]

Since 2007, the demand of making China a full SAARC member has gradually gathered momentum among India's neighbours, particularly Pakistan and Nepal. India has been resisting this under the pretext that status of the Observer countries in the SAARC has not been defined. It may also be kept in mind that since 2005 China has keenly moved to improve its credentials for closer engagement with the SAARC. It has set up a China-South Asia Business Forum which held its ninth annual meeting in June 2014 in Kunming, and was inaugurated by the Bangladesh Prime Minister Shiekh Hasina Wajid.[6] Possibly with the view of building public opinion in favour of its closer engagement with the SAARC, China has also been holding the meeting of South Asian think tanks in Kunming. Prior to the 17th SAARC Summit held at Male in 2011, Kunming also hosted a conference sponsored by the China Institute of International Studies, Beijing, the Yunnan Academy of Social Sciences, Kunming and the Institute of Policy Studies, Islamabad, on "China-SAARC: Towards a Better Understanding through Enhanced People-to-People Exchanges" during July 26-27, 2011.[7]

At the 17th Male Summit, the ADDU Declaration issued on November 14, 2011 undertook "a comprehensive review of all matters relating to SAARC engagement with Observers, including the question of dialogue partners, before the next session of the Council of Ministers" (Para 19). The reference to "Dialogue Partners" in this declaration was interesting and must have come up to avert the pressure for elevating Observers like China to the full membership level. The inspiration for this has obviously come from the Association of Southeast Asian

Nations (ASEAN) and other regional groupings. India's strong reservations about China becoming a full member of the SAARC emanate from the legitimate fear that SAARC's decision-making may get undermined in view of the veto rights its members are accorded. Obviously, India may not want regional decision-making to be held hostage to China's political and economic preferences. Will India or the other SAARC members find an alternative to full membership for China in SAARC+1 Summits, on the lines being held by ASEAN, remains to be seen. China's efforts to deepen its engagement with SAARC and express its interests and commitment to its processes, however, continue. China had organised a SAARC Officials Exchange Programme with the China Foreign Affairs University from October 21-November 01, 2012. SAARC has not yet firmed up its consensus on the role of Observers. There was no reference to the proposed review of this question at the 2012 session of the SAARC Council of Ministers. No SAARC summit has been held after Male. There is also no certainty if this issue will be resolved by the next summit expected to be held in Kathmandu in November 2014.

In contrast to the approach of its other neighbours, India has reservations because if the neighbouring countries are trying to use China as a counterweight to its own strategic space in South Asia, obviously India cannot but resist it. Gradually, however, this resistance has been diluted. For example, as mentioned earlier, India accepted China as an Observer in SAARC. An important factor behind this has been China's rise as a formidable economic power opening up economic opportunities, and one South Asian country which has taken the most advantage of it is India. How can India then grudge its other neighbours for doing the same, i.e., enhancing their economic engagement with China? Indian economy has also become stronger over the years, and there is increased confidence in the government as also the corporate sector to engage with China to their advantage. This confidence can be seen in the multifaceted engagements between India and China (e.g., the Bangladesh-China-India-Myanmar [BCIM] forum, which was initiated by China to help expand the reach of its Yunnan region to South Asia). India at first stoutly resisted from participating in the forum. But in 2013, India agreed to work with China in developing the BCIM economic corridor. According to the Joint Statement issued at the end of the then Indian Prime Minister Manmohan Singh's visit to China during October 22-24, 2013:

> Pursuant to the understanding reached between the two leaders in May 2013, India and China have each established a Study Group on the BCIM [Bangladesh, China, India and Myanmar] Economic Corridor. The visit of the Chinese delegation to India in this regard was noted as a positive step. Further discussions on concepts and alignment of the economic corridor are envisaged. Both India and China would continue to discuss with the other parties to this initiative, and hold the first BCIM Joint Study Group meeting in coming December to study the specific programs on building the BCIM Economic Corridor.[8]

The Indian and Chinese prime ministers have in principle and in practice also agreed to collaborate on enhancing connectivity with Bangladesh, Myanmar, and also Northeast of India in order to develop that region. Another reason behind the Indian shift is also the initiative to develop India's Northeast region and link it with the Look East Policy. There was no such link initially when the Look East Policy was launched in the early 1990s. It is important to note in this respect that some of the Southeast Asian countries like Singapore and Thailand, as also Japan, have been quietly prodding India to develop its Northeast region in view of expanding Chinese influence in Myanmar and Bangladesh. To facilitate its greater and easy access to South Asia, China has also been proposing that joint development effort should be encouraged between India, China and Nepal. The idea of trilateral cooperation was highlighted by a senior Chinese official in Kathmandu in the last week of August 2014. China has already promised to link Kathmandu with Tibet through the Tibet rail link in Shigatse. This is compatible with the idea of the former Maoist Prime Minister of Nepal, Baburam Bhattarai, to develop Nepal as an economic link between India and China.

Some Pakistani analysts have also proposed that India could become a partner in China-Pakistan economic corridor that would connect Pakistan's Gwadar sea port developed by China to China's Xinjiang Province through Karakoram Highway. India may not find it easy to respond to such proposals positively, at least in the near future. But all these moves fit in with the Chinese keenness to have smooth and expanded access to South Asia in view of its interests and stakes outlined earlier. India will have to evolve a fitting response to deal with China in South Asia. There are surely areas where the two will continue to compete, but there may also be issues on which the two Asian giants can cooperate and coexist in South Asia to their respective mutual advantage.

It is, therefore, clear that India or any other country in South Asia cannot wish away China, particularly its growing economic and strategic interest in the region and its desire for greater role and participation in the SAARC activities. India is learning slowly and hesitatingly to cope with the growing Chinese presence in the region which is of critical strategic significance, and is increasing its engagement with China both bilaterally and in regional affairs. However, this engagement need not be considered synonymous with a full membership of SAARC for China, and in this context, not only India but also other SAARC members must think through seriously. Simply in economic terms, China's engagement with the South Asian countries has been growing steadily, and will continue, irrespective of China becoming a full SAARC member. If China is elevated to full membership from its present Observer status, other Observers will also ask for the same, and that raises the question of the expansion of SAARC. Can SAARC accommodate all the Observer countries as its full member? Will it become unwieldy and meaningless to call it SAARC then? Will it not open SAARC to avoidable strategic competition, for instance, between China on the one hand and Japan and the US on the other? Will it in any case benefit the original SAARC members or will it tend to polarise them?

There is also a strong possibility of SAARC getting further divided with China's co-option as a full member. SAARC was originally planned as a forum for development cooperation that would in due course of time also soften the intra-regional political and strategic conflicts. This has actually not happened as the process of development cooperation has been stifled. Moreover, SAARC is not progressing not because of the lack of economic theories or economic analyses or economic data or the prospects and opportunities which the economists are bringing out. SAARC is not progressing essentially because of political hurdles that operate at two levels: firstly, in terms of bilateral relations amongst the SAARC countries and, secondly, in terms of internal politics and instability within the SAARC countries. The major bilateral hurdle is the India-Pakistan hiatus. China is a part of the problem in the India-Pakistan hiatus rather than a part of the solution. Therefore, China's entry as a member of SAARC is not going to diminish this hiatus, if at all it will enhance it. China's presence in the SAARC will also encourage other smaller neighbours of India to play China card to counter-balance India even in matters related to development cooperation.

Internally, the South Asian countries are struggling to consolidate and establishtheir democracies, and SAARC would not really gather its full developmental momentum unless these democracies get firmly institutionalised, ensure stability and orient respective internal political dynamics towards development, away from inflated nationalist or emotional issues with reference to regional relations. China has no sympathy either for democracy or for developmental politics. In fact, China is characterised by its preference for strong, assertive, centralised regimes on its periphery. One must look around to see if China has ever helped or encouraged democratisation in any of its neighbouring countries. South Asia's democratisation is forcing China to come to terms with democratic processes, and in some cases like Nepal and Myanmar, it is getting sucked into the depths of domestic politics to create supportive constituencies. In Nepal, for instance, China is encouraging resistance to ethnicity-based federalism. China's fear is that if its close neighbours get democratised, they may start distancing themselves from China, as is evident in the case of Myanmar.

While considering a SAARC membership to China, the South Asian countries need to look closely at China's participation in other regional groupings. Strong arguments have been made to underline China's increasing comfort level with multilateral diplomacy and its strategy towards multilateralism at the global level.[9] Multilateralism at the global level, however, is different from the role in a given regional organisation where critical national interests are at stake. In this context, for instance, it would be worthwhile to consider China's approach towards ASEAN. When China's core interests came in conflict with ASEAN regional harmony, China did not hesitate to break it. In July 2012, the ASEAN Summit unity was breached by Cambodia under the Chinese influence on the question of South China Sea. While some ASEAN members like Vietnam and Philippines wanted ASEAN to take a strong position on the South China Sea dispute contrary to China's interests, the regional unity was shaken as the Summit could not even adopt a declaration under the Cambodian Chair.[10] With China's presence in SAARC, such a regional breakdown is more likely because internal SAARC cohesion is far more fragile than what we see in ASEAN. Some of India's neighbours are ever prepared and looking forward to using China against India on regional issues. That being so, who will care about building SAARC unity and advancing regional cooperation under its umbrella.

ENDNOTES

1. "Spreading the Net," *The Economist*, London, August 09, 2014, at http://www.economist.com/news/china/21611110-new-episodes-violence-and-repression-have-heightened-tensions-xinjiang-spreading-net (Accessed August 10, 2014).
2. S.D. Muni, "China's Strategic Engagement with the New ASEAN," *IDSS Monograph No.2*, Institute of Defence and Strategic Studies, Nanyang Technological University, Singapore, 2002.
3. Mohan J. Malik, "South Asia in China's Foreign Relations," *Pacific Review,* 13 (1), February 2001, pp. 73-90.
4. The APEC participation was offered by the Chinese President Xi Jinping in his meeting with India's new Prime Minister Narendra Modi at Brazil BRICS summit in July 2014. Indrani Bagchi, "Xi Calls Modi to Apec Meeting, Scores over US," *The Times of India*, New Delhi, July 16, 2014, at http://timesofindia.indiatimes.com/india/xi-calls-modi-to-apec-meeting-scores-over-us/movie-review/38448569.cms (Accessed July 24, 2014)
5. See "Foreign Minister Li Zhaoxing Addresses Opening Ceremony of the 14th SAARC Summit," *Ministry of Foreign Affairs of the People's Republic of China*, April 03, 2007, at http://www.fmprc.gov.cn/mfa_eng/wjdt_665385/zyjh_665391/t308922.shtml (Accessed July 24, 2014).
6. "9th China-South Asia Business Forum (CSABF), 7 June 2014, Kunming, Yunnan, Peoples Republic of China," at http://www.saarcchamber.org/index.php?option=com_content&view=article&id=472:9th-china-south-asia-business-forumcsabf-7th-june-2014-kunming-yunnan-peoples-republic-of-china&catid=3:main-news-articles&Itemid=911 (Accessed July 12, 2014).
7. For the papers presented at the conference, see *Policy Perspectives,* 9 (1), 2012, Institute of Policy Studies, Islamabad. Also, see the special Issue on "China and SAARC."
8. Para 04 of the text of the Joint Statement. See "Joint Statement—A Vision for Future Development of India-China Strategic and Cooperative Partnership," *Ministry of External Affairs, Government of India*, October 23, 2013, at http://mea.gov.in/bilateral-documents.htm?dtl/22379/Joint+Statement+A+vision+for+future+development+of+India China+strategic+and+cooperative+partnership (Accessed October 25, 2013).
9. Jagannath P. Panda, "China in SAARC: Evaluating the PRC's Institutional Engagement and Regional Designs," *China Report,* 46, 2010, pp. 299-310. Also, see Elmie Konwar Rengma,

"Soft Power Game: A Study of China, India and South Asian Association for Regional Cooperation (SAARC) Tripartite," *Emerging Scholars Papers 2012*, India China Institute, New York, at http://indiachinainstitute.org/wp-content/uploads/2010/03/Elmie-Soft-Power-Game-A-Study-of-China-India-and-SAARC-Tripartite.pdf.

10. Patrick Barta and Carlos Tejada, "Sea Dispute Upends Asian Summit," *The Wall Street Journal*, July 23, 2012, at http://www.wsj.com/news/articles/SB10001424052702303919504577524133983292716?mod=_newsreel_1 (Accessed June 24, 2013).

15

India's Trade with Neighbours: Perceptions and Reality—With Special Reference to India-Pakistan Trade

Indra Nath Mukherji

Introduction

This paper brings out the role of perceptions of Pakistani stakeholders in its trade relations with India. While some of these perceptions cut across other neighbouring countries of India, the focus of this paper is primarily on Pakistan. It brings out the background to regional trade liberalisation, in particular, the deliberations at the official level meetings under the previous Pakistan Peoples' Party (PPP) Government in Pakistan and the previous United Progressive Alliance (UPA) Government in India. It was expected that once the electoral process is over and new governments have been formed, the earlier long drawn dialogue process would chart out the steps towards fulfilment of trade normalisation between the two countries. Yet many commitments remain unfulfilled and a rethinking process is on among a section of Pakistan's stakeholders, strongly asserting that unless a level playing ground is provided by India, the grant of Non-Discriminatory Market Access (NDMA) to India should be kept in abeyance. This paper examines the Pakistani perceptions from an assessment of ground reality.

Background to Regional Trade Liberalisation

Over the past decade, India has been moving towards greater trade liberalisation or normalisation with its neighbours, both through bilateral free trade agreements as well as through regional approaches, such as South Asian Preferential Trading Agreement (SAPTA) activated since2005 and, its successor, South Asian Free Trade Agreement (SAFTA) activated since July 2006. India used its bilateral approach to have free trade with its traditional trading partners such as Nepal and Bhutan, long before bilateralism came to be accepted as the most popular instrument of foreign trade policy of both developed and developing countries. The India-Sri Lanka Free Trade Agreement, signed in December 1998, has been in operation since March 2000. Under this Agreement, India and Sri Lanka engage in free trade, barring products in their respective sensitive lists. India has used the regional framework of SAFTA to offer all contracting Least Developed Countries (LDCs) duty-free, quota free access to its market barring only 25 items. It has pruned its sensitive list for Non-Least Developed Countries (NLDCs) to only 614 items.

All South Asian Association for Regional Cooperation (SAARC) members are signatories to the World Trade Organisation (WTO), with the exception of Bhutan, and as such are obliged to give Most Favoured Nation (MFN) treatment to each other. The only exception to this has been Pakistan's non-acceptance of this principle in its market access to India. Till 1965, India-Pakistan trade was governed by positive list[1] approach under which only products specified by each country in their respective positive lists were allowed to be exported by the other. With the outbreak of hostilities between the two countries in 1965, any formal trade between them during 1996-1974 ceased.In accordance with the Shimla Agreement of 1972, a Protocol on Resumption of Trade was signed by India and Pakistan on January 23, 1975 which provided that the trade would be on MFN basis as provided for in General Agreement on Tariffs and Trade (GATT). India accorded MFN status to Pakistan in conformity with its general approach. However, Pakistan continued with the positive list strategy, which is, allowing only selected items for import from India.

The PPP Government of Pakistan appeared well disposed and reconciled to granting India the MFN status in November 2011,[2] and considerable time and effort in attaining the same was reflected in the long drawn official level meetings both at the secretarial and ministerial levels that was initiated in 2004 under the composite dialogue process. With the initiation of composite dialogue process, Pakistan de-linked, for the first time, trade issues from Kashmir. The Composite Dialogue between India and Pakistan from 2004 to 2008 addressed all outstanding bilateral issues. It had completed four rounds and the fifth round was in progress when it was paused in the wake of Mumbai terrorist attacks in November 2008.

As a result of their meeting in April 2010 in Thimpu on the sidelines of the 17th SAARC Summit, the then Indian Prime Minister Manmohan Singh and his Pakistani counterpart Yusuf Raza Gilani mandated their foreign ministers and foreign secretaries to hold discussions on the modalities to pave way for a comprehensive and sustained dialogue on all issues of mutual interest and concern.[3] The meeting of the then Indian External Affairs Minister S.M. Krishna and his Pakistani counterpart Hina Rabbani Khar in New Delhi on July 27, 2011 marked the culmination of the first round of the resumed dialogue.[4]

The 7th Round Table on Commercial and Economic Cooperation (RTCEC) reiterated that the road map for liberalised trade drawn in earlier ministerial meetings would be "scrupulously" adhered to.[5] Both sides developed a long-term plan of trade liberalisation during the 7th RTCEC: It was noted that Pakistan then had 936 tariff lines at 6-digit under its SAFTA sensitive list, as against 614 tariff lines at 6-digit of India. It was agreed that after Pakistan had notified its removal of all restrictions on trade by Wagah-Attari trade route, India would bring down its SAFTA Sensitive List by 30 per cent before December 2012 keeping in view Pakistan's export interests. At present, Pakistan allows only 137 items to move via the land route.[6]

According to the 7th RTCEC: As Pakistan would transition fully to the MFN status for India by December 2012, as agreed earlier, India would thereafter bring down its SAFTA sensitive list to 100 tariff lines by April 2013. As India notifies the reduced sensitive list, Pakistan, after seeking approval of the cabinet, will also notify its dates of transition to bring down its SAFTA sensitive list to a maximum of 100 tariff lines within the next five years (i.e., before the end of 2017). Moreover, before the end of year 2020, except for this small number of tariff lines under respective SAFTA sensitive lists, the peak tariff rate for all other tariff lines would not be more than 5 per cent.[7]

Growing and Persistent Trade Imbalance

One of the major issues in India's trade relations with its neighbours is the persistent and growing trade imbalance with India. While it is true that South Asian Countries' (SACs) trade imbalance with India has been increasing, their similar imbalance with the world has been increasing even faster, such that the share of India in SACs global trade deficit has declined from 41.02 per cent in 2000 to 21.08 per cent in 2011 (see Figure 1).

Examples of country-specific trade imbalance of some SACs such as Sri Lanka, Bangladesh and Pakistan with China (another developing Asian country) show that their trade imbalance with China is far more pronounced than that with India. An illustration of Pakistan's trade imbalance with China, India and world is presented in Figure 2. As observed, Pakistan's trade deficit with China in 2012 was around four times of that with India. A counter factual to this is that SACs trade deficit with the world could have been much higher had they not sourced their essential requirements from India.

Figure 1: South Asian Countries (Excluding India) Trade Deficit with India and World (US$ Million)

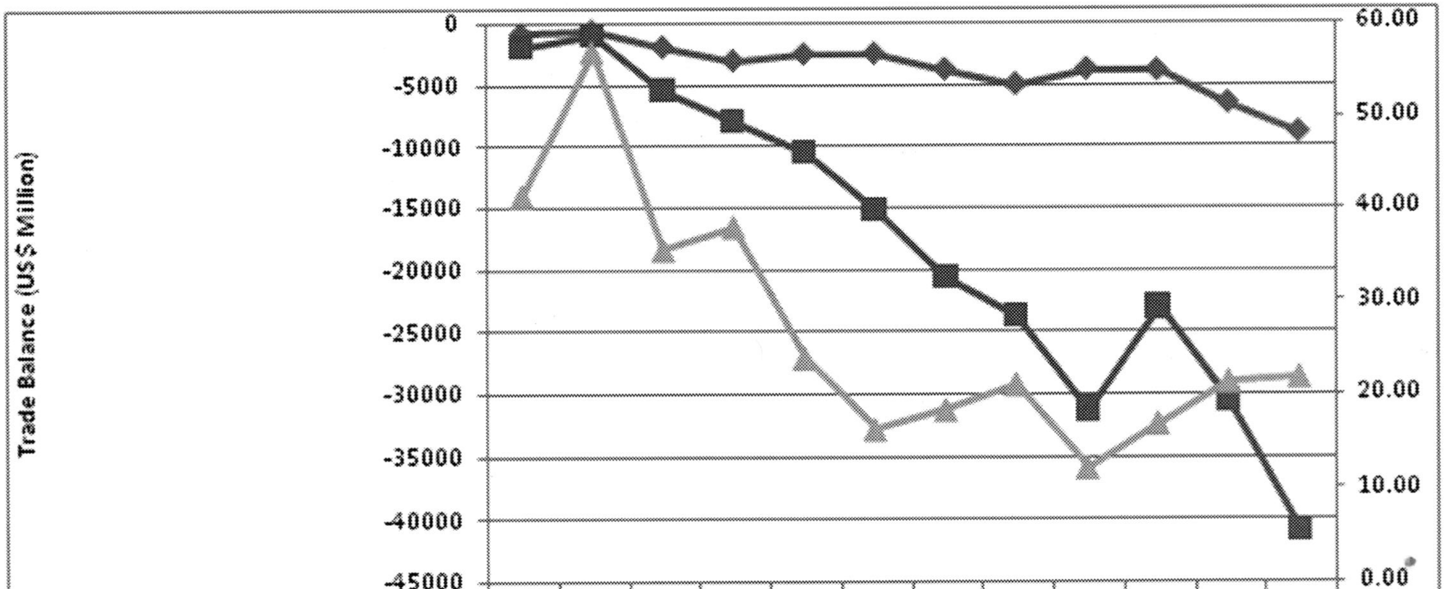

	2000	2001	2002	2003	2004	2005	2006	2007	2008	2009	2010	2011
Trade Balance with India	-825	-571	-1916	-3036	-2506	-2461	-3776	-4989	-3777	-3877	-6520	-8891
Trade Balance with World	-2002	-1005	-5415	-8014	-10532	15212	20694	23772	31263	23064	30642	40870
Trade Deficit with India as % World Deficit (Right Axis)	41.22	56.82	35.38	37.88	23.79	16.18	18.25	20.99	12.08	16.81	21.28	21.75

Source: Based on author's estimates from UN Comtrade Data, World Integrated Trade Solution (WITS), World Bank, at wits.worldbank.org.

Figure 2: Pakistan's Trade Deficit with China, India and World (US$ Million)

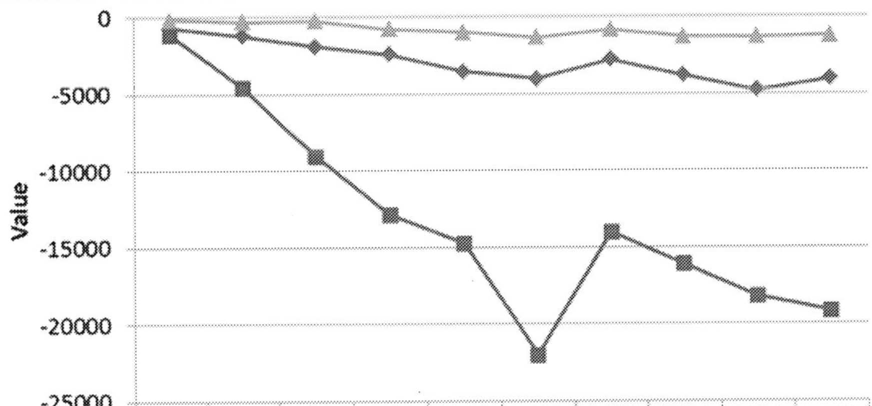

	2003	2004	2005	2006	2007	2008	2009	2010	2011	2012
China	-698	-1188	-1914	-2408	-3550	-4011	-2782	-3812	-4792	-4068
World	-1119	-4570	-9046	-1289	-1475	-2204	-1402	-1612	-1823	-1920
India	-143	-296	-239	-788	-975	-1337	-845	-1285	-1334	-1225

Source: Based on author's estimates from UN Comtrade Data, World Integrated Trade Solution (WITS), World Bank, at wits.worldbank.org.

Another dimension of trade deficit is to observe trade not merely in value terms, but also in terms of its content. According to Figure 3, Pakistan imports mainly capital and intermediate goods from China (around 80 per cent in 2012).

Pakistan's imports from India are dominated by intermediate goods and raw materials (around 90 per cent in 2012).The share of consumer goods and capital goods combined was10.75 per cent in 2012 from India compared to 57.84 per cent from China (see Figure 4). There can be little doubt the pattern of market access realised by India and China has much to do with Pakistan's positive list approach to India, combined with preferential access to China (discussed later).

Tariff and Non-Tariff Barriers

It is contended by Pakistani stakeholders that India imposes high tariff barriers against Pakistan's imports. Figure 5 demonstrates that overall tariff incidences in both India and Pakistan are not very dissimilar, both applied and final bound.[8] The difference arises in that while Pakistan imposes lower tariffs on agricultural goods, it imposes higher on non-agricultural goods as compared to India.

Pakistani stakeholders have more often expressed concerns of the prevalence of opaque Non-Tariff Barriers (NTBs) being faced by exporters in Pakistan. The NTBs are those costs, other than tariffs, that have a bearing on the trader. This

Figure 3: Pakistan's Imports from China by End Use Classification (Per Cent of Total Imports)

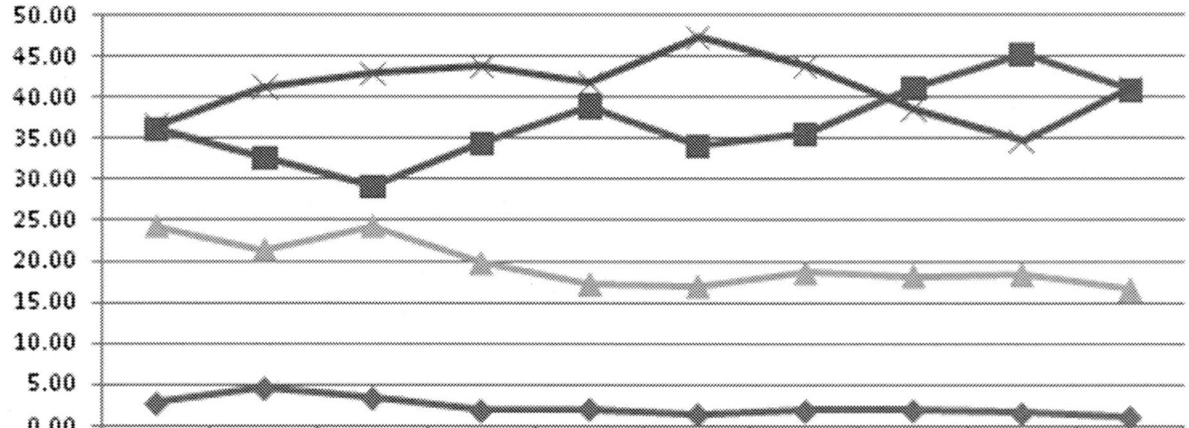

	2003	2004	2005	2006	2007	2008	2009	2010	2011	2012
Raw Materials	2.80	4.62	3.45	1.93	2.12	1.47	1.91	1.97	1.60	1.14
Intermedite Goods	36.29	32.68	29.26	34.47	39.01	34.27	35.69	41.17	45.28	41.02
Consumer Goods	24.34	21.43	24.40	19.78	17.22	16.97	18.57	18.23	18.38	16.58
Capital Goods	36.57	41.27	42.90	43.82	41.65	47.29	43.83	38.63	34.74	41.26

Source: Based on author's estimates from UN Comtrade Data, World Integrated Trade Solution (WITS), World Bank, at wits.worldbank.org.

Figure 4: Pakistan's Imports from India by End Use Classification (Per Cent of Total Imports)

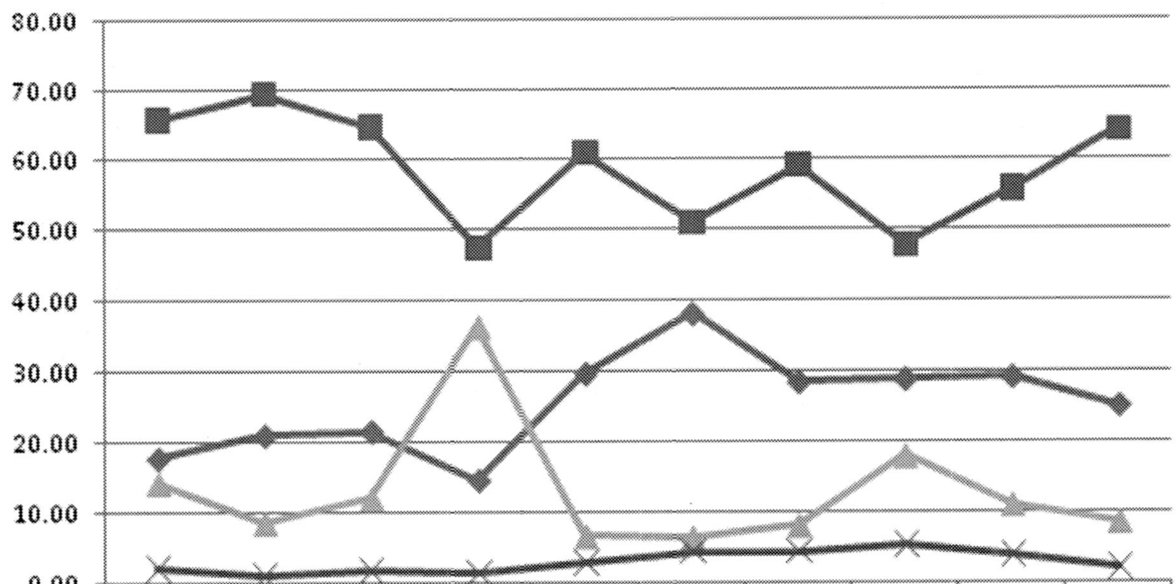

	2003	2004	2005	2006	2007	2008	2009	2010	2011	2012
Raw Materials	17.72	20.96	21.53	14.55	29.75	38.21	28.50	28.90	29.23	25.10
Intermedite Goods	65.75	69.33	64.62	47.51	60.84	50.97	59.02	47.77	55.80	64.15
Consumer Goods	14.25	8.54	11.99	36.37	6.57	6.33	8.04	17.96	11.01	8.54
Capital Goods	2.28	1.17	1.86	1.57	2.84	4.49	4.44	5.38	3.96	2.21

Source: Based on author's estimates from UN Comtrade Data, World Integrated Trade Solution (WITS), World Bank, at wits.worldbank.org.

Figure 5: Tariff Profiles of Pakistan and India

Pakistan

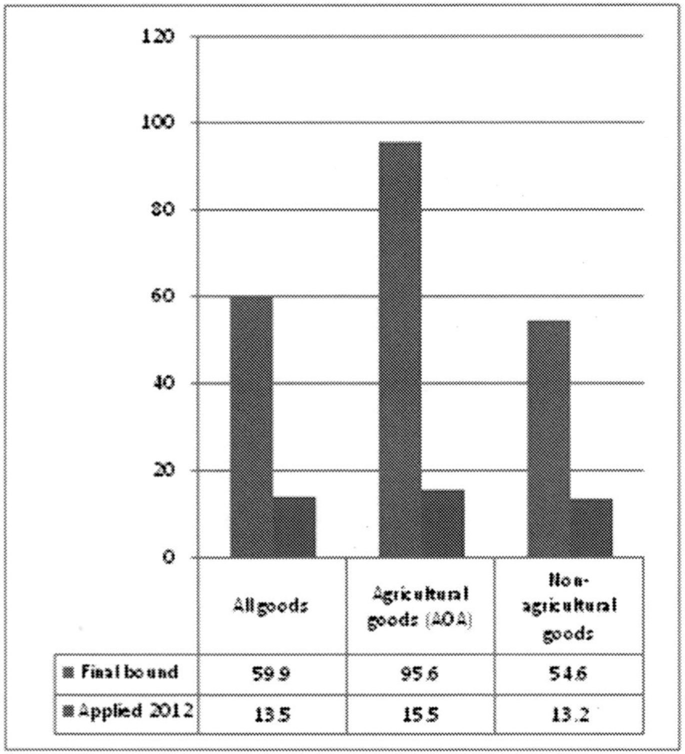

India

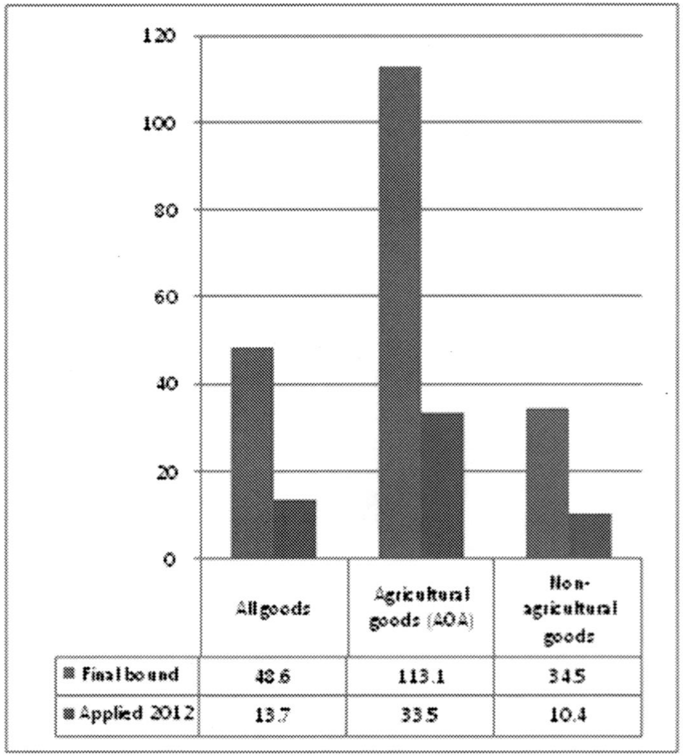

Source: "Tariff Profiles," WTO.

term is quite often used synonymously with Non-Tariff Measures (NTMs). These measures designed to protect health, safety or environment, are quite legitimate under the WTO rules provided they are non-discriminatory as between domestic and third country suppliers and implemented in a transparent manner. When these conditions are not met, these measures could take the shape of barriers.

The NTBs generally go beyond border issues and often extend to trade facilitation measures covering customs clearance procedures, transport and transit infrastructure logistics, etc. To the extent that a cheaper available alternative is not provided when available (e.g., use of port facility or land route), in trader's perception, this could constitute an NTB. There always remains the possibility the when NTMs are not implemented in a transparent manner, or within a reasonably accepted period of time, these could translate to NTBs.

A recent study by the Pakistan Business Council (PBC) expresses concerns of the agricultural lobby and domestic manufacturers, particularly automobiles and pharmaceuticals. With only a limited number of products allowed on the sensitive list under the SAFTA regime, the cheaper Indian products, the study observes, could hurt domestic interests. India, on the other hand, continues to protect its interests with its systematic network of para-tariffs, non-tariff barriers and subsidies, not offering reciprocal treatment to Pakistan.[9]

The PBC study further recommends that the Government of Pakistan as a prelude to trade normalisation with India, establish a strong regulatory and safeguard mechanism and strengthen regulatory bodies such as National Tariff Commission (NTC) and Pakistan Standards and Quality Control Authority (PSQCA) to protect its local interests, while negotiating with the Indian side for a level playing field for Pakistan's exports into the Indian market. Such a level playing field can be achieved if Pakistan's decision to grant MFN/NDMA status to India and opening of the Wagah border for all items is reciprocated by India, categorically addressing its non-tariff barriers that have played a significant role in limiting Pakistan's export potential.[10]

In order to discuss in detail the concerns of Pakistani stakeholders on non-tariff and tariff barriers, a comprehensive discussion, "Nuts and Bolts of Trade Facilitation," was organised in Delhi by Federation of Indian Chambers of Commerce and Industry (FICCI) on September 29, 2011. Participants included Pakistani and Indian business delegates, technical experts, representatives of Indian regulatory bodies and senior government officials. The seminar, according to the feedback received, was most useful in addressing issues raised by businesspersons and in dispelling various misapprehensions. It was clarified that all standards and specifications were non-discriminatory, viz., they applied to all countries exporting goods to India. The discussions also explained how insistence on specific standards by importers was due to commercial considerations and not because of any governmental requirement.[11]

In the 6th Round of India-Pakistan bilateral trade talks held in Delhi from November 14-16, 2011, a special slot was allotted for discussing the 'non-tariff barriers' perceived by the Pakistani side in respect of exports to India in sectors such as textiles, leather, cement, agriculture and surgical instruments.[12] A summary of issues raised and addressed under the comprehensive discussion was appended to the talks under the 6th Round of trade talks. These relate to:

(i) Compulsory certification/long time in renewal of Bureau of Industrial Standards (BIS) for cement
(ii) Opacity of sanitary and phytosanitary (SPS) measures /import permit/ non-availability of labs
(iii) Food products: testing and packaging requirements
(iv) Marking and labelling requirements
(v) Surgical instruments: Indian conformity assessment certificate mark
(vi) Valuation procedure

The Indian side clarified that BIS is mandated to give license within six months and inspection visit has to be completed within one to two months after an application is registered. Delay occurs in cases where the Indian inspection team is not allowed certain site visits owing to security reasons. Moreover, renewal license was being given to all manufacturers who have applied for the same.

Regarding textile consumer protection regulation, it was clarified that testing labs for azo dyes in Mumbai/Delhi were available. A certificate by accredited certification bodies/labs of the Pakistan National Accreditation Council was acceptable.

Regarding marking and labelling, BIS has not prescribed any mandatory standard on textiles. However, marking and labelling is a national requirement.

Regarding SPS measures, the Indian side clarified that fresh fruits and vegetables are tested at the lab at Attari, and all perishables are cleared the same day; further, no delays were being reported. Regarding food products testing and packaging requirements, the Indian side agreed to send a team for educating the exporters as and when a request is made.

Part of the perceived problems arises from underdeveloped consumer protection legislation in Pakistan. While Punjab enacted Consumer Protection Act in 2005, other provinces have yet to enact the same. On SPS risks, there is yet absence of a legal framework for quality control system in its domestic and global markets. A national level authority to deal with harmonised food safety control system is yet to take shape in Pakistan. Inadequate information is another factor.[13]

Concerns of Farmers

A major concern of farmers in Pakistan is that India's agriculture is heavily subsidised and more protective. Liberalising agricultural trade would call to question Pakistani farmers' livelihood concerns. The influential farmers lobby has been most vocal in opposing free trade with India. Their contention is that Pakistan's agriculture would suffer from highly subsidised farm imports from India.

It is contended that the farmers of Pakistan were taken on board while taking the decision to grant MFN status to India. Such a decision should not have been hastily taken without prior cost-benefit analysis of the two countries' respective agricultural subsidies. It appears that the ground reality of Pakistan's apprehensions is somewhat more complex. According to Kugelman, some food producers "actually relish the prospect of acquiring foodstuffs from India because they believe such products will be of higher quality than their own, and hence generate greater profits."[14]

A study sponsored by International Trade Centre (ITC), as part of its Technical Assistance Programme to Pakistan, on "Enhancing Pakistan's Agricultural Sector Exports to India" has brought out that Indian agriculture is more protected than in Pakistan. While India's SAARC Sensitive List contains 122 agricultural products, there are only 57 such products under Pakistan's sensitive list. Further, the average applied and bound tariff rates on agricultural products are substantially higher in India as compared to those applicable in Pakistan. Similarly, subsidies in agriculture are substantially higher in India.[15]

It must be considered here that India's food security programme is not to subsidise exports of food grains, but for the domestic consumption of its impoverished population. In case, Pakistan feels threatened by cheap food imports from India, the solution is not to ban such imports, but to include the same under its sensitive list. A look at notifications issued by the Government of Pakistan shows that out of 16 agricultural products in Pakistan's negative list, eight are already in its sensitive list. The remaining products could likewise be brought under its sensitive list after bilateral negotiations.[16] As suggested under the ITC study, Pakistan could further consider managed trade liberalisation in agricultural trade with India. Before full trade liberalisation in agricultural sector, the study suggests import quota regime under the Pakistan Safeguard Ordinance 2002.[17]

Concerns of Industrialists

Pakistan uses its negative list for restricting its imports from India for avowedly protecting its domestic industries from competition from India. If this objective is followed to its logical conclusion, the country would similarly limit its imports from all competing third countries. The data presented in Table 1 relating Pakistan's imports from China, India and the world shows that no effort has been made to limit such imports. On the contrary, Pakistan's free trade agreement with China offers preferential access to China in those very products restricted to India. The table shows that China is making deeper penetration in Pakistan's market for those very products in Pakistan's negative list. Imports from the world are considerable. Chinese products, under the selected groupings including pharmaceutical products, iron and steel, paper and paper board, electrical machinery, and vehicles, benefiting from restricted entry of Indian goods, are making deeper inroads in Pakistan's industrial market. More notable is that India is suffering a double whammy in respect of products under the grouping organic chemicals and mechanical appliances. While India is prohibited from entering into Pakistan's industrial market, China has been granted duty-free access. A logical consequence of India not getting a level playing ground and China benefiting from first mover advantage is an increase in China's share in Pakistan's industrial market.

Table 1: Pakistan's Imports of Products in its Negative List for India from China, India and World (US$ Million)

Year	*2008*	*2009*	*2010*	*2011*	*2012*	*Remarks*
Organic chemicals (HS 29)						
Import from China	222	276	321	395	371	a
Import from India	456	339	261	373	308	
Import from World	1761	1518	1721	2213	2032	
Pharmaceutical products (HS 30)						
Import from China	40	35	32	31	28	b
Import from India	22	7	22	20	14	
Import from World	433	539	498	534	598	
Iron and steel (HS 72)						
Import from China	216	104	243	268	358	c
Import from India	44	31	29	29	28	
Import from World	1629	1683	1695	1680	1848	
Paper and paperboard (HS 48)						
Import from China	39	52	55	92	85	d
Import from India	1	1	1	1	1	
Import from World	439	377	440	528	467	
Electrical machinery and equipment (HS 85)						
Import from China	1392	990	1245	1366	1741	e
Import from India	18	8	7	7	4	
Import from World	3782	2619	2442	2430	2750	
Vehicles other than railway or tram (HS 87)						
Import from China	80	77	111	152	172	f
Import from India	0	0	0	0	0	
Import from World	1184	969	1308	1502	1583	

Year	*2008*	*2009*	*2010*	*2011*	*2012*	*Remarks*
Nuclear reactors, boilers & mechanical appliances (HS 84)						
Import from China	856	604	802	856	872	g
Import from India	34	33	43	25	23	
Import from World	3943	3140	2962	2978	3084	
All selected products						
Import from China	1989	1534	2008	2304	2755	h
Import from India	540	386	320	430	355	
Import from World	9229	7706	8104	8887	9277	

Here,

a Pakistan offers China duty-free access on 118 products under this category. 30 products under this category are included under Pakistan's negative list for India.

b 23 products under this group are in Pakistan's negative list for India.

c 97 products in this group fall under Pakistan's negative list for India.

d 94 products under this group have been placed under Pakistan's negative list.

e 106 products in this category are in Pakistan's negative list for India

f 180 products in this category are in Pakistan's negative list for India.

g Pakistan has offered China duty-free access on 268 products under this category while keeping 197 such products in its negative list for India.

h This is the total of all the selected negative list products categories.

Note: Most products under the two-digit HS classification are under Pakistan's negative list for India. Pakistan's imports of products under these categories from India are likely to have taken place for those not in the negative list. Besides, sometimes Pakistan relaxes import of products from India even though they are in its negative list.

Source: Based on author's estimates from UN Comtrade Data, World Integrated Trade Solution (WITS), *World Bank*, at wits.worldbank.org.

Figure 6 shows the trend when all the selected product categories in Pakistan's negative list are aggregated. It is observed that overall, while the share of India in Pakistan's world imports for products under its negative list for India has remained stagnant at around 4-6 per cent, the same for China has gone up from 21 per cent to 30 per cent during 2008-12.

Concluding Observations and the Way Forward

Overall tariff incidence in both India and Pakistan is not very dissimilar, both applied and final bound. The ground reality is that while Pakistan imposes lower tariffs on agricultural goods, it imposes higher on non-agricultural goods as compared to India.

Most South Asian countries perceive that India imposes non-tariff barriers on their exports. It has been clarified under official India-Pakistan trade dialogue that all standards and specifications are non-discriminatory as they applied to all countries exporting to India.

Figure 6: Pakistan's Imports of Major Products in its Negative List from China, India and World

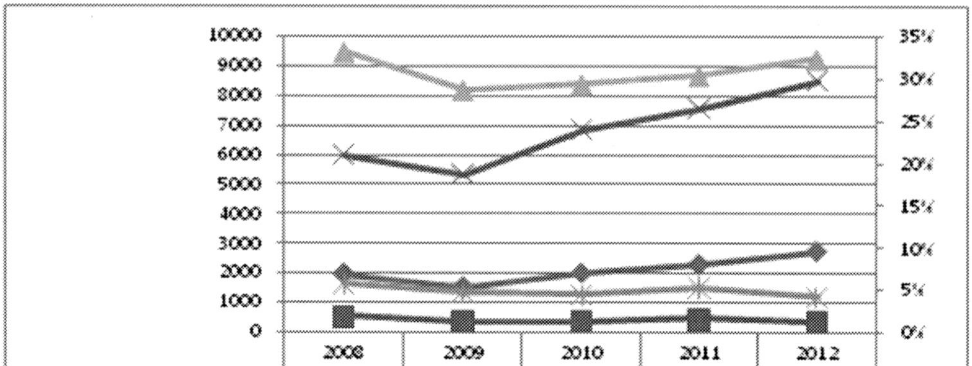

	2008	2009	2010	2011	2012
Import from China	1989	1534	2008	2304	2755
Import from India	540	386	364	461	384
Import from World	9476	8197	8392	8685	9258
% share China	21%	19%	24%	27%	30%
% share India	6%	5%	4%	5%	4%

Source: Based on author's estimates from UN Comtrade Data, World Integrated Trade Solution (WITS), *World Bank*, at wits.worldbank.org.

Consumer protection legislation is still at a formative stage in Pakistan as compared to India, and accordingly, so are standards. The solution lies in Pakistan upgrading its own standards, rather than expecting India to comply lower ones.

It is true that agriculture in India is more protected than in Pakistan and also subsidies are higher. But in India, subsidies are targeted mainly at the domestic poor as a core element of country's food security policy. Rather than ban such imports, Pakistan has the option to negotiate to put such products in its sensitive list, or else apply import quotas on them. If considered necessary, it can, on valid grounds, even raise its applied rates.

Pakistan's concerns for surge in industrial imports of products included in its negative list are misplaced as the country is importing in large quantities the same products from the rest of the world and in particular from China, the latter, in fact, benefiting from its free trade agreement with Pakistan. Here the question of providing India a level playing ground for industrial imports in Pakistan arises similar to Pakistani farmers seeking the same with respect to agricultural imports from India.

The two most prominent NTBs applied by Pakistan on India's exports need to be removed. Under its first NTB, Pakistan needs to move forward in its commitment to grant India NDMA status by dismantling its negative list since its perception of threat of surge in imports from India is highly exaggerated. In sectors where India is competitive, imports from India will only replace more costly imports from third countries. In any event of a sudden surge in imports from India, Pakistan can always apply SAFTA-specific safeguard measures. Under the provisions of the WTO, it can also raise its applied rates so long as they are below the bound ones.

Under its second NTB, Pakistan allows only 176 products to be imported from the Wagah border. As committed, it needs to open up for all products. It also needs to strengthen land customs stations on its side of the border as India has done on its side. In fact, more land and rail routes need to be opened up.

As a means to overcoming India's NTBs, the two countries signed the following three agreements in September of 2012:[18]

(i) Cooperation and Mutual Assistance in Customs Matters;
(ii) Bilateral Cooperation Agreement between BIS and PSQCA; and
(iii) Redressal of Trade Grievances

However, these three agreements are still to be formally implemented.

In final analysis, all bilateral perceptions, including those on trade, are ultimately shaped by the overall relations between the concerned countries. Under very adverse bilateral security environment, quite often the NTMs are likely to be implemented in a more trade restrictive manner translating into the NTBs.

ENDNOTES

1. Under positive list approach, products so listed are permissible for trade, the remaining are banned.
2. The present government of Pakistan has changed this nomenclature to a more politically satisfying Non Discriminatory Market Access (NDMA) connoting the earlier meaning that India would be getting the same market access terms as those being offered to any third country member of the World Trade Organisation (WTO).
3. "Saarc Summit: PM Manmohan Singh Meets Gilani," *The Times of India*, November 10, 2011, at http://timesofindia.indiatimes.com/india/Saarc-summit-PM-Manmohan-Singh-meets-Gilani/articleshow/10676482.cms
4. "SM Krishna to Meet Hina Rabbani Khar Today, Terror Top Agenda," *IBN Live*, July 28, 2011, at http://ibnlive.in.com/news/sm-krishna-to-meet-hina-rabbani-khar-today-terror-top-agenda/289488-3.html
5. "Joint Statement of the 7th Round of Talks on Commercial and Economic Co-operation between Commerce Secretaries of India and Pakistan," *Department of Commerce, Ministry of Commerce & Industry, Government of India*, September 21, 2012, at http://commerce.nic.in/pressrelease/pressrelease_detail.asp?id=2978
6. Ibid.
7. Ibid., para 12.
8. Under WTO rules a member country is permitted to raise its applied tariffs up to the maximum permissible limit of its bound rate in case of a sudden surge in imports threatening its domestic industry/agriculture.

9. "Preliminary Analysis of Pakistan India Trade and a Viable Roadmap for Trade Liberalization," *Pakistan Business Council* (PBC), at http://pbc.org.pk/preliminary-analysis-of-pakistan-india-trade-and-a-viable-roadmap-for-trade-liberalization
10. Ibid.
11. "Joint Statement of the 6th Round of Talks on Commercial and Economic Co-operation between Commerce Secretaries of India and Pakistan," *Department of Commerce, Government of India,* November 15, 2011, at http://commerce.nic.in/writereaddata/pressrelease/Joint_Statement_India_Pak_Round6th.pdfand "India Pakistan Trade Talks: India, Pakistan Make Rapid Progress in Round 6," *FIEO News*, December 2011, at http://www.fieomail.org/uploads/files/1323671993ojut97ii3d1lesd4lu20q0v2r5India-Pakistan.pdf
12. Ibid.
13. *Trade Time*, 2 (2), Quarterly Newsletter, Trade Related Technical Assistance (TRTA II) Programme, ITC and WIPO, June 2012, at http://trtapakistan.org/wp-content/uploads/2012/05/TRADE-TIME-5.pdf
14. Michael Kugelman and Robert M. Hathaway (eds.), *Pakistan-India Trade: What Needs to be Done? What Does It Matter?*, Wilson Centre, 2013.
15. "Enhancing Pakistan's Agricultural Sector Exports to India," *EU funded TRTA II Programme*, International Trade Centre (ITC), Islamabad, 2012, at http://www.academia.edu/5125748/enhancing_pakistans_agricultural_sector_exports_to_india_trade_related_technical_assistance_programme_the_ programme_is_implemented_by_unido_in_association
16. List of items not importable from India (negative list), *Trade Development Authority of Pakistan*, at http://www.tdap.gov.pk/pdf/SRO-280-I-2012.pdf and Pakistan's Revised Sensitive List under SAFTA, December 12, 2011, at http://saarc-sec.org/uploads/document/07%20Pakistan%20-%20Revised%20Sensitive%20List%20(Phase-II)_20120319120622.pdf
17. Ibid.
18. no. 5.

16

Seizing New Opportunity for Regional Cooperation and Understanding

Shahmahmood Miakhel

History writing in every age is a biased operation. This is because no historian, no matter how much they try, can be free of all bias. Therefore, there are different versions and books on history, since if one could write an 'unbiased' and 'objective' version of history, all the other historians would be out of business.[1]

Introduction

Myths and (mis)perceptions are invisible and inseparable parts of eastern culture, especially within South Asia. Unfortunately, South Asian politicians have often turned to exploiting historical myths and misperceptions within the region in order to divert the attention of people from the real problems. While this may be an effective populist tool for re-election or consolidation of power, it has historically led to a fractured regional politics.

In a conference organised in 2012 by the National University of Singapore, I had spoken about myths and perceptions about Afghans amongst the international community, and vice versa.[2] It is important to mention that these myths have not only become a part of the popular narrative, but have also significantly influenced policy formulation, albeit negatively. As the former Interior Minister of Afghanistan Ali Ahmad Jalali once said, "The Afghan government and international community are both partners in Afghanistan, but unfortunately neither side understands the other very well."

Fortunately, the 7th Annual South Asia Conference organised by the Institute for Defence Studies and Analyses (IDSA) was dedicated to exploring regional perceptions in South Asia. I strongly believe that these myths and (mis)perceptions have had an adverse impact on security, economic growth, governance and regional cooperation amongst all the regional states. Changing these deleterious perceptions will depend on sincere efforts by political leaders and elites of the respective countries to work towards removing unsubstantiated allegations against each other. Politicians and elites of the region should justify their argument and policies based on the needs of the 21st century, and not on the myths and perception of the past. South Asia's political leaders must move away from the rhetoric of the Cold War or the old Great Game in the region, and look towards developing a new political culture that embraces modern challenges as well as opportunities for the region. The regional leadership must move away from the politics of blaming neighbours and foreigners for their failure to provide good governance and stability in their respective countries. There is a strong need for elites and politicians of the region to change their mindset.

In this paper, I will share a few examples of (mis)perceptions since 2001 about Afghanistan's relationship with India and Pakistan. I believe the key to improving relationship among states in our region lie in improving governance in each of the countries, and an increased role of a new generation of leaders who have the energy and the vision to look at the region from a fresh and new perspective.

Historical Background about Afghanistan and India

India and Afghanistan are distant neighbours, but have enjoyed very close historical, cultural, economic and political ties over the centuries. Since the inception of Pakistan in 1947, successive Afghan governments have had much stronger relations with India compared to Pakistan. Even people-to-people relationship between Afghanistan and India was strong till the 1978 coup in Afghanistan. Both the countries were members of the Non-Aligned Movement (NAM), and had close relationship with the former Soviet Union as well. At the time when India and Afghanistan were looking up to the Soviet Union, Pakistan was part of the Southeast Asia Treaty Organisation (SEATO) and Central Treaty Organisation (CENTO)[3] and had close links with the US and other Western countries.

The dynamics of the India-Afghanistan relationship changed after the coup of 1978 and the Soviet invasion of Afghanistan in 1979. Millions of Afghans rose against the Soviet occupation and millions immigrated to Pakistan and other regional countries. Pakistan's influence in Afghanistan affairs increased, while India's influence declined as it supported unpopular communist regimes until 1992 when the government led by President Najibullah finally collapsed.

Before 1978, traditionally, India had close ties with Pashtuns on both the sides of the Durand Line and supported Afghanistan's Pashtunistan policy towards Pakistan. During the partition, Mahatma Gandhi and Bacha Khan (Khan Abdul Ghafar Khan) had close ties and supported the Pashtun cause.

After the collapse of the Najibullah Government in 1992, India was in an odd position because most of the Pashtun groups were then supported by Pakistan, and India had shifted its support to the non-Pashtun groups, such as the Northern Alliance. Pakistan used this relationship as a tool of propaganda to support the Taliban inside Afghanistan, which analysts and experts argue still continues in the form of support to a select group of Taliban insurgents, while at the same time portraying itself as a supporter of Pashtun nationalist movement. In reality, the rivalry between India and Pakistan has had a considerably negative impact on the stability of Afghanistan.

After 2001, India pledged its support to the new government led by President Hamid Karzai and took an active part in rebuilding of Afghanistan. Today, India is the fifth largest bilateral donor in Afghanistan and its assistance totals up to $2 billion.[4]

Some activities of India in western or south-eastern parts of the country might have alarmed Pakistan, but in most cases these concerns are exaggerated. Pakistan has publicly criticised India's large presence in the country and has raised its concerns with Afghan authorities in various forums. At one point, there were even exaggerated reports coming from Pakistan claiming that India has 32 consulates in Afghanistan.[5] This exaggeration about India's presence in Afghanistan was rooted in historical mistrust and misperception between these two countries, and was not based on reality and facts. Rather, it is based more on strategic depth policy between India and Afghanistan since the inception of Pakistan. There is no doubt that the difficult relationship between India and Pakistan has a direct impact on peace, stability and economic growth of Afghanistan. Though free trade and transit between Afghanistan, Pakistan and India would benefit the people in the region, but due to the past hostilities, myths and misperceptions there has been very little progress on the issue and, as a result, millions of people continue to suffer from poverty. William Dalrymple, the British historian, had aptly titled his article published in *The Guardian*, "Forget NATO v the Taliban. The real Afghan fight is India v Pakistan."[6]

Relationship of India with Afghanistan and Reaction of Pakistan Since 2001

As mentioned before, Pakistan is very suspicious about India's presence in Afghanistan. I have seen these reactions first hand during various track two and track one-and-a-half dialogues between Afghanistan, Pakistan and India, which I have attended since 2008.[7] Pakistan's argument is that India would like to support anti-Pakistani elements in Afghanistan, especially Balochistan Liberation Army (BLA), a separatist movement in Pakistan. Most recently, the ministry of foreign affairs of Pakistan openly stated that such outstanding issues as India's interference in Baluchistan, needs to be addressed. But India denies Pakistan's claim and has stated repeatedly that they are involved in Afghanistan at the behest of the Afghan Government to contribute to its reconstruction and rebuilding efforts. Undoubtedly, India's assistance is very diverse in nature—supporting agriculture, civil service commission, hydroelectric lines from Tajikistan and Uzbekistan, scholarship programmes, and road construction and so on. However, at the same time, Pakistan sees India's involvement in Afghanistan as an attempt to enhance its strategic depth. Pakistanis are especially very suspicious about India's projects close to the borders of Pakistan, such as building Zarang-Dilaram road. Pakistanis were always suspicious about India's soft power projects such as scholarship programmes and support to the civil service commission. In fact, offering military assistance and training to the Afghan National Security Forces (ANSF) in the long run may increase India's influence in Afghanistan.

Therefore, Pakistan has repeatedly requested the Afghan Government to allow it to support the same kind of programmes such as offering scholarship, training of the ANSF and involvement in other key areas. Moreover, it has even encouraged Afghanistan to cut ties with India and instead sign a strategic partnership agreement with Pakistan.[8] But the government of Afghanistan has been reluctant to send Afghan students or ANSF personnel for training to Pakistan or sign a strategic partnership with Pakistan.

In July 2004, after long discussions among the leadership of Afghanistan, the then Interior Minister Ali Ahmad Jalali visited Pakistan and agreed to send some token number of Afghan police personnel for training there. However, Pakistan always wanted a more robust relationship. Even though the Afghan Government was ready to have a better relationship with Pakistan, but due to worsening security situation in the country since 2005, it openly began blaming Pakistan for supporting and harbouring Taliban. Pakistan constantly denied these accusations. Though many high level meetings between Afghanistan and Pakistan took place in various countries, mediated by the US, the UK, Turkey and other countries, but to no effect.

Many examples illustrate that some of the engagements between Afghanistan and India are based on reactions from Pakistan. In October 2011, when India and Afghanistan signed the Strategic Partnership Agreement,[9] Pakistan was alarmed. Just few days before, the Chairman of High Peace Council Burhanudin Rabbani was killed by a suicide bomber at his residence in Kabul. Afghanistan openly stated that the assassination plot was planned in Pakistan.[10] Additionally, Pakistan wanted Afghanistan to sign a strategic partnership agreement, but there has been no progress to date.[11] The signing of the partnership agreement between India and Afghanistan and Rabbani's assassination may have been a mere coincidence, but Afghans perceived it as a plot originating from Pakistan. As a result, it further contributed to negative perception about Pakistan. At the same time, when the security situation got tense after skirmishes between Afghanistan and Pakistan at a border post in the eastern Goshta District, President Karzai visited India and asked for lethal and non-lethal arms.[12] Again, many interpreted Karzai's request as openly hedging bets on hostile matters, such as the Durand Line, and instigating negative view against Pakistan.

Peace and reconciliation with Taliban is another sensitive issue. Pakistan has been trying to keep it on the top of the agenda and is open to dialogue with Afghanistan, but India has always been concerned about these talks, especially with the Haqqani network.[13]

Pakistan sees strong relationship between Afghanistan and India against its strategic interest. Moreover, there are several other unresolved issues between Afghanistan and Pakistan, such as Durand Line, trade and transit and water issues. In order to improve the relationship between these two countries, there is a need for direct negotiation. Pakistan sees the current scenario in Afghanistan as a golden opportunity to approach these contentious issues, thinking that the Afghan Government is in a weak position and may accept its terms and conditions. However, a key factor that may hinder such efforts is lack of strong support for the current Afghan Government within the country.

Conclusion

There is a famous saying that you can pick your friends, but not your neighbours. By default, each country has close and distant neighbours. One thing that the three neighbours—Afghanistan, India and Pakistan—might agree is that the instability in Afghanistan will have an adverse impact on the entire region. For the three countries to reject the status quo and improve perceptions about each other, sustained dialogue is the essence. Continued bloodshed in Afghanistan has impacted millions of lives in the region. The recent wave of terrorism resulting in loss of thousands of innocent lives in Pakistan, and collective Pakistan-Indian concerns about violence in Kashmir and Balochistan, will not serve either country's interests.

It is important to steer the region towards peace in the post-2014 period. While Western forces will withdraw, Afghanistan, Pakistan and India must seize the opportunity that would follow to work together. The three countries must enter into a sincere dialogue and address even the most contentious of issues, such as the role of the Taliban in Afghanistan and the border disputes, and shift the focus to working towards the economic prosperity of the region. If the three neighbours miss this opportunity to restart negotiations, it will further reinforce negative perceptions in the region and people will continue to view each other from the prism of suspicion.

ENDNOTES

1. Yaqoob Bangash, "Historical Myths and Realities," *The News International*, September 15, 2013, at http://jang.com.pk/thenews/sep2013-weekly/nos-15-09-2013/pol1.htm#1.
2. The proceedings of the conference were published as a book. See Shahmahmood Miakhel, "Myths and Impact of Bad Governance on Stability in Afghanistan," in Shanthie Mariet D'Souza (ed.), *Afghanistan in Transition: Beyond 2014?*, Pentagon Press, New Delhi, 2012.
3. Mohammed Ayub Khan, "The Pakistan-American Alliance," *Foreign Affairs*, January 1964, at http://www.foreignaffairs.com/articles/23567/mohammed-ayub-khan/the-pakistan-american-alliance (Accessed September 12, 2013).
4. "India-Afghanistan Relations," *Indian Ministry of External Affairs*, August 2012, at http://mea.gov.in/Portal/ForeignRelation/afghanistan-aug-2012.pdf (Accessed September 12, 2013).
5. Anita Joshua, "Indian 'Consulates' Theory Incorrect: Pakistan," *The Hindu*, March 22, 2013, at http://www.thehindu.com/news/international/indian-consulates-theory-incorrect-pakistan/article3155622.ece (Accessed September 12, 2013).
6. William Dalrymple, "Forget Nato v the Taliban. The real Afghan fight is India v Pakistan," *The Guardian*, June 26, 2013, at http://www.theguardian.com/commentisfree/2013/jun/26/nato-taliban-india-pakistan
7. "Islam, Politics and Security in South Asia" (Afghanistan, Pakistan, India and Bangladesh),Track one-and-a-half annual meetings supported by IISS-NESA; Track Two Dialogue between Afghanistan, Pakistan and India, supported by The Delhi Policy Group; and Ottawa Dialogue between Afghanistan, Pakistan and India, supported by University of Ottawa, Canada.
8. Anita Joshua, "Pakistan Denies Asking Afghanistan to Snap Ties with India,"*The Hindu*, March 29, 2013, at http://www.thehindu.com/news/international/south-asia/pakistan-denies-asking-afghanistan-to-snap-ties-with-india/article4562463.ece (Accessed October 05, 2013).
9. "India-Afghanistan Sign Strategic Partnership Agreement," *Outlook*, October 04, 2011, at http://news.outlookindia.com/items.aspx?artid=737276 (Accessed October 05, 2013).
10. Ghanizada, "Rabbani's Assassination Plotted in Pakistan," *Khaama Press*, September 25, 2011, at http://www.khaama.com/rabbanis-assassination-plotted-in-pakistan (Accessed October 05, 2013).
11. Ali Hussain, "Security matters: Pakistan, Afghan parliamentary panels hold talks today," *Business Recorder*, September 10, 2013, at http://www.brecorder.com/general-news/172:pakistan/1229658:security-matters:-pakistan-afghan-parliamentary-panels-hold-talks-today?date=2013-09-10 (Accessed October 07, 2013).
12. "Karzai's Wishlist," *The Indian Express*, May 23, 2013, at http://www.indianexpress.com/news/karzais-wishlist/1119306/ (Accessed October 05, 2013).
13. Indrani Bagchi, "Afghan peace talks: India voices concern," *The Times of India*, June 21, 2013, at http://timesofindia.indiatimes.com/india/Afghan-peace-talks-India-voices-concern/articleshow/20704621.cms?referral=PM. Also, see Indrani Bagchi, "India wary as Haqqanis may join peace process," *The Times of India*, June 21, 2013, at http://timesofindia.indiatimes.com/world/south-asia/India-wary-as-Haqqanis-may-join-peace-process/articleshow/20692396.cms? (Accessed October 07, 2013).

The Way Forward: Key Recommendations

In this section, key recommendations have been collated based on the proceedings and outcomes of the roundtable discussion* held among key country participants in the Concluding Session of the 7th South Asia Conference.

It was pointed out that perceptions are influenced and shaped by diverse factors in the region. Perceptions prevalent within and among countries in the region are mixed and there is no one or single dominant determining factor. However, negative perceptions outweigh positive perceptions in the region, a fact that has to be factored in while addressing issues pertaining regional integration and cooperation. In general terms, negative perceptions or misperceptions are preponderant and play a crucial role in shaping inter-state relations, particularly vis-à-vis India.

Key reasons broadly identified for negative or misperceptions prevalent within the region are:

(i) Historical memories or baggage from the past. Contesting identities, conflicting histories and unresolved border disputes have distorted perceptions in the region.
(ii) Internal developments in countries grappling with political and social transition.
(iii) Poor knowledge about the region and of each other particularly among the youth.

---

*The roundtable discussion in the Concluding Session of the conference, held on October 31, 2013, was moderated by the then Director General, IDSA, Dr. Arvind Gupta. Key country participants were Dr. Yaqoob Khan Bangash (Pakistan), Mr. Shahmahmood Miakhel (Afghanistan), Dr. Dayan Jayatilleka (Sri Lanka), Ambassador Humayun Kabir (Bangladesh), Ambassador Phae Thann Oo (Myanmar), Ambassador Dinesh Bhattarai (Nepal), Mr. Pema Tenzin (Bhutan) and Dr. Ashok Kumar Behuria (India).

(iv) India's failure to respond to several aspirations in the region in keeping with its size and preponderance which remains an unavoidable fact.
(v) Failure of regional integration due to India's inability to deliver on promises and agreements has seriously dented its image among its neighbours.
(vi) Negative role of media in creating and reinforcing myths and misperceptions.
(vii) Social media often contributes to creating misunderstandings at a much rapid pace than the print media.
(viii) Lack of media coverage to positive stories coming out from the region, stories of various achievements and growing people-to-people contacts.
(ix) China's increasing footprint is changing perceptions in the region particularly vis-à-vis India, which is largely perceived both as a reluctant power and an unsteady partner in its neighbourhood.

KEY RECOMMENDATIONS

Following are some of the key takeaways from the roundtable discussion which may be of policy as well as academic relevance:

Need to Nurture Public Intellectuals

Public intellectuals are a key constituency and must be nurtured. As South Asia becomes more democratic, rather than less, the role of public opinion becomes more salient. The role of opinion makers, the opinion moulders and thought leaders become absolutely strategic in such a scenario. It is lamentable that despite greater connectivity, due to huge advancement in the field of information technology, there was a greater degree of commonality and mutual acquaintance between opinion makers and intellectuals of the earlier generation than the present one.

The previous generation of public intellectuals in India's neighbouring countries were often educated in Indian universities and would return to their countries with greater understanding of India and its philosophy. There are still some such inter-connections but those are on the fringes such as the cultural intelligentsia and university academics. If a university academic is also a public intellectual, i.e., someone with significant national audience, then she/he has to be counted as one. A singer or a film maker or a newspaper editor, who has a national audience and someone who is read by the elite of the country, should also be regarded as a critical/target constituency. The connectivity among these constituencies, which somehow existed in previous decades, has now thinned out.

There is an urgent need to explore why it has happened and how to address it. If the countries of the region could collectively address the issues and re-grow the connectivity among the public intellectuals in the region, then the region will also have a common corpus of ideas and concepts and develop a common South Asian discourse, which in turn can lead to a common idea of and for the region. An idea of not only what it is to be an Afghan, a Sri Lankan, a Pakistani, or an Indian, but also a South Asian, just as there was an idea of what it was to be European, long before the idea of European Union was conceptualised. That is the trajectory that the region must get back on.

Need for Clarity in India's Policy

There is a need for greater clarity in India's foreign and security policy. India is generally seen as a reluctant power by its neighbours. This view was generally endorsed. It was pointed out that this is not only in the context of South Asia, but also at the wider global level where often questions on what exactly is India's strategy, what does India see for itself, what role India is going to play in international relations, and why India is unable to come up with a clear position or mission statement on its security and foreign policy, are bring asked. The continuing ambiguity about India's security and military policy often reinforces misperceptions in its neighbourhood.

It was also argued that after making a good start in bilateral relations and emphasising on non-reciprocal relationship often India develops a 'statist mindset' or 'statist perspective', which makes it difficult for India as well as the neighbouring countries to sustain the momentum of their engagement.

India Should Take the Lead

By and large there is positive perception about India's rising stature and profile in the region and also at the global level including in the Indian Ocean Region. India's reach is now not just confined to South Asia. To create positive perceptions, India should be helping neighbouring countries to build their capacities but at the same time should not be seen as interfering. India's soft power is well acknowledged in the region and could go a long way in a creating a more positive perception about India. India must expand the scope of its soft power in its neighbourhood. India must take the lead in initiating joint reconstruction projects with its neighbours.

There are diverse views about India in the region. In some cases, there are clearly very negative perceptions. Nevertheless, there was consensus among participants that a rising India, a more sensitive, capable and strong India, will create positive perceptions in the region. India should not be reluctant to use its leverages in a positive way. South Asia is perceived as one of the least integrated, highly deprived, and also one of the most militarised regions in the world. If we have to correct perceptions or misperceptions, we will have to focus on, and collectively address, socio-economic issues, particularly poverty, harnessing of natural resources including water resources which are abundant. None of this would be possible unless India takes the lead.

It was also argued that democracy is a precondition to several contentious issues in the region. When democracy brings people to the centre of governance, it goes a long way in correcting perceptions. India's democratic strength and credentials also add to its soft power in its neighbourhood.

India's Global Reach is Beneficial for the Region

India has always had some sort of global reach including in the Indian Ocean Region. Global image of India has always been there and it worked to a great extent for a long time. That kind of an idea where India can take its neighbours along as it used to in earlier times need to be resurrected.

Even under the British, India had lot of influence in and around West Asia, Africa and Southeast Asia. If that is tapped into, things can go forward and India can become a much stronger world power with a much clearer vision and with a lot more comfortable neighbours. At the moment, neighbours are apprehensive about the way India is moving ahead. If India would choose to bring transparency into its strategic outlook and let it be communicated effectively, things will get better between India and its neighbours.

India Must Reassure and Intellectually Support Pakistan

For some reasons, there is a perception among a section of people in Pakistan that India hasn't yet accepted its existence. It was suggested that India must keep reassuring Pakistan that it has accepted its existence. Unilateral concessions are often not taken as something positive. Pakistanis often think Indians want to undo the partition. Former Prime Minister Atal Behari Vajpayee's visit to Minar-e Pakistan is cited in Pakistan as a lone positive move on the part of India, which needs reiteration given the extreme insecurity persisting in Pakistan about Indian behaviour for all the wrong reasons.

Pakistanis do understand that 2008 Mumbai attacks were India's 9/11 which really changed India's attitude towards them. However, what is lacking from the Indian side is the understanding that Pakistan itself is the largest victim of these terrorist groups. They are now carrying out attacks both against the armed forces and the civilian population in an indiscriminate manner and tearing into the social and political fabric of the country. Pakistan has lost to a large extent its ability to control several such groups which it had helped create. They have become

Frankenstein's monsters and are posing a serious threat to the very existence of the country. This is something that needs to be understood more from the Indian side. Perhaps, there is a need to explore how India could help Pakistan in this regard. India should at least render intellectual support in terms of ideas to deal with terrorism, which would go a long way in building bridges with the people of Pakistan and diluting negative perceptions about India.

The strength of India-Pakistan relationship lies in helping Pakistan strengthen its position against several odds that it is faced with. India's intellectual support could go a long way in helping Pakistan handle its threats better. A more destabilised Pakistan would affect India badly. A more stable Pakistan means a less violence-prone and less-extremist Pakistan, which is likely to change its outlook, if India were to contribute to its stability and growth.

Provincialise Contacts at Sub-regional Level

To further strengthen India-Pakistan relations, it was suggested that there is a need to provincialise lot of issues. Both Indian and Pakistani Punjab(s) want to cooperate on several issues. Students exchange at college and university levels, for instance between Lahore University and Panjab University in Chandigarh, and provoncialising contacts at a lower level where it is more possible, where lot of things can move positively, can help change entrenched negative perceptions. Indian universities must open up to students aspiring to come to India for higher education from Pakistan. This would further boost India's soft power and help develop a constituency for peace and greater understanding among the youth.

Engage Media

There is a need to engage media in a more robust and meaningful manner. Role of media including social media is very critical in reshaping and correcting misperceptions. Media must give wider coverage to positive stories coming out from the region, including on growing people-to-people contacts. Joint ventures among leading media groups whether at the bilateral, trilateral or multilateral levels could play a significant role in dispelling misperceptions and in building peace constituencies in the region.

Specific reference was also made to lack of media coverage to the news and developments pertaining SAARC. This often creates confusion and somewhere it has also reinforced the perception that SAARC is irrelevant. Therefore, there is a need for greater dissemination of information regarding several initiatives taken at the level of SAARC and achievements made by its various bodies over the years.

At the same time, it was argued that we are depending too much on media and are often misguided and misled by negative reporting. As it is difficult to manage media which is a very dynamic and vibrant sector, perhaps, a more institutional approach to disseminating correct information and countering disinformation is required. One way of doing this is to establish more research centres and country chairs in universities across the region. It was stated that there is not a single research centre on India Studies in the neighbouring countries. This remains a major missing link in the region.

It was also suggested that South Asia needs a common perception survey mechanism to gauge changing perceptions. Pew Global Research Centre, which does various kinds of survey and in several countries and regions across the world, was cited as an example. Establishing something like Pew Centre in South Asia was proposed which could be a good tracking mechanism to see how people are thinking, which policies are working and how and what policy adjustments need to be made.

Address Gaps in Bilateral Relations

It was stated citing India-Bangladesh relations that although concept-wise the bilateral relationship is well woven into the psyche of the people in both the countries, there are still major gaps which both sides have not been able to address. How to rectify gaps in bilateral relations, remains a major challenge. Similar observations were made about India and its other neighbours including India and Nepal where often there is no clarity on each other's policy. Often neighbouring countries too do not have anything called 'India Policy'. At the broader regional level, the big concept of how regional countries want to look at South Asia is important. India is definitely the leader in the region and both India and its neighbours would have to find ways to overcome gaps in their bilateral engagements.

It was also suggested that there is a need to look beyond the rhetoric of politicians and foreign services officials. Unless clarity and consistency in foreign policy is enhanced, it will have no credibility. Foreign policy goals should be pursued through institutional approach particularly in view of emergence and rise of various illegitimate actors trying to determine bilateral relations.

Gujral Doctrine Stays Relevant

The value and relevance of the Gujral Doctrine was repeatedly referred to. It was said that the doctrine resonated through every section of society and was welcome by all in South Asia. It was generally endorsed and accepted in India's neighbourhood. None of the successive Indian governments abandoned the Gujral Doctrine. They simply modified it and without using the same name continued to follow the principles of the doctrine. But the question is why are we so hesitant in telling our neighbours as to what we want or expect from each other. If we have a set of ground rules we know what we expect from each other and based on that set up our relationship and move forward. In that case, lot of confusion and misperception that often clouds the relationship could be avoided or removed.

Economy Should Drive Foreign Policy

It was further stated that South Asia region has entered into a new phase of relationship with the rise of India. India is now an upcoming economy, an emerging giant, and would definitely play a positive role in the context of economic relationship with neighbouring countries. South Asia has a huge population and is itself a big market. It presents several mutually beneficial opportunities, which need to be explored.

India has been trying to advance economic tools to consolidate or improve its relationship with its neighbours, but there also India is kind of hesitant. Economy should be the driver and India could be more generous in dealing with its smaller and immediate neighbours. However, it was pointed out that strict reciprocity should not be insisted upon given the asymmetry.

Create Peace Constituencies

There is also a need for creating peace constituencies in the region by strengthening people-to-people contacts. The states can help through relaxation of visa regimes, encouraging more and more of dialogue and interaction.

Often bilateral relations in South Asia, for instance between India and Nepal, are premised and founded on people-to-people relations. It is regular and healthy interaction among the people that promotes cohesion and removes misunderstanding.

Shared cultural values should be duly acknowledged and used as an asset by the countries of the region to build people-to-people contact. It should not be manipulated to divide people along sectarian, ethnic and religious lines.

Peace education should be integrated into the school syllabus and college systems. Peace tours among school children of different countries of the region could be useful in dispelling misperceptions among the youth.

The idea of regionalisation of the UN peacekeeping and whether it can come on the SAARC charter may be explored.

Develop Diplomatic Capacities

It was pointed out that the diplomatic corps of regional countries are not well prepared to deal with several complex challenges of the 21st century. The foreign policy establishment of respective countries must reinforce their diplomatic capacities both quantitatively and qualitatively.

Familiarise Youth about South Asia

The issue of lack of common socialisation process in the region was highlighted by several participants. It was said that there are different discourses on the issue among South Asia countries. At the SAARC level, countries have been talking last few years about harmonising of syllabuses, acceptance of degrees at regional level, but there is a need to go down perhaps at the school and college level and assess how youth are looking at the region. There is no such mechanism whereby socialisation among youth in the region could be coordinated.

It is important to take into account the fact that South Asia has a huge young and enterprising population. It was stated that nearly 1700 youth everyday on an average leave Nepal for various reasons. They are in different settings and often come back with a different exposure, understanding and orientation. Youth also often question the traditional relationship among countries of the region. It is important to make them understand our traditional relationship. The region cannot afford to ignore its youth population and needs to collectively address issues relating to them urgently.

In history textbooks in some of the countries, often India does not exist, even neighbourhood does not exist. Same is the issue with the Indian textbooks. We need to look at how are we going to familiarise our younger generation, who would be different and operating in a different context than the present generation. How are we going to groom them, what kind of information we need to provide to them. If we could do some work on coordinating school syllabus, study tours, etc., it would be a good idea to work on.

Similar sentiments prevail among youth in Myanmar, which in the past shared close cultural and political and economic linkages with India. The present generation in Myanmar think that they belong to Southeast Asia just because Myanmar is a member of ASEAN. They do not know much about SAARC, BIMSTEC or South Asia. They know much more about ASEAN though Myanmar was initially reluctant to join it. New generation tend to look further towards Southeast and East Asia particularly Japan, Korea and China.

Myanmar belongs to the eastern part of South Asia. Like in old days, Myanmar would like to consider itself as a member of South Asia and intensify not only government-to-government but also people-to-people contacts particularly with India and Bangladesh. India can play a very constructive role through Myanmar in Southeast Asia. However, India has been a reluctant partner compared to China.

Myanmar does not see speedy and actual realisation of India's Look East Policy (LEP).

There is a perception that South Asian countries tend to look more westwards as was the case in previous centuries. India has a huge soft power in view of its old cultural and religious linkages with countries in Southeast Asia. Training in English language and exchange of students could further boost India's soft power in the Southeast Asia region. At the moment, majority of ministers in Southeast Asian countries are graduates from Australia which plays a role in shaping perceptions about that country in the region.

Improve Air Connectivity

Improving air connectivity within the region was said to be critical to building people-to-people contact at grassroots level and thereby perception management. There are either no direct flights or the frequency of flights are low between various regions in South Asia. Still there are no direct flights between India and Myanmar (one has to travel via Bangkok, Kuala Lumpur or even Singapore). It was reiterated by several participants that stronger intra-regional connectivity is essential to building trust and confidence at the regional level.

Change of Mindset

When the gap between reality and rhetoric increases, the results could be disastrous. Even a small incident could stir negative perceptions. The South Asian countries would have to shed their historical baggage which has led to certain mindsets which need to be changed. It was argued that though mindsets are products of history, but it is possible to change mindsets without compromising our respective national interests. Reference was made to the Maoists in Nepal who had submitted a 40-point demand in 1996 in which nine points directly related to the India-Nepal relations. They talked of American imperialism and Indian expansionism and had called for abrogation of even the 1950 Indo-Nepal Treaty. But such is not case with their latest manifestos where hardly such things are mentioned.

Strengthen Informal Channels Within SAARC

It was stated that SAARC has a very productive and meaningful window, and that is retreat. SAARC has not been able to hold even such informal meetings. The grouping has missed 11 such meetings between leaders in retreats which are held in an informal way.

Common Regional Approach Against Terrorism

There is a need to study and enhance our understanding of various dimensions of security. There is a changing concept of security which the region needs to understand. Nearly all South Asian countries have suffered on account of terrorism and some have long been victims of various forms of terrorism. The region must have common approaches in dealing with terrorism, drug trafficking, smuggling, etc. Terrorism must be condemned in all its forms and manifestations. However, this is not possible without clarity and consistency in the foreign policy of the regional countries.

Factor in China

Rise of China has to be factored into the broader regional discourse. China has grown phenomenally in profile and influence. Today it is the world's second largest economy and in close proximity to South Asia. China's rise is not without geo-political implications which need to be scrutinised and studied by all South Asian countries.

Promote Inter-cultural Learning

Though South Asia is a region of contested histories, of unresolved borders and protracted rivalries, and that regional countries are haunted by negative perceptions of each other, but the discussions revealed a huge consensus on the need to find a way out. The common urge to rid the region of misperceptions or negative perceptions itself could be seen as a positive perception. It was reiterated again and again that countries and people need to talk to each other and try to reshape perceptions about one another.

It was pointed out that IDSA has been organising South Asia conferences for the last seven years, and if one looks at the outcome of each of them, there is not much difference among them. But what is reassuring is the fact that even if same things are being said again and again, there is a deeper conviction that we all are thinking the same thing the same way. That way we are all together in this struggle to make a better South Asia and with a stronger regional consciousness. The geo-political reality is changing and if the regional countries do not work together, the world is not going to help the region.

Gradually, people in general and from different walks of life, economists, politicians, historians and businessman, all are realising the need for each of us to know more about the other. There is a value in inter-cultural learning and greater interaction provides an impetus to our inherent instinct to know each other in better ways. Informal meetings and discussions play a big role in dispelling myths and negative perceptions about each other. South Asians live in a larger common cultural matrix that people may not be aware of. There is a value in coming together and discussing contentious issues again and again. It provides an opportunity to convince ourselves of our own convictions.

Changing the 'Governmentality'

Reference to the term 'governmentality' was made in the context of 'statist mindset' that India's political and bureaucratic elite often display in their approach to neighbouring countries. It is not something limited to South Asia region alone. People in other regions and parts of the world too often allege that they are victims of 'governmentality'. However, it was argued that it is important to understand and shape 'governmentalities' as it too is informed and influenced by prevalent perceptions.

There is thus a value in changing perceptions. It was further stated that there is a contention among two different points of view. Many people are of the view that since conflicts and differences among nations creates negative perception of each other, so the conflicts and tensions have to be resolved before perceptions change. But there is a contrarian view as well, which is that perceptions have to change first to create conducive atmosphere for governments to be able to take up issues in much more constructive ways.

It was a commonly held view that series of conferences like the one organised by IDSA should be held at regular intervals, bringing policy analysts, academics or former foreign policy officials together on a common platform. The ideas that are generated in such interactive conferences could go a long way in correcting and clearing misperceptions.

Another key takeaway from this conference was that at the civil society level, at track 1.5 or track 2 level, it is important to churn out consensual models and practical way forwards that can be fed into governmental structures so that 'governmentality' can change.

Index